She Has Done a *Good Thing*

Lydia Harder

Lois Y. Barrett

Gayle Gerber Koontz

Brenda Isaacs

Reta Halteman Finger

Emma L. Richards

Grace R. Brunner

Dorothy Nickel Friesen

Charlotte Holsopple Glick

Ruth Naylor

Pauline Graybill Kennel

Joyce M. Shutt

Ruth Brunk Stoltzfus

Mary K. Oyer

Bertha Fast Harder

Marlene Y. Kropf

Shirley Hershey Showalter

June Alliman Yoder

Miriam F. Book

Donella M. Clemens

Marian Franz

Shirley Byler Yoder

Alice M. Roth

Carol J. Suter

Lee Snyder

Marilyn Miller

Mary Swartley

Linda Keener

She
Has Done

a
Good
Thing

Mennonite Women Leaders Tell Their Stories

Edited by
Mary Swartley
& Rhoda Keener

Herald
Press

Scottdale, Pennsylvania
Waterloo, Ontario

Library of Congress Cataloging-in-Publication Data
She has done a good thing : Mennonite women leaders tell their stories
/ edited by Mary Swartley and Rhoda Keener
    p.   cm.
    Includes bibliographical references.
    ISBN 0-8361-9112-9 (alk. paper)
    1. Mennonite women—United States—Biography. 2. Mennonite
women—Canada—Biography. 3. Women in church work—Mennonite
Church. 4. Women in church work—United States. 5. Women in church
work—Canada. I. Swartley, Mary, 1934-   . II. Keener, Rhoda, 1951-
BX8141.S54   1999
289.7'092'2—dc21
[B]   99-21765

Bible text is used by permission, all rights reserved, and unless otherwise noted is
from the *New Revised Standard Version Bible,* copyright 1989 by the Division of
Christian Education of the National Council of the Churches of Christ in the USA.
NIV, from the *Holy Bible, New International Version* ®, copyright © 1973, 1978,
1984 by International Bible Society, Zondervan Publishing House. Mark 14:6-9, from
NAB, *The New American Bible with Revised New Testament,* N.T. copyright © 1986
by the Confraternity of Christian Doctrine, Washington, D.C. NEB, from *The New
English Bible,* © The Delegates of the Oxford University Press and the Syndics of the
Cambridge University Press 1961, 1970; KJV, from *King James Version of the Holy
Bible.*

Degrees: B.A./A.B., bachelor of arts. B.S., bachelor of science. B.Th./Th.B., bachelor
of theology. D.Min., doctor of ministry; M.A., master of arts. M.Div., master of divinity. M.Mus., master of music. M.Th./Th.M., master of theology. Ph.D., doctor of
philosophy. Th.D., doctor of theology.

SHE HAS DONE A GOOD THING
Copyright © 1999 by Herald Press, Scottdale, Pa. 15683
    Published simultaneously in Canada by Herald Press,
    Waterloo, Ont. N2L 6H7. All rights reserved
Website for Herald Press: www.mph.org
Library of Congress Catalog Card Number: 99-21765
International Standard Book Number: 0-8361-9112-9
Printed in the United States of America
Cover and book design by Gwen M. Stamm

08 07 06 05 04 03 02 01 00 99 10 9 8 7 6 5 4 3 2 1

This book is dedicated to
Edith Nyce Lapp and
Doris Sell Shenk,
our mothers

Jesus said, "Let her alone.
Why do you make trouble for her?
She has done a good thing for me. . . .
She has anticipated anointing
my body for burial."

—Mark 14:6

Contents

Foreword • *Anne Stuckey* 9
Vision for This Book • *Mary Swartley* 12
Acknowledgments 20

Theologians

Reaching for a Blessing • *Lydia Neufeld Harder* 23
From a Distance • *Gayle Gerber Koontz* 31
Nudged by God • *Lois Barrett* 40
Standing in the Gap • *Reta Halteman Finger* 47

Pastors

Pioneer Pastor • *Emma Sommers Richards* 59
By the Grace of God • *Grace Brunner* 65
Rooted, So I Could Sway in the Wind •
   Dorothy Nickel Friesen 74
God's Smile • *Brenda Isaacs* 81
Ode to Joy • *Charlotte Holsopple Glick* 87
Proceed with Much Prayer • *Ruth Bundy Naylor* 97
God's Mysterious Doors • *Pauline Graybill Kennel* 106
I Never Intended to Be a Pastor • *Joyce Shutt* 114
By God's Providence • *Ruth Brunk Stoltzfus* 124

Educators

The Holy Ghost over the Bent World Broods •
   Mary K. Oyer 137

Go and Teach Christian Education •
    Bertha Fast Harder 144
Way Leads on to Way • *Marlene Kropf* 153
Two Stories on a Continuing Journey •
    Shirley Hershey Showalter 165
It Just So Happened • *June Alliman Yoder* 178

Administrators

For Such a Time as This • *Miriam F. Book* 189
Birthing a New Denomination • *Donella M. Clemens* . . . 197
I Can't Make That Much Potato Salad •
    Marian Claassen Franz 207
How Will I Learn to Dance? •
    Shirley Buckwalter Yoder 218
Six Decades in God's Global Family • *Alice M. Roth* . . . 231
Blazing the Leadership Trail • *Carol J. Suter* 240
Red Poppies • *Lee Snyder* 247
The Alabaster Jar • *Marilyn Miller* 256

Epilogue

Little Girl in Pigtails • *Rhoda Keener* 267

The Editors 271
    Mary Swartley
    Rhoda Keener

Foreword

THE WEEK I was to be ordained, I looked at the wall of my church study and saw that the picture had fallen. This in itself would not be noteworthy except that it was a watercolor painting of a feed mill in Waterloo County, with two Mennonites standing in front of the mill. With abstract brush strokes, the painter portrayed the relationship of the man and the woman as they turned their heads to talk to each other, with their backs turned to the world. Even in this ordinary setting, they were joined in holy conversation. This was a picture of my home and of my people.

When the painting fell, the frame didn't leave the wall. The artwork merely tilted within the mat, presenting a visual image askew for anyone to see. I was a little unnerved by the timing of this occurrence. I hoped that the picture's drop was not a comment on my ordination to the ministry of the gospel in the Mennonite Church. I wondered whether my Mennonite brothers and sisters were also upset or askew over my call to pastoral ministry. Again I asked God what he wanted.

These are questions we hear repeatedly in the women's stories of this book. Their words are testimonies of God's call to pastoral ministry, theology, education, and administration within the church. However, each woman also carried a heightened awareness that such faithful steps could affect important relationships within the family, the community, and the church. Each one knows that ministry is about relationships.

Lois Barrett says, "Theology follows relationships," and Marilyn Miller resounds with "relationships are the most important." It is no wonder, then, that these women live and serve in ministries that honor the relational God, who wants to be with his people. That reality is borne out as we listen to the stories of these women. They express who they are as eloquently as what they do.

The ministries of these women have certainly been shaped in relationships with friends, colleagues, grandparents, mothers, fathers, aunts, uncles, husbands, and children. Encouragers within the church have cared for these women and provided places for them to grow. That made a huge difference for this generation of leaders.

However, past relationships do not tell the whole story. There is also an awareness that the next generation of women leaders are primarily the responsibility of this generation. All who still struggle to be what God has designed, recognize that they are the mentors and role models for women who follow.

As Carol Suter claims, "Some of us have spent our whole lives searching for mentors. In the process, we didn't notice that we ourselves have become mentors needed by others. . . . We must share our experiences with those coming along behind and beside us. We must encourage and exhort less-experienced and younger women to follow their own callings to leadership." Relationship thinking continues as it extends to new generations and a broader circle.

Yet in these stories we can't help but marvel how often God called with the extraordinary request right in the midst of the ordinary. Lee Snyder was doing the weekly laundry when she was called to consider the presidency of Bluffton College. Lydia Harder was carrying roles that go with housekeeping and childcare when she was encouraged to do some self-reflection alongside biblical interpretation. Marilyn Miller's first congregation was a hen house full of chickens, to whom she would preach. Shirley Yoder learned about leadership while seated on a pilothouse stool in the Chesapeake Bay ferry captained by her father. Even in the ordinary, God was at work preparing women for leadership.

Without a doubt, the joy and certainty of the abiding presence of God surfaces in a measure equal to the pain of the journey toward church leadership. Think of the 1950s, when selected arts were present with uneasy acceptance, but not yet embraced with freedom, joy, and pleasure, according to Mary Oyer. The leadership of women in the church has followed a similar path.

From Oregon to Virginia, Alberta to Ontario, many of the stories describe the safety of a home where these individual women were loved. These homes were linked with community and congregational restrictions that pushed them out to serve in other places. In every story, fear stands alongside faithfulness. Empowerment to serve stands with self-doubt.

Nevertheless, these are also love stories. Love for God and for the church infuses each page. These women leaders rejoice that the work of the Holy Spirit to affirm life has always been there "through all the deadening arguments and dull nagging fears," as Oyer claims. Such rejoicing is the strength of all of these women.

These stories are for women who follow wherever God leads and for the sons and the daughters of the church. They give strength to those on the journey and a light for those who will yet come. These are not just the stories of the twenty-six writers in this book. They are the stories of women who have been "the first one" in a church conference, congregation, office, or classroom.

Shirley Hershey Showalter concludes, "What special strength can women give to women? We can pronounce each other good. We can share our life stories. We can in trust reveal our fears. We do not have to understand each other. Love is enough."

For the woman who came to pour ointment on Jesus' head, this was all that she was asking for, too. She wanted to know that what she did was good. She did not want to be scolded for it. She wanted to reveal her fears of Jesus' impending death and burial. She wanted to be loved. Jesus answered each one of her internal questions when he proclaimed that she had done a good thing.

So have the women whose stories we read today. By God's grace and call, each one of them has done a good thing.

—*Anne Stuckey*
Minister of Congregational Leadership
Mennonite Board of Congregational Ministries

Vision for This Book

You ARE HOLDING in your hands a gift to you by twenty-six Mennonite women leaders. In this volume they tell their own stories of how God called them into leadership positions within Mennonite churches and organizations.

One of the writers refers to the glass ceiling that has traditionally separated women from leadership roles in the church. As women responded to God's call to church leadership, they became the ones to puncture this glass ceiling. The writers in this book, as well as many other women leaders, know the thoughts and feelings that go into coping with this ambiguous opportunity.

The title, *She Has Done a Good Thing*, is from Jesus. He spoke these words in response to people criticizing the woman who broke an alabaster jar of expensive perfume and poured it on Jesus' head. Jesus declared, "She has done a good thing. . . . Wherever the gospel is proclaimed to the whole world, what she has done will be told, in memory of her" (Mark 14:6-9, NAB).

In the last chapter of this book, Marilyn Miller writes, "Each of us, like the woman in the Bible story, is gifted with an alabaster jar. . . . We can choose to measure that perfume out little by little, sharing it only with those we think will appreciate it. Or we can do as the woman in the Bible story, and offer it all to Christ."

You are about to read stories told by women who have many gifts and have used those gifts to do a good thing. Just as Jesus applauded the woman with the alabaster jar, so he applauds all of us today as we use our gifts to serve God's reign.

Blessed by One Who "Did a Good Thing"

In my own experience, I would not be where I am today were it not for a woman in my life who courageously helped me, risking the possible disapproval of my parents. That woman was Grace Bower (now Good), from Plains Mennonite Church in Lansdale, Pennsylvania, where my father was pastor.

When I was a teenager, I prayed daily that my parents would allow me to finish high school. After much praying and appealing, they finally agreed to let me continue my education at Eastern Mennonite High School (Harrisonburg, Va.) for my junior and senior years.

However, permission was not all I needed. I was not capable of making decisions and preparing for dormitory life. My mother had seven younger children and wasn't able to give attention to this.

Happily, Grace Bower (Good), a member of my home church, intuited my need and offered to take me shopping in Philadelphia, to help me select things I would need: bedspread, curtains, towels, and clothes. In addition to all this, she bought me a suitcase and gave it to me as a gift. I still have that suitcase. Without her help, my years in the dormitory would have been far more difficult. Thank God, Grace took the risk to do a good thing for me. She prepared me for life.

A New "Sowing Circle"

Several years ago, a group of Mennonite women leaders in Elkhart County began getting together quarterly for the purpose of networking and support. One of the significant contributions we have made to each others' lives is to share our enthusiasm for new books we are reading. One recommended in 1995 was *Rattling Those Dry Bones: Women Changing the Church*, edited by June Steffensen Hagen.

As I read it, I began thinking about what Mennonite women would say if they wrote their stories. I envisioned a similar book, featuring Mennonite women leaders who would share their own stories.

I recognize how far we have come in the Mennonite Church in affirming the leadership of women. Sharon Klingelsmith has researched the history of "Women in the Mennonite Church, 1900-1930" and summarized the "rules" for this era:*

[The] rule of thumb [for women] meant in practice that women could be teachers of children and younger women but not of men, for that would be a violation of the authority/submission positions. It also meant that women could fill no leadership functions, since that would put them over men. Thus, with rare exceptions, women did not serve as choristers, secretaries, or chairmen of the

---

* *Mennonite Quarterly Review* 54 (July 1980): 181.

Sunday school conferences. They could be writers but generally not editors. And women did not serve on denomination-wide church committees.

This history describes the milieu in which many of the writers of this book grew up. My own vision also connects with this time period. As a young child, it appeared to me that there were almost no opportunities for women in the church. Yet I felt a distinct awareness that God had a place for me. Two books opened a window into the lives of other women. My Sunday school teacher, Grace Delp, gave me *Ten Girls Who Became Famous*, telling about Fanny Crosby, Susannah Wesley, Florence Nightingale, Mary Slessor, and others. I also eagerly read *Girls' Stories of Great Women* and began to see rays of hope for myself.

In the 1970s, as I was again feeling that there was no place for me in the church, I discovered the book *All We're Meant to Be* (1975), by Scanzoni and Hardesty. I found hope as I came to realize I was not alone in these feelings. Probably the most positive lift came in the 1980s. I discovered that women's sense of integrity can be intertwined with an ethic of care, according to Carol Gilligan in her book *In a Different Voice* (1982). Women do have a different way of thinking, prioritizing, and ordering their lives. The urgency for gender balance in the church hit me with new force.

Identifying with Leaders

I grew up as the daughter of a Mennonite Church leader in Franconia (Pa.) Conference, John E. Lapp. Since Mennonite church leaders visited in our home, I learned to know them by name. On the phone, I recognized the voices of people like A. J. Metzler, Orie O. Miller, Harold S. Bender, John C. Wenger, John R. Mumaw, and many others. When they came to the door, I knew them. I was not intimidated by them; instead, I identified with them.

As a high school senior at Eastern Mennonite High School in 1952, my roommate and I had many conversations about "what we want to be when we grow up." We confided to each other, "What I'd really like to be is a minister." But we both saw that as being so far from the realm of possibility that we hardly dared to whisper the thought. At that time, even the young men in our class were suspect if they aspired to become ministers.

Already in 1957-58, my first year of teaching at Christopher Dock Mennonite High School (Lansdale, Pa.), I remember that I was carefully observing the leadership style of Richard C. Detweiler, our principal. Later I taught at Eastern Mennonite High School and studied the style of Harold D. Lehman.

By the time I taught at Bethany Christian High School, I was quick to point out to John M. S. Steiner some of the positive points of Detweiler and Lehman. I'm sure it was evident to Steiner and later to William D. Hooley, that I was identifying with him as principal. Yet I never dreamed that one day I would be a principal.

In 1979, as a novice on the board of directors of Mennonite Mutual Aid, again I found myself observing the leadership style of the chair—Bill Dunn first, and then George Dyck, Arthur Jost, and others. It never occurred to me that one day I would have the opportunity to try out my leadership style with this board.

In the early 1970s, I recognized my interest in administration and started looking at possibilities for enrolling in a program for a master's degree in business administration. In that process, I first realized a deficiency in the academic counsel I had received as an undergraduate. I had not been encouraged to meet basic mathematics requirements for such a degree. So my advisers in the master's program encouraged me to stay in education. In retrospect, I would have done well if I had gone back and taken the undergraduate math, but I didn't know that then.

At Wilfrid Laurier University, Waterloo, Ontario, I did, however, take courses in organizational management. Later, at Sacred Heart University in Fairfield, Connecticut, I studied educational administration. I found the study of organizational behavior, capital management, and school finance to be valuable and helpful in many areas of life. Administration was clearly my interest.

Special Interest in Women

As a business teacher in Mennonite high schools as well as Eastern Mennonite College, I found myself taking special interest in women students: their plans for college, the academic counsel they received or lack of it, and their leadership potential.

In the late 1980s for one of my graduate courses, I did an extensive study of the trends in SAT scores and GPA scores for men and women, comparing trends at Bethany Christian High School with national averages. This became the basis for a presentation to our faculty and a means of sensitizing all of us to gender issues in education. In the 1990s my concern became the issue of how we teach classes, give unfair advantage to men students, and unfair disadvantage to women students.

Inspired by Women Leaders

In 1973 at a churchwide Mennonite conference held on the campus of Eastern Mennonite College, I heard the report of how one congregation came to consensus on calling a woman to be congregational chairperson. I was deeply moved and gratified to know that God is working within the Mennonite Church in this way. I affirmed Doris Janzen Longacre for sharing this story.

I have been blessed through the sermons and the leadership of Mennonite women. I am inspired by the stories of their call to leadership. In the 1970s I was also moved when I heard Ruth Brunk Stoltzfus, then in her sixties, ask a Sunday school class at Park View Mennonite Church in Harrisonburg, Virginia, "How long do I have to wait for the *church* to recognize my call?"

I also felt personal affirmation from God at a baptismal service. This came through Mary Mininger, a seminary intern at my home church, Belmont Mennonite. She put a cross around the neck of a young woman being baptized and read a promise from God:

> I have called you by name, you are mine. When you pass through the waters, I will be with you; and through the rivers, they shall not overwhelm you; when you walk through fire you shall not be burned, and the flame shall not consume you. For I am the Lord your God, the Holy One of Israel, your Savior. (Isa. 43:1-3)

I am studying at Associated Mennonite Biblical Seminary (AMBS), usually taking one course a semester. I savor each new course, sometimes wishing I had studied theology when I was younger. I am blessed to be located where I can continue studying at AMBS without inconveniencing my family. But even today, I cannot declare that I am serious about this study, with a clear intention or expectation that I might use it somewhere.

The issue of women in ministry in the Mennonite Church is still ambiguous. In spite of the twenty-five years since Emma Richards was ordained, we need only to read the church press to realize that women in ministry is still a live issue.

Since receiving these stories, I am even more aware of the courage and spiritual strength it has taken for women to hear and respond to God's call for leadership in the church. This is true because of our conflicted emotions concerning women who lead, much resistance to their leadership, and controversy about their role. I marvel that Mennonite women in leadership have been able to understand the Bible, its message, and its mission as including them fully.

Mission to Do This Book

Although my mother often mischievously said, "I could write a book," it was something she never did, and it was never one of my goals. However, when the vision for this book hit me, I could not let it go. I dipped my toe into the water and found it warm. So I sought out a good friend and former colleague who has recognized editorial abilities. I am most grateful that Rhoda Keener was willing to take time to work with me in an editorial capacity.

Rhoda has provided more than editing. She and I have had many similar interests and experiences in the church, and we share similar reactions to them. She has provided additional insights and understandings that have contributed to the total project.

About co-editing this book, Rhoda writes,

When Mary asked me to help her with this book, I was intrigued with the idea. I thought, "Yes, these stories should be told." I only knew a few of the writers personally, so I approached each story as an editor looking for what "caught" me. As I worked with commas, semicolons, and paragraph formation—sitting at the computer with Mary—something else happened. I realized that I saw myself in these women's stories.

As we edited, I smiled, I nodded, I lifted an eyebrow, I cheered, I cried. Most of the women in this book have lived more years than I have. As we worked, I wondered if our daughters and granddaughters will someday be able to embrace the full range of their potential and ability when they ask, "What is God calling me to?" My hope is that this book will be another step in that direction. I am grateful to Mary for giving me the opportunity to be a part of this project.

Selection of Contributors

In the birthing stages of this volume, an extensive list of possible contributors was developed. Since there were many more qualified persons than one volume could contain, I was forced to find ways to narrow the list. The first suggestion came from the publisher, who encouraged me to choose writers whose stories had not been included in the book *Godward*, edited by Ted Koontz (1994). A few exceptions were made to this policy. While the direction of those stories is a bit different, you still may want to refer to it and read stories by Wilma Bailey, Carolyn Holderread Heggen, Sarah Wenger Shenk, and others.

Next I chose to give priority to those born before 1950. Thus, the stories primarily include women born between 1915 and 1950. The geographic area of ministry provided another step in narrowing the list. Dorothy Yoder Nyce has published *To See Each Other's Good* (1996), recognizing Mennonite women in mission. Hence, the focus of this book is on North American church leadership.

Whenever the project was mentioned, everyone suggested names of persons who must be included. I regret that it was impossible to invite all of these "must include" persons.

Finally, there has been some self-selection. Not all persons invited to contribute were able to accept the assignment. Some found the path too sacred or too painful to share. In the telling of these stories, there are elements of risk and vulnerability, fears and doubts. Some contributors wondered whether they indeed can be called leaders. These stories are told with a great deal of humility.

Organization

The essays are arranged in groups by profession: theologians, pastors, educators, and administrators. Many of the writers qualify to be in several of the categories, so the groupings are somewhat arbitrary. Each writer was given six starter questions:

• How have you gotten to where you are now without giving up?
• What have been the challenges and obstacles along the way, and

how have you handled them?
- What/who inspires you? What compels you to go on?
- What rays of hope have you found for yourself, for Mennonite churches, and for other women in the church?
- What thoughts can you offer Mennonite women who may be growing weary in the struggle?
- In what ways have you influenced the church to change?

Vision

Twenty-five years ago most of us never envisioned the opportunities and challenges that would become options for women in church leadership today. Most of the writers in this book were raised in homes and churches that were quite patriarchal. The very concept of women as leaders would have been considered an oxymoron. Women were only expected to make their ideas and concerns known indirectly, through their fathers, husbands, or brothers.

The writers of these chapters are pioneers. Most of them were without mentors or role models. They are now the role models and mentors for the next generation. Their movement into leadership has required a great deal of courage, humility, and grace. For many, the path is still lonely.

These stories are shared as a way of celebrating the new openness to women as leaders in Mennonite churches. They document an important time in Mennonite history. Most of all, they proclaim the mighty acts of God who has called us all. These experiences may also provide insights to help us deal with lingering concern and distrust of having women in leadership.

Just as the church has told the stories of women in the Bible, we can learn from the experiences of these Mennonite women of faith who responded to God's call. As you read their stories, you may begin to see God working in your life in new ways. God may be calling you to be courageous and willing to risk the unknown, with the confidence that God will also be your strength and guide.

These stories can be used as a springboard for discussion regarding the church's participation with women in leadership. They also encourage other women to share their own stories.

I commend to you these stories of Mennonite women theologians, pastors, educators, and administrators. I hope you can identify with them and thank God for them. Most of all, I invite you to pray for them in the work to which they have been called. My prayer is that this book will speak to women and men who are still trying to find their place in the life of the church, and that God will empower each of us to courageously do a good thing for Jesus.

Mary Swartley

Acknowledgments

THIS BOOK grows out of a wide variety of interactions and relationships. The first source of support came from "The Sowing Circle": Miriam F. Book, Charlotte Holsopple Glick, Gayle Gerber Koontz, Alice Roth, Shirley Hershey Showalter, and Shirley Buckwalter Yoder. Shirley Buckwalter Yoder helped to launch the project by submitting the first chapter and kept prodding us to complete the book.

We acknowledge the many women—mothers, grandmothers, aunts, daughters, sisters, nieces, granddaughters, teachers, students, colleagues, and friends—who have inspired us and stirred up our interest in learning to know the experiences of women leaders in the Mennonite Church.

In the birthing stages of this book, Michael King was the editor who provided us with enthusiastic encouragement to move ahead on the project. David Garber followed the project through to completion, giving prompt and helpful advice along the way.

We offer thanks and love to our husbands, Willard Swartley and Robert Keener, for their blessing on our work, their support for us in our journey, and their continued encouragement, even when the project became almost all-consuming.

—*Mary Swartley and Rhoda Keener*

Theologians

You are a chosen race,
a royal priesthood,
a holy nation,
God's own people,
in order that you may proclaim
the mighty acts of him
who called you out of darkness
into his marvelous light.

—*Peter, in 1 Peter 2:9*

Reaching for a Blessing

LYDIA NEUFELD HARDER

LYDIA HARDER has been a full-time home-maker, volunteer in church and community, and a teacher in schools ranging from elementary to university level. Her present role as director of the Toronto Mennonite Theological Centre, as well as her involvements in her local church community and conference committees, allow her to further her vision of a mutual relationship between scholarship and congregational life.

Lydia's partnership with her husband, Gary, includes co-teaching courses on church and ministry, participating with him on the preaching team in their church, and helping to can vegetables he grows.

She earned a B.Th. from Canadian Mennonite Bible College, a B.A. from Goshen College, an M.Th. from Newman College in Edmonton, and a Th.D. at Emmanuel College at the Toronto School of Theology. Lydia is the author of the book *Obedience, Suspicion and the Gospel of Mark* (Wilfred Laurier Press, 1998), articles in the *Conrad Grebel Review* and *The Mennonite Quarterly Review,* and curriculum for the Foundation Series. She served on the Associated Mennonite Biblical Seminary board for eight years, and is on the editorial council of the Believers Church Bible Commentary.

Lydia delights in her three adult children, Mark, Kendall, and Kristen, and her five grandchildren, who provide good reasons for laughing and playing. A good novel, a few apples, and a chair under a shady tree beside a lake—these continue to represent the utmost in pleasure and enjoyment for her. But she also values long talks with close friends, cross-cultural interactions, and traveling to unfamiliar places.

WHEN I WAS a little girl, I found it difficult to answer questions about what I wanted to be when I grew up. My standard response was "a teacher"—an acceptable answer. However, buried deep within me was another answer I never dared whisper, even to myself. My dream seemed too presumptuous. So I chose between the three usual vocations for women before marriage: teaching, nursing, or clerical work. I went to teachers' college and spent several years teaching elementary children. However, the inner urgings continued.

A Secret Dream Unfolds

Though unaware of it, my family and congregation had nourished my secret dream since early childhood. Playing church was a favorite game in our home. With my brother, I planned and led pretend worship services and programs, to the delight of my parents. I do not know why I did not play the role of my mother, who took care of children in the *Stübchen* (nursery) at the back of the church. Instead, I identified with my father, a lay minister and teacher in the church.

Theology was everyday language in our home. I remember heated discussions about how to interpret Genesis, while we were perched on ladders, picking cherries in the orchard. These debates were interspersed with lively hymn singing, the lead taken first by those in one tree and then those in another.

I listened to stories of Mennonite life in Russia during the terrible events of the Revolution. This gave me a concrete context for debates about pacifism and nonresistance. I thrived on opportunities to teach Sunday school and to become involved in daily vacation Bible school and camp programs. I enjoyed committee work and youth service projects.

At age seventeen, I attended my first Canada-wide Mennonite conference in my hometown along with fifty other youth. Despite the fact that women and youth could not vote, I felt the excitement of being involved in the church and its mission. (Years later I hung over my desk a photo of the delegates of that conference, all male. When I became discouraged about the lack of support for women, I remembered with hope how much had already changed since that day!)

A Struggle for Faith

During my first year of college studies, I merely enjoyed the intellectual stimulation and the pleasant social context. However, soon my studies led to a struggle for faith: life experiences and intellectual questions began to overlap. During a vacation break, I came home to a congregation in conflict over differing understandings of leadership, worship, and lifestyles. I heard my father being discredited and disgraced by people whom I had respected and loved. I saw my mother trying to carry on her supportive role as she experienced rejection by a congregation.

Canadian Mennonite Bible College encouraged critical reflection. This allowed me to phrase my questions in theoretical language, without betraying the hurt lying just below the surface. My real questions, ones I never quite dared to speak out loud, were ultimate: Where was God if the Bible was produced in a human process, and if the church was made up of sinful human beings? How could I even be sure that God was real?

In studying 1 Corinthians, I gradually discovered a God who chooses to communicate with us, not outside of human efforts, but through human writers of the Bible and even through a sinful church. I recognized how God, in grace and love, could then also use me. That became the encouragement and comfort I needed. Now I had a theological foundation for the sense of calling that I continued to feel.

In my last year of study, another theme began to emerge. Our class chose a graduation motto: "Freed to Obey." The tensions created by putting these two words together were replayed many times for me, in various contexts. I began to experience the subtle but dominating influence of the various cultural and church contexts within which I tried to follow my calling.

For example, professors were urging my brother to continue studying because of his good grades. Yet everyone assumed that I would not continue into graduate work, even though I also had good grades. The equality and mutuality of relationships between students during college days began to change as different opportunities presented themselves to men and women. Marriage increased these differences, since both my husband and I assumed that his career goals would determine our future direction.

The tension this created within me climaxed in the year Gary participated in pastoral internship training in London, Ontario, as part of his seminary training. We lived in a small basement apartment with our two infant children. Gary's work was intense. He spent much time becoming self-aware in settings of small learning groups, in the hospital and in the church where he received supervision. No conscious decision on my part was needed to know that I could not continue to work with him in congregational settings as I had in the past.

My role had become housekeeping and childcare. Depression and unhappiness began to surface more and more. Slowly I began to admit my own feelings of being left out, and my jealousy of Gary and his opportunities to study and minister. I realized that we had begun a pattern in which I tried to work through my husband's profession, knowing there would be no affirmation of my own sense of calling. This did not contribute to a healthy marriage partnership. It also did not allow me to do my work joyfully, using my own gifts and abilities.

Several key people encouraged me in the task of self-reflection during this time. One woman from the church offered to care for our children during the Sunday school hour so I could teach an elective course, the first opportunity I ever had to teach adults. The chosen theme was a study of the book by Lois Gunden Clemens, *Woman Liberated* (1971). This allowed me to explore my own issues in the context of women and men serious about searching for new and more faithful interpretations of the Bible.

Gary's supervisor arranged a small-group experience where interns and spouses could interact. In this context, Gary and I could begin to name dysfunctional communication patterns in our marriage and start to create new ones. Though this was a stressful time, I began making more conscious choices about my role in the church and in our family.

Toward Mutuality in Marriage

My struggle to respond to God's call took a different turn when Gary became pastor in Edmonton. In a church where lay involvement was encouraged, I was free to be part of many areas in church life. In women's Bible study groups and adult Sunday school classes, I began to articulate publicly my convictions and questions. The central issues we worked with included raising children and growth within marriages, as well as questions about God's presence during domestic violence, accidental death, or suicide.

Volunteer activities included working for a distress line, on a daycare board, and teaching Sunday school. These broadened my horizons but also raised questions about the value of my activities when compared to my husband's full-time job as pastor.

The shift to a more mutual relationship in our marriage did not come easily. Sometimes I struggled with feelings of unworthiness and guilt. One such occasion was when I left our three preschool children with Gary while I spent a week in an orientation session to prepare for writing a quarter of the Foundation Sunday school curriculum.

A significant turning point came for us as a couple when we were in Paraguay during Gary's sabbatical year from the pastorate. We decided that we would each teach half-time at the seminary while sharing parenting and household tasks equally. I began to admit how much I enjoyed the teaching. Meanwhile, Gary realized how much parenting he had missed by his total commitment to public ministry.

Naming the Dream

Back in Canada, I again began to explore various career paths. In my search for direction, I asked advice from a former professor. When I told him of my interest in further studies in theology, he encouraged me, suggesting that I was lucky that I could take courses "just for fun."

Somehow, I felt crushed and humiliated. Why had I imagined that my gifts could be used to serve the church! However, I cautiously began exploring further studies by applying at a university to secure a bachelor of education degree. I was discouraged by the lack of credit I would receive for my past education.

Finally I decided to do what I really wanted to do—study theology. Unexpectedly, I received the equivalent of a master of divinity degree for my various undergraduate degrees and occasional courses, a not-so-small miracle! I could enter directly into a master of theology program at Newman College, a small Catholic school in Edmonton.

There I learned to dialogue with the larger Christian community about my own faith questions. I discovered feminist theologians who read the Bible self-consciously as women. I found role models, such as Sister Lina Gaudette, who taught me to value my own integrity and commitments. After graduation, I was even hired to teach Bible courses in the same college.

Several key experiences during those years helped me to own my gifts and offer them to the larger community. I remember a weekend retreat with Katie Funk Wiebe, a Mennonite author. She shared the story of how she finally named herself an author, because that meant accepting responsibility for the influence her books might have on others. It would have been much easier for her to say that she just wrote a few little articles "for fun."

After that retreat, I struggled for a long time but finally, secretly, named myself a Mennonite theologian. I knew this meant accepting my share of responsibility for the direction Mennonite theology was taking.

My Mother's Blessing

I remember weeping as I listened to the tape of the ordination to ministry of my brother and also my sister-in-law, Doreen Neufeld. She was the first woman ordained in the United Mennonite Conference of Ontario, in 1980.* What moved me most deeply was hearing my mother's words at the end of the service. My father had been asked to speak, but when he finished, she decided she also wanted to say something. She spontaneously offered her own blessing.

I wept because of my mother's courage. I wept because of the many gifts that she had, which had not been used in the church. I wept for myself, admitting that I too longed for affirmation from my faith community.

However, I was not left without a blessing. When I was finishing my master's thesis, I was asked to speak at a conference on power

---

*Doris Weber was the first woman ordained in the Western Ontario Mennonite Conference, in 1979. Martha Smith Good was the first woman ordained in the Mennonite Conference of Ontario and Quebec, in 1982. These three conferences integrated in 1988 to become the Mennonite Conference of Eastern Canada.

and authority. I still have a vivid memory of standing before former professors and respected church leaders. I was wondering if I would be able to get any words out, even after the many hours of hard work I had put into preparing the lecture.

I received courage from the lines of a song that kept ringing in my ears throughout that weekend. Our choir had been practicing a Bach cantata which set the words of Psalm 115:12-15 to music. Certain lines kept repeating themselves to me: "Der Herr segne euch, . . . euch und eure Kinder!" (the Lord bless you, . . . you and your children). I accepted those words as a commissioning by God for my task, a promise that my family would also be blessed as I responded to the inner call.

Soon I discovered a fact of life: not everyone agreed that women's voices were needed in Mennonite theology. I became discouraged when my tentative contributions were discounted. I remember one consultation in particular. I was completely overwhelmed when I noticed political maneuvers happening, participants completely ignoring women's concerns, and exclusive language being used.

At one point I could not hide my tears, so I went downstairs to hide in the washroom. There I found the other two women attending this conference of approximately one hundred leaders. They also were crying. What redeemed this conference for me was a letter by one of our male church leaders. He encouraged me to continue to speak, in spite of the suspicious atmosphere and exclusivity that he admitted had been so apparent at that meeting.

"The Lord Has Been Mindful of Us"

Many people did wonder about the wisdom of my next major decision. Why would a homemaker approaching fifty move her family across the country to begin a six-year doctoral program in theology? My husband's commitment to mutuality and his willingness to move for the sake of my studies opened this possibility for me. However, to take this step, I also had to overcome a lifetime of conditioning telling me that practical service and theoretical work are separated along gender lines.

The years of study in Toronto were full, rich years. I had intense involvement with a friend struggling to affirm her own gifts after years of sexual abuse. This experience encouraged me to name the authority and power issues within church institutions.

After graduation came the real test of whether I believed in my calling. Gary and I had arranged for a small group of people to help us discern our future direction. Before the meeting could take place, we received an invitation for me to come to Canadian Mennonite Bible College to teach there for one year. Rather quickly, we assumed we would say no because Gary would not be able to arrange a year's leave from the church he was pastoring.

Surprisingly, the discernment group thought otherwise. They affirmed my gifts and suggested that I go by myself for the first four months. Perhaps Gary would be able to join me for the second half of the year. This created a great inner turmoil for me since I could not imagine going without Gary. I finally accepted the group's counsel as God's leading and phoned Canadian Mennonite Bible College with my acceptance.

Now it was their turn to hesitate. If I was there alone, what message would that give to younger women in college? I was devastated. However, after reconsidering, Canadian Mennonite Bible College decided to invite me to teach all year, with Gary coming for the second semester. Opportunities to teach and preach have continued to appear for me after that year of working in a Mennonite institution.

Do I now know what I will be when I grow up? I continue to find the question relevant as I begin to think about retirement. Perhaps the call to ministry I have felt throughout my life was a call to further growth. Perhaps it was really an invitation to be a disciple, following the God who leads us, nudging us on to further maturity amid various obstacles, external and internal.

If this is true, then no human institution can stand in the way of our receiving the blessings God has in store for us. For "the Lord has been mindful of us; [God] will bless us" (Psalm 115:12). This can be our confidence as women responding to God's call.

Lydia Harder

From a Distance

GAYLE GERBER KOONTZ

J. Tyler Klassen

Gᴀʏʟᴇ Gᴇʀʙᴇʀ Kᴏᴏɴᴛᴢ is professor of theology and ethics at the Associated Mennonite Biblical Seminary, Elkhart, Indiana. Both Gayle and her husband, Ted, joined the AMBS faculty in 1982.

In 1990-95 Gayle was academic dean. Upon the sudden death of president Marlin Miller in November 1994, Gayle became acting president until June of 1995.

Both Gayle and Ted served in the Philippines with Mennonite Central Committee (MCC), as visiting professors at Silliman University Divinity School in 1988-90.

Earlier, Gayle taught religion at Goshen College in Indiana, worked for MCC Information Services for four years, served as administrative assistant for the Boston University Institute for Philosophy and Religion, and taught high school English in Massachusetts.

After attending Bluffton College in Ohio, Gayle graduated from Bethel College in Newton, Kansas. She received an M.A. in religion from Lancaster Theological Seminary in Pennsylvania, and a Ph.D. in philosophy of religion and social ethics from Boston University in 1985.

Gayle has been a member of the MCC Peace Section task force for women, and she is currently on the Higher Education Council for the General Conference Mennonite Church. She has published articles in *The Mennonite, Conrad Grebel Review*, and *Mennonite Quarterly Review*.

Gayle and Ted are the parents of Rachel, Timothy, and Peter. Along with parenting, Gayle likes to bake bread, swim, garden, and occasionally write poetry.

AN ENORMOUS PAINTING by Chuck Close hangs in a hall at the Chicago Art Institute. As I walk down the corridor and pass close to the painting, the canvas appears to be covered with random dots and swirls of color. But when I back away from the painting and stand across the hall, the fragments of paint melt into an incredibly detailed, almost photographic image of a man's face.

Living my life year by year, close to the canvas, so to speak, I saw only random dots and swirls—places bright with color, places devoid of color, flowing into one another, lacking pattern, direction.

As a child, then a student in high school and college, I thought of being a high school teacher or missionary. I did not dream of being an information services director for a church agency. As a married woman working in a church agency and a graduate student in my twenties, I never once imagined myself growing into a seminary professor. As a doctoral student, a college faculty member, and a seminary professor in my thirties and early forties, I did not consider myself being prepared for a major administrative role in theological education.

However, when I step back and look from some distance at the fragments of my life, I see a pattern of development. I see an ongoing rhythm of call and response, encouragement and risk, affirmation and growing confidence, dead ends and new choices, failure and forgiveness—small steps each, small brush strokes that in some larger picture, beyond my view, were connected.

God, whose providence and artistry still confound my imagination, layered stroke upon stroke, loving me, calling me, redeeming me beyond what I was toward someone other than I imagined.

I was a girl child born to a General Conference Mennonite family in a small Ohio town in the midforties. So what brought me to the point where, even though I am a woman, I could say, "I am a seminary professor," or "I am a theologian and a dean"?

I believe God was drawing me toward this present through innumerable invitations to take small steps, most of which I have forgotten. Reviewing memories still preserved, as if scanning old slides on a screen, I can clearly see that I am a woman in leadership *not* by virtue of my own intent and effort.

The strength and ability to lead in the church has been a gift granted to me and nurtured by others: family and congregations, church colleges, camps and conferences, artists and teachers and church leaders. I believe that God, moving before and beside and among the communities of Christians I know best, drew me into the Christian story and gradually into Christian leadership.

Looking back at the pattern of my life, I notice basic features in my experience of family, home congregation, and the wider church. I believe some of those basic qualities drew me into church leadership and eventually into seminary teaching and administration.

Religious Inclinations Nurtured, Questions Welcomed

I grew up in a home where I was loved and valued, respected and forgiven. With this gift of original blessing, it was not difficult for me to trust that I was also loved and valued by God. I further learned to see the amazing creation in which I lived as God's artistry. My father saw the world with the eyes of a photographer—the color and texture of flowers and bread, the beauty of weathered faces and trees, the play of light on water, the delicacy of a spiderweb.

As a small child, I remember waking at night during a crashing thunderstorm, fearful, running to my parents. My father took my hand and led me out to the front porch, enclosed on three sides with windows. As lightning flashed and thunder cracked, he held me safe as we watched the storm spend itself.

My father began to reinterpret what I saw and heard. He talked about the beauty of God's lightning and how God created storms to water the earth. My fear began to turn into respect for God's creation and curiosity about it, opening the way for development of a mature spirit of gratitude. Through such experience and reinterpretation, repeated again and again in relation to a variety of fears and questions, my trust in God grew.

My mother read to me—Bible stories and many other stories and books. I learned to love reading. Through stories, I learned to notice human frailty and foibles, to laugh at ourselves, and to understand those who are different. I learned about the ravages of human sin, the re-creating work of forgiving love, and the power of courageous hope.

I further saw, watching and listening to my parents, how Christian faith made a difference in their lives. As a conscientious objector in World War II, my father worked in a mental hospital; my mother joined him there. Their stories opened my eyes to the way American society dealt with the mentally disabled at that time. Their example encouraged me to interpret as "normal" and "good" the actions of a man and woman who chose to follow a culture of peace rather than a culture of war.

I listened to my parents struggle with ethical issues they faced in their small photography business: Should they forgive unpaid bills? Should they change their policy and agree to take pictures during wedding services? They understood weddings to be times of worship and therefore not to be interrupted by picture taking.

Often I observed them relating to the congregation of which we were members: participating in simple suppers in homes on Good Friday, questioning the appropriateness of a Mennonite pastor wearing a robe, preparing to teach Sunday school to both children and adults.

I remember my father expressing ambivalence with tears at one family meal. He was not sure if he should be part of a service of prayer and healing at the home of a seriously ill member of the congregation. He didn't know if his faith was strong enough.

My parents were not, however, comfortable with the religious questions I began to entertain as an adolescent. During one extended family meal, practicing the virtue of honesty but lacking in political sensitivity, I declared that I didn't believe in heaven and hell.

My mother said, "Don't you ever say that again! If you think like that, I'll feel like I've been a total failure as a parent." I did not discuss heaven and hell with my mother again.

However, I did find space within the wider church to follow my questions honestly. The youth group and pastor of the First Mennonite Church in Bluffton, Ohio, permitted this space. Through three summer voluntary service assignments and in courses at Bluffton College, I met a number of serious, articulate, good-humored Christians not threatened by religious questions.

We freely discussed war and peace, racism, abortion, agnosticism, suffering and death, and the meaning of Christian community. I was given mentors able to ask me fruitful questions and offer insights that deepened my understanding. Such dialogue allowed my faith in the saving power of Jesus Christ to live and grow.

Through this process, I came to feel that honestly following one's deepest questions about the meaning of life can lead to stronger rather than weaker faith in God. I was drawn into an ongoing theological journey that eventually included spending years of my time and energy in graduate school. On this journey, I was considering in detail some broad questions.

What is good and right and true for us as human beings here in this time and place? What do we know about these through Jesus Christ? What does it mean for our life together in the church and in the world? I listened particularly to the different "Mennonite" ways in which Mennonite theologians responded to these questions.

By 1969 I was also asking explicitly, What is good and right and true for me as a Christian *woman* here in this time and place? I witnessed the first woman preaching at Harvard Memorial Church in Boston—Mary Daly. I began the arduous task of re-examining Christian faith with the painful question in hand: What is God saying to us as women through this Scripture, in this Christian church?

At this time, the Mennonite denominations as a whole were not able to be of much help to me with questions of faith and sexuality. Mostly there was silence on the topic. Raising the question openly, particularly among Mennonites, was somewhat like questioning heaven and hell with my mother at the dinner table.

However, once again I was drawn into space hospitable to honest questions, space first within other-than-Mennonite theological communities, and later within the Mennonite church itself. In time I found ways to stand with integrity and love as a Mennonite Christian woman before God in the midst of the church.

Encouraged to Develop Leadership Skills

I was offered opportunities for writing, speaking in public, working in committees, listening and negotiating, problem solving, and creative thinking. Perhaps most important were the gifts of expectation and trust—expectation that I could do things I was afraid to do, trust that I would make good decisions.

Looking back, I recognize one of the things I have struggled to overcome for many years in relation to leadership. I am reluctant to initiate—actions, projects, even phone calls. I do not like to take risks, to put myself forward. I fear being presumptuous. I want to be liked. I do not want to fail. It is emotionally easier for me to be passive than to embrace the initiative and risks involved in leadership.

Perhaps without understanding its significance, I received encouragement given with integrity by members of my original congregation, as well as by many teachers and members of the wider church. That gift was critical in my formation as a woman in leadership.

I still remember the editor of the *Bluffton News* who read an article I had written as a high school student for a church paper, then sent me a warm and encouraging note to keep writing.

I recall a church member I respected who, after hearing a speech I gave on campus as a college student, said it was an outstanding presentation. That inspired me to try again.

I remember the time a leader for a church-sponsored high school work camp handed me the key to a VW bug and expected me (with license but little driving experience) to be able to figure out how to drive this strange car.

I have forgotten many similar encouragements. Six years ago, while I was sorting through old boxes from my parents' house, I found a letter from a Bluffton College religion professor. He wondered, given my interests and questions, if I might want to consider seminary study sometime.

Such small expressions at formative times in my life built my confidence to try again, to continue to risk, to develop my talents for leadership rather than hiding them quietly and safely in the earth.

Of special import was an invitation to join a year-long General Conference Mennonite Church voluntary service project following my junior year in college. Five of us college-age students traveled and worked with youth and youth sponsors in selected Mennonite congregations. While there was adult leadership at intervals, we usually worked by ourselves, with no particular leader. We had unending opportunities to learn about leadership dynamics and skills the hard way and the best way—through practice.

One later encouragement specifically related to seminary teaching came when I was expected to help teach seminary students during my doctoral study. I was surprised to find myself in this unanticipated role and surprised to find myself thinking at the end of the semester, *I can imagine being a seminary professor.*

Examples of Christian Leadership I Could Embrace

This gift from the church saved me from cynicism about leadership. From counselors at our church camp in Michigan to Martin Luther King Jr., I saw effective leadership at work in many situations. I saw leaders who were persuasive, respectful, and compassionate. They exemplified integrity, were good listeners, could get groups to work together, were courageous in the face of unfair criticism, and were creative and thoughtful in connecting their Christian commitments with the way they led.

I saw enough of such leading styles that I developed a basically positive attitude toward leadership and its potential. As I moved into administrative assignments myself, I valued the leadership I saw and experienced while working with Don Ziegler at Mennonite Central Committee in Pennsylvania and Marlin Miller at the Associated Mennonite Biblical Seminary in Indiana. Both of these men understood and valued collegiality between women and men.

Early in life, I also learned that leadership initiatives in smaller groups are often shared among members even when one person is designated as leader. For years I practiced leadership in many settings in these informal ways.

While the Mennonite church gave me numerous positive examples of leadership, few of them were women. As a youth, I didn't know any women serving as pastors, congregational chairs, college religion teachers, seminary professors, or heads of church agencies, schools, or conferences. I never imagined becoming one of them.

I am grateful for the models of women in leadership that were in my view. I treasure them because they are few.

I remember Anna Juhnke, one of my Bethel College professors in Kansas. She combined profound Christian faith and incisive intellectual ability, while attending to both a professional career and family life. Her judgments about quality meant a great deal because they were never flattery. She modeled receptivity, not only to new ideas, but also to a transformed spirit before God and others.

Dorothy Nickel Friesen, a friend and colleague in the church for many years, modeled creative problem solving and offered the gift

of trustworthy counsel as we worked together in seminary administration.

Even now, however, I lament the scarcity of Mennonite women
mentors and peers for me in theological education and as a theologian of the church.

Extraordinary Practical Help and Care for a Young Family

This concrete assistance, some of it the gift of congregational
members and seminary students, made it possible for me to prepare
for and serve as a seminary professor and administrator.

From the beginning, Ted and I held equality and mutuality as
ideals in our marriage. We were committed to sharing responsibilities for our life together in mutually agreeable ways. We assumed
that it would be normal for me as well as Ted to have a Christian
vocation outside the home, and that we would find ways to work
out household and family life with this in mind.

We were married eleven years and had completed all formal
course work for our doctoral work before we added children to our
family. But during the next fifteen years, we received a variety of assistance. Some persons were hired and some were volunteer. They
extended our household in ways that made commitments to church
work and family life (usually) feasible.

Threaded into this web of support, our family was upheld by—

- a woman in our congregation who, having just retired, volunteered to care for our infant daughter half days for several
  months while we prepared thesis proposals.
- Ted's major professor, who offered him a research assistantship
  requiring minimal responsibility but providing us financial support for a year of doctoral research.
- a Mennonite neighbor, slightly disabled from a stroke, who
  cared for children, including one of ours, in her home in Indiana.
- a college student and several Mennonite Central Committee exchange visitors who lived in our home and helped with household work and childcare.
- two single seminary students who, in consecutive summers, each

cared for our children as Ted and I wrote our dissertations. They wanted the flexibility in their summer schedules that this job provided, but they were also motivated by a desire to support women in church leadership. They understood the difficulty of a pair of parents completing doctoral work.

- the Mennonite Biblical Seminary administration, which agreed to hire us in a joint appointment, counted us as full-time in relation to benefits (though each of us usually worked part-time), but permitted flexible hours. They hosted a cooperative child-care facility on campus. Also, they agreed to hire an assistant dean, so that when I became dean I could continue to teach during the year and be at home with our children during the summer months.
- my parents, who drove to spend time with our family and help with household projects. In 1990 they moved into our household and remained until their deaths in 1994 and 1995.
- members of the Hively congregation, where my parents attended. As my parents grew more frail and ill, a number of people in the congregation generously kept visiting, providing transportation, and staying with them when we could not be there ourselves and could not hire other assistance.
- friends, colleagues, and members of the small groups in our congregation, who have been sources of emotional and spiritual renewal and witnesses to the power of love and hope in Christ.

From a Distance

Dots and swirls of color as well as empty spaces mark the canvases of our lives. Whether up close or at a distance, we Christians interpret these mysteries in faith. Who can see a pattern? Who can see the artist at work?

Gayle Gerber Koontz

Nudged by God

LOIS BARRETT

LOIS BARRETT is executive secretary of the Commission on
Home Ministries, General Conference Mennonite Church,
Newton, Kansas. Earlier she was
pastor of Mennonite Church of
the Servant, Wichita, Kansas,
and served as associate editor of
The Mennonite.

She is author or coauthor of
six books. The latest is *Missional
Church: A Vision for the Sending
of the Church in North America*
(Eerdmans, 1998). Occasionally
she teaches history and theology
courses in the Great Plains Seminary Education Program, North Newton,
Kansas.

Lois holds a Ph.D. in historical theology from the Union Institute,
Cincinnati; an M.Div. from Mennonite Biblical Seminary, Elkhart, Indiana; and a B.A. from the University of Oklahoma, Norman, Oklahoma.

For twenty years, she has served the broader church on a variety of
committees. These include the Inter-Mennonite Confession of Faith Committee, the Joint Committee on Violence, the coordinating council of the
Gospel and Our Culture Network, the advisory council of the Institute
for Mennonite Studies, the committee for volume 5 of *The Mennonite
Encyclopedia,* the Mennonite Central Committee Peace Theology Working Group, and the steering committee of New Call to Peacemaking.

Lois and her husband, Thomas Mierau, live in Wichita, Kansas, and
have three children, Barbara, Susanna, and John.

IN MY YOUTH I never really considered becoming a minister. Even though my father was a minister and I had occasionally heard my mother "give the message," it never occurred to me that I should be a minister.

As a college freshman searching for a major, I took a vocational preference test. The results suggested that my personality resembled that of a history teacher or a nun. I presume in those days "minister" or "pastor" was not even on the test's list of vocations for women. I did not consider a church vocation because I had no intention of becoming a nun and I didn't think becoming a Protestant minister was an option.

The First Nudge

My first nudge in the direction of a church vocation came from a year spent in Mennonite Voluntary Service in Wichita, Kansas. That year marked my first involvement with a Mennonite congregation. I was glad to discover, during the midst of the Vietnam War, a church that not only had a pacifist view of war, but also had a theology in which to ground its peace stance.

More than that, I found a different understanding of the church from what I had known in the past. These Mennonites thought of themselves as a community of God's people, willing to give and receive counsel.

The next year I spent a semester at a seminary in Fort Worth, Texas, one of five full-time women students in a student body of two hundred. The classes were exciting, but I still couldn't envision myself as a pastor. I had no desire to be a pioneer, which a woman in ministry certainly was in 1970, in any denomination. But God had other plans in mind for me.

I came back to Wichita and entered an environment that was going to lead me into what I did not foresee—ministry in the church. Deciding to go to seminary ten years later was not exactly a precipitous decision. In fact, I kept talking about "going back to seminary someday."

Finally Tom, my husband, asked, "When are you going to quit talking about it and do it?"

"Next fall," I answered.

Wichita gave me opportunities to practice ministry and leadership skills. For seven years I was part of a small Christian intentional community where leadership was shared.

I was a charter member of Mennonite Church of the Servant, a congregation of house churches. I held a variety of leadership positions there in settings small enough not to be threatening. During the year before I returned to seminary, the pastor, David Habegger, supervised a pastoral internship for me and gave me encouragement and opportunities to practice tasks of ministry.

Trying to Be a Superwoman

My third baby was born in the middle of my first semester of study at Associated Mennonite Biblical Seminary in Elkhart, Indiana. I took him to class with me for five months as I juggled caring for three small children, taking three courses a semester, finishing writing a book, and chairing the seminary coop nursery committee.

I worried whether any congregation would ever call me to be its pastor, even with a graduate degree. During this time, I learned a lot and gained confidence for ministry. I thought, *I've got the same tools for biblical interpretation as every other seminary-trained pastor out there.* A Tuesday noon women's support group meeting at the seminary helped me to not feel alone.

However, I was trying to be superwoman and wasn't paying much attention to my physical or spiritual health. During my senior year, I developed hypoglycemia (low blood sugar). It took me five months to get it under control. During that time, I learned that to be well spiritually and physically, I had to set aside regular time for prayer and meditation. I couldn't claim that I didn't have time to pray. Prayer was a necessity.

Theology Follows Relationships

After graduation, I went back to Wichita to Mennonite Church of the Servant, the congregation that had sent me to seminary. Although I was later given the title *pastor*, my first title was *mentor*. The congregation was young, nontraditional, and informal.

The members were rather leery of any leadership. A woman pastor was not the issue. Instead, they debated leadership and structures, in the anti-authority stance of many baby boomers. This formed a marked cultural contrast with the area conference ministerial committees I needed to face to be licensed and ordained to ministry.

I remember a discussion about licensing and ordination interviews with Kansas Mennonite pastors. To the amazement of the women in the group, every man there said that his interview had been no big deal. None had doubted that the committee would approve him. For all of us women pastors, there had been a large measure of doubt. We had been asked questions we thought were inappropriate. We had been grilled and challenged. We had not been sure that we would be approved for ministry.

My licensing and ordination interviews with the Western District Conference ministerial committee were somewhat anxiety producing. But I was approved, and I thought that was the end of the ordeal. Mennonite Church of the Servant was affiliated with both the Western District Conference and the South Central Conference. The two conferences had a reciprocal agreement that each would honor the other's ministerial credentials. Thus pastors of dually affiliated congregations did not have to satisfy two committees.

However, there was a problem. South Central Conference had never had a woman pastor in its midst before. They had not expected that the reciprocal agreement with Western District Conference would bring them two new women pastors in one year.

On the same year Dorothy Nickel Friesen, then pastor in Manhattan, Kansas, and I were introduced as new pastors at South Central Conference. Some of the delegates got up and started protesting that having women as pastors was unbiblical. One of them accosted me in the hall between sessions with the admonition, "Don't take this personally."

South Central Conference decided to address the issue by holding a special session of conference on the subject of women in church leadership. The conference was put together well. It gave Dorothy and me opportunity to tell about our calls to ministry.

It also gave our congregations a chance to talk. Several people from Mennonite Church of the Servant came to the conference. However, because of the culture gap, I had a hard time convincing them that women in ministry was a problem for some people.

Paul M. Miller, who had once written a book advocating the

prayer covering for women, gave the biblical teaching and shared: "Every time I read the Bible, I receive new light. And on the issue of women in church leadership, I have received new light, brothers and sisters."

I learned that it was important to take this issue "personally." One of the members of our congregation reported on a conversation in his small-group discussion at the conference. A man in the group had gone on at some length with an abstract discussion of why women should not be in ministry.

Finally, in exasperation, the member from our church asked him, "Then do you think we should fire Lois?"

"Oh, no," he replied.

It dawned on me that the first step in helping people to accept women in ministry was not a theological discussion. Instead, the key was letting them get to know real women in ministry. When "women in ministry" was a general issue, this man was against it. When it was Dorothy and Lois, he could accept us as pastors in the South Central Conference. Theology often follows relationships.

Learning Leadership

The people of Mennonite Church of the Servant taught me a lot about what it means to be a pastor, even when they didn't want to give me the title. They helped me learn to receive from the congregation as well as give. I also learned that relationships with members of the congregation cannot always be as mutual as I had hoped, because I did have authority.

During the early years of my ministry at Mennonite Church of the Servant, all of us together were discovering a lot about prayer. We learned that no problem is too small to bring before God. We learned to pray for healing. We learned that God does answer prayer, sometimes in dramatic ways.

In one stimulating example, the congregation was offered a building—free. The building was usable, with some remodeling needed, but not in the right location. It was hidden from the main roads and hard to find. No one was sure how to respond. To heighten the pressure, the company offering the building gave us a deadline for the decision.

We met as a congregation and could not come to consensus.

Some wanted to take the building, some didn't, and others were un-decided. A few days later, we met again, with a different strategy. We would share any new information at the beginning of the meet-ing, then spend twenty minutes in silent prayer together before any further discussion.

At the end of the prayer time, each person in the circle shared. Amazingly, every person had come to the same conclusion. God had been at work among us! The experience was very energizing for the church and for our confidence that God was acting in our midst.

Another Nudge

When I felt it was time for me to leave my position as pastor of the congregation, I had a similar experience of God speaking in the midst of confusion. There was no open door for what I had pre-pared to do and for what I wanted to do. Even my second and third choices were falling through. My only job offers were part-time, and I wanted something full-time. If I had been male, would it have made a difference? I was discouraged.

One morning after Tom and the kids were gone, I sat down in the living room and prayed an angry and impolite prayer. I screamed at God, demanding a solution. Like the psalmist, I told God, "Wake up! Get with it!" I complained, "Look, I've been doing what I thought you wanted me to do. So why haven't you come through for me and provided me with a new job?"

At that moment, the doorbell rang. I dried my tears and opened the door. There were two Jehovah's Witnesses. They said, "We're here to teach people about the Bible."

Trying to get rid of them, I said, "That's nice. I'm a pastor, and I teach people about the Bible, too."

They saw that I was likely not a potential convert. As they pre-pared to leave, one of them said, "We'd like to leave a Scripture verse with you. Read Ephesians 2:17."

Immediately I had a clear sense that this verse had something to do with the new job I would have. I got my Bible and looked it up: "So [Christ] came and proclaimed peace to you who were far off and peace to those who were near." I didn't yet know how this re-lated to that new job, but I was certain it did. I was confident that God was going to take care of me.

What Keeps Me Going

A few weeks later, I was offered a full-time position as executive secretary of the Commission on Home Ministries (CHM) of the General Conference Mennonite Church. The job does involve proclaiming the gospel of peace across the United States and Canada, to those far off and those who are near.

I am the first woman to hold that position. Most of the time my gender is not an issue. The CHM staff is great to work with. But in other settings, I am often the only woman or one of only a few women in meetings. I've discovered that sometimes my gender makes me invisible when it comes to being consulted or assigned responsibilities. I know I view the mostly male meetings in a much different way than do the men.

Once I was one of two women at a meeting of a dozen or so mission executives. In the meeting, some of the men talked at length about how great the meeting was. They said they could really "let their hair down" in a group like this. Later, back in our room, the other woman and I agreed that such a group would be one of the last places where we would expect to feel as relaxed and supported as these men did.

I am able to "let my hair down" and get emotional and spiritual nurture from other women, and from groups within my home congregation. I have been particularly blessed by a Wednesday night prayer group. A lot of listening and praying and healing has happened there over the years. Such people, plus my family, keep me going. God keeps me going by answering prayer and turning problems into possibilities.

Within myself, what keeps me going is my love for the church. This is not a naive or glib statement. I have experienced plenty of pain in the church, because of my gender and also for other reasons. However, I have also experienced much healing within the church. I cannot imagine being anywhere else.

Even though I don't know the future of my service in the church, I trust that the God who has led me thus far will keep on leading me.

Lois Y. Barrett

Standing in the Gap
The Bible and Feminism

RETA HALTEMAN FINGER

RETA HALTEMAN FINGER teaches New Testament at Messiah College, Grantham, Pennsylvania, and lives in Harrisonburg, Virginia, with her husband, Tom Finger, who teaches theology at Eastern Mennonite Seminary.

She received her B.A. from Eastern Mennonite College, her M.A. in theological studies from Northern Baptist Seminary, and her Ph.D. from Northwestern University and Garrett Theological Seminary in Evanston, Illinois.

Reta wrote *Paul and the Roman House* 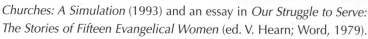 *Churches: A Simulation* (1993) and an essay in *Our Struggle to Serve: The Stories of Fifteen Evangelical Women* (ed. V. Hearn; Word, 1979).

Many of Reta's articles and book reviews have appeared in *Gospel Herald, The Mennonite, The Other Side,* and *Sojourners;* and in *Daughters of Sarah,* which Reta edited from 1979 to 1994.

The Fingers have two sons, Ted and Brent.

THE LETTER, from a Mennonite pastor and teacher I used to know in college, was addressed to me as editor of the Christian feminist magazine, *Daughters of Sarah.* "If you say you publish a Christian feminist magazine, why do you call yourselves 'daughters of Sarah'? According to 1 Peter 3:5-6, Sarah obeyed Abraham and called him lord. That certainly doesn't sound like what you are promoting."

In the Image of God

It was a typical question directed toward the mission of our magazine. Before I responded, I looked up the text anyhow. The meaning seemed quite clear. In the context of telling wives to submit to the authority of their husbands, the author of 1 Peter uses the weight of sacred Hebrew Scripture to convince Christian women of his churches to obey their husbands:

> It was in this way long ago that the holy women who hoped in God used to adorn themselves by accepting the authority of their husbands. Thus Sarah obeyed Abraham and called him lord.

For anyone seeking a proof text to keep women in their place, this statement is perfect. The hitch is that we have the same access to ancient Scripture as Peter did. We can read Genesis and reflect on *how* these holy women like Sarah, Rebekah, and Rachel obeyed their husbands. When we do so, we find a blurring of the prescription identifying absolute right and wrong in their marital relationships.

For better or worse, Sarah managed her own household without a lot of input from Abraham. Genesis 16:2 says he "listened to" his wife's voice, and in 21:12, God tells Abraham, "Whatever Sarah says to you, do as she tells you."

Rebekah's plan of manipulating and deceiving her blind husband in Genesis 27 succeeds. In Genesis 30, Jacob's wives, Leah and Rachel, treat him merely as a sex object in their childbearing contest. The "holy women" of Peter's Scriptures had a curious way of accepting the authority of their husbands!

Such tension occurs here and there between certain prescriptive texts in the canonical epistles and narrative accounts in both testaments of the Bible. In 1 Corinthians 11:7, Paul alludes to Genesis 1:26-27 and says that "a man" is "the image and reflection of God." But the original Genesis text says that *both* "male and female" humankind are made "in the image of God."

Here Paul completely changes the thrust of the Old Testament Scripture to strengthen his argument that Corinthian women ought to wear something on their heads for worship. This is an interpretive method we would not consider appropriate today.

Interpreting the Sacred Texts

I did not learn about these scriptural tensions from my parents, Wilmer and Perle Halteman; nor at Salford Mennonite Church and Sunday school in Harleysville, Pennsylvania; nor at Christopher Dock Mennonite High School and Eastern Mennonite College. What I did learn, however, was a comprehensive knowledge of the Bible and a great love for it that has never let me go.

I knew little about the range of methods for interpreting the Bible until I was in my thirties. Yet I often took Scripture texts to mean something different from what others understood. My father was an ardent (though not rigid) premillennialist in a church of amillennialists, an original thinker despite his lack of formal education. Unless we avoided a religious discussion, few evening meals would go by without a trip to the bookcase for a Bible, concordance, Bible atlas, commentary, or the *Martyrs Mirror*.

Daddy was never afraid to point out religious fallacies promoted by our preachers, the Sunday school quarterly, or even the bishop! He could demolish a church pillar's theology faster than he could polish off Mom's fried potatoes. However, it was all done in a good-natured and humorous way. Daddy never undermined our warmth or respect for Elias Landis, Rein Alderfer, Henry Ruth, or John E. Lapp as persons. From this experience, I learned that one can debate and argue ideas without lobbing personal attacks onto others.

Thus it has happened that from childhood, I have embraced what most people find to be peculiar and mutually exclusive. Christians or non-Christians, feminists or non-feminists, and liberal or conservative—many disagree with me. Yet every cell in my body is unalterably feminist, *and* I possess an equal passion to understand the Bible as the story of God's people and the good news on which we base our faith and hope in eternal life.

I believe these two positions are inseparable. The nature of the gospel itself is radically egalitarian. Nevertheless, most people on both the religious right and left, now and throughout church history, have had a hard time grasping that. Hence the vital importance of properly interpreting and applying our sacred texts.

Into the Foray

Ironically, my first introduction to the current wave of Christian feminism came through the Mennonite church and in the *Gospel Herald*. In 1972-73 my husband, baby son, and I were living in Germany. In January of 1973, our church publication had printed Phyllis Pellman Good's one-page article on "Woman's Place." It challenged sex-stereotyped occupations in a way that instinctively resonated with me.

I was marveling that the Mennonite church was taking so broadminded an approach. Then I started reading the barrage of angry letters blasting Good's thesis. What ignited the fire in my belly was the way these letter writers quoted Scripture (wildly out of context). They tried to show that since God intended for women to be "weaker vessels," they couldn't possibly be electricians, carpenters, or tillers of the ground. They claimed that Phyllis had a "severe inferiority complex."

With this provocation to my feminist instincts and my Bible, I determined to find out what the New Testament actually did say about gender roles. I searched for English resources in a German library.

Study and reflection eventually resulted in two articles to the *Gospel Herald:* "A Woman's Place Is in Christ" (Jan. 14, 1975), and "Who Does the Dirty Work in the Kingdom?" (June 24, 1975). My biblical feminist writing career, such as it was, was taking off—and now the angry letters were directed at me!

By the fall of 1976, through circumstances I could never have planned, I began doing volunteer work for the infant newsletter *Daughters of Sarah*. By this time my husband and two small boys and I had moved to Chicago. Thus I began eighteen years of centering my work energies around that publication, including fifteen years as its editor. I saw it grow from an eight-page newsletter to a quarterly magazine of sixty-four pages.

Learning to Think Biblically in Creative Ways

Working for *Daughters of Sarah* was anything but lucrative. I could never have done it without my husband's full-time teaching job and our simple standard of living. Yet there were considerable perks.

For one thing, there were my co-workers. Our organization attracted bright, articulate, thinking women, full of humor and often
bossy, pushy, or assertive. Their passion for promoting Christian
feminism equaled mine. They told sad stories of struggles with Fun-
damentalism, racism, sex discrimination in church or workplace,
and marital abuse. Their experiences were far more traumatic than
mine.

Friendships were forged during our office hours, monthly pot-
luck-and-discussion meetings, and three-hour editorial meetings.
These have proved to be some of the most stimulating and enduring
relationships I have ever known.

The second perk was ecumenicity. A wide range of denominations was represented by our local group and our subscribers. Over
the years, our core people hailed from denominations as varied as
Evangelical Covenant, Assemblies of God, Baptist, Methodist,
Lutheran, Roman Catholic, Wesleyan Methodist, Christian Reformed, Seventh-Day Adventist, Plymouth Brethren, Church of the
Brethren, and Mennonite.

I thrived on this variety. I had grown up culturally sheltered in the
Franconia Mennonite community of southeastern Pennsylvania
during the 1940s and 1950s. I had attended Mennonite schools
from first grade through college, followed by three years as dean of
girls at Eastern Mennonite High School.

By 1965 I had overdosed on Mennos and needed a wider world.
This drive led me to Gordon Divinity School (now Gordon-Conwell
Seminary) and Boston University in New England, a whole new ge-
ographical and cultural region for me. I worked as assistant dean of
students at a Roman Catholic women's college in Massachusetts.

Then in 1969, I married Tom Finger, a seminarian of no particu-
lar denomination, whom I had met at Gordon. He thought of
Menno Simons as a hayseed farmer with pitchfork, suspenders, and
Amish hat—until my father set him straight with the right books on
Anabaptists.

Not till 1980 did Tom make his decision to join the Mennonite
Church. We began attending the tiny Oak Park Mennonite congregation. During those intervening years, I had enjoyed wandering
from state to state and church to church. I found rich spiritual sustenance in other places, even though I was convinced that as an eth-

nic Mennonite, I could never be anything else.

I clung fiercely to Anabaptist values of community, peacemaking, simple lifestyle, and a nonhierarchical tradition of leadership. Though proud of my Mennonite heritage, I could appreciate my denomination better when I wasn't close enough to see all its warts and blind spots.

For a number of years, *Daughters of Sarah* became my church in a more meaningful way than the worship services we attended on Sundays. Within this circle of women, I grew theologically and ethically, learning to be accountable to others, to debate ideas with diverse people, to participate in stimulating Bible studies, and to articulate my Christian feminism in reader-friendly ways.

The third perk was the interdisciplinary nature of *Daughters of Sarah*. I had a passion for making intellectual and practical connections, and integrating thinking and doing. From its beginnings, our newsletter shone its feminist lens on biblical, historical, and social questions.

Usually we chose a different theme for each issue, and then sought material that was biblical, historical, and personal-social. We insisted that no topic was off-limits, whether abortion, incest, sexuality, witchcraft and goddess religions, or whatever. The crucial thing was *how* we handled it. I was constantly challenged to think biblically in creative ways about feminist issues. One cannot honestly deal with women and the Bible without confronting a range of methods of biblical interpretation.

Clearly, the message of our Scriptures is not uniform when it comes to women's status in church and society. The biblical documents have emerged from highly patriarchal cultures, and they reflect androcentric assumptions. What kind of "hermeneutical circle" can rightfully exist between feminist theory and biblical interpretation?

Standing in the Gap Editorially

Two important things became clear to me as I wrestled with these issues. First, most Christian women had no expertise in this area and were hard pressed even to see the problems. Some with backgrounds more evangelical stressed egalitarian emphases in the Bible and tended to play down patriarchy. Others with a less biblically based orientation were often poorly informed about the content of Scripture. They paid little attention to it, or were selective about what they emphasized.

A typical approach was to contrast Jesus as a liberator of women against Paul as a misogynist. Similar attitudes existed toward theology. Often women were ignorant of various denominational theologies not immediately supportive of women or impatient with such church stances.

I often saw my role in these discussions and arguments as standing in the gap—helping people not throw out too much baby with the bath water. In our editorial practice, when we could not agree, we would publish a range of positions on a particular topic. However, I often had to struggle with how wide a range I could live with.

For example, in 1992 Joanne Carlson Brown sent us an article asserting that Jesus' death was essentially child abuse—God killing God's only child. My first reaction was to groan, "Give me a break!" Yet other women seemed to be taking Brown seriously. So we printed four different responses to her article, offering opinions on the meaning of atonement through Christ.

Before that, our biggest theological tussles had been over a 1983 issue called "Unveiling the Goddess" and a two-issue series on lesbians in 1988. However, by 1994 we were enmeshed in the controversy surrounding the Re-Imagining Conference at Minneapolis in the preceding fall. As a Christian feminist, it was the worst polarization I had ever seen involving feminism and the mainline U.S. churches.

Conservative wings of Presbyterian and Methodist denominations ranted on about the non-Christian heresies and rank lesbianism promoted at Re-Imagining. Feminist attendees raved about the wonderful spirit of acceptance and openness and truthfulness the conference had exemplified.

Most of the editorial board of *Daughters of Sarah* believed we had an ideological commitment to support Re-Imagining and all those who had been hurt by the conservative fallout. I could not agree. I certainly was thoroughly disgusted at the knee-jerk Fundamentalist rhetoric against Re-Imagining. Yet I thought we had a journalistic and theological responsibility to critique what had been said there.

I had not been able to attend, but I listened to all the tapes of plenary addresses and worship services. Much was inspiring and creative and not against Christian theology. Nevertheless, a few speeches had pushed far beyond the bounds, moving into religious syncretism and sometimes scorn for an exclusive Christian faith.

In my opinion, that syncretism needed to be challenged openly in our magazine. However, I was strongly opposed by some. Once again, I was standing in the gap and appreciated by neither those on the right or the left.

The second thing these theological struggles impressed upon me was my ignorance of biblical interpretation and theology, and my passion to understand them better. By taking one seminary course a term at Northern Baptist Seminary, where Tom was teaching, I received my master of arts in theological studies in 1987. I wrote my thesis on Elisabeth Schüssler Fiorenza's biblical feminist hermeneutics.

However, I was not sure about a doctoral program. The road seemed too long and hard. Would I really need it?

The Academic Leap

Geography again intervened in 1989, when Tom was hired at Eastern Mennonite Seminary, in Virginia. I had to do some long-distance, monthly commuting to keep both my *Daughters of Sarah* job and some semblance of family life. But I soon realized this arrangement could not work forever.

By now I was in my late forties. As my fiftieth birthday loomed, I pondered my situation. I was healthy, energetic, and I loved life. I planned to live to a be hundred—at least! If I quit editing *Daughters of Sarah* and moved to Harrisonburg, what would I do with the second half of my life?

How could I get another job using my interests in Bible, theology, feminism, writing, and editing? Would I have to settle for office work? Go back to elementary school teaching, my college major? Or just wither on the vine and feel worthless?

I concluded that I had lived only half my life. If I didn't take the leap now, I knew I never would. So I applied to doctoral programs in New Testament, choosing the joint program in theological and religious studies of Garrett Seminary and Northwestern University in Evanston, Illinois.

Yes, the journey was long and hard, and I didn't finish writing my dissertation until the fall of 1997. But I never regretted my choice for a minute. The program centered my life around my passions and gave me a goal to work for. (Maybe I'll shoot for 110 years instead of merely 100!)

In 1995 I was hired to teach New Testament at Messiah College, a Brethren in Christ institution near Harrisburg, Pennsylvania. I commute three hours each way once a week. But that seems like small potatoes compared to the nineteen-hour train trip I used to take between Chicago and Harrisonburg.

Called to Stand in the Gap

However, a funny thing happened on the way to teaching undergraduates at Messiah. In my Chicago milieu as a *Daughter of Sarah* and member of Oak Park Mennonite Church, I often felt like the last conservative holdout. After all, what cutting-edge postmodern person would take the Bible that seriously anymore?

However, at Messiah I soon discovered that students generally viewed me as a flaming radical. Simply being a woman teaching Bible threatened some of the male students, especially freshmen.

An anonymous note from the roommate of one student blasted my Romans textbook. He thought it absolutely "bizarre" that Phoebe in Romans 16:1-2 should be considered a leader in the early church, since women by nature could never take that role.

My attempts to use race, class, or gender analysis on biblical texts thoroughly bewildered my first class on introduction to the Bible. The chair of my department received a long letter from a couple who were youth leaders in a local Evangelical Free church.

The letter included a *Daughters of Sarah* article I had written in 1987, heavily underlined to show him how heretical I was. The writers said they could only hope and pray that Messiah did not know what I was like before they hired me!

A copy of the same article was briefly pinned to the student opinion board, along with some nasty comments, until some faculty or administrator mercifully removed it. I was accused of teaching that "God is a woman, and Jesus is a woman" (which I don't) and of making students buy an NRSV Bible with the (noncanonical) Apocrypha (which I do).

It was good I'd had practice standing in the gap and getting along with people with whom I don't agree. In this case, the students were near one end of an ideological spectrum, my Chicago friends at the other end, and I was in the middle.

I also had to learn that eighteen-year-olds don't have much life experience. Many are not yet developmentally able to do much critical thinking. In the three years I've been at Messiah, I've learned to soften the rhetoric. I hope I still encourage young women to be all God means them to be, and still challenge those ready to listen and grow.

At the 1998 commencement, two male graduates personally expressed appreciation for how I had helped them change their minds about women's leadership in the church. And (though I don't know if this is good or bad) my most recent student evaluations contained not one criticism about my "heretical" feminist persuasions.

It is never easy to stand in the gap between the traditional and the cutting edge. But it can be fun—and sometimes even downright funny! Nevertheless, it is a biblical practice to learn to get along with people when we don't agree, while debating intensely at the same time. Most of the New Testament documents were written out of experiences of conflict and offer exhortations toward unity and accommodation.

In any case, I feel I am called to such oddball, standing-in-the-gap places—even if I do live to be 110!

Reta Halteman Finger

Pastors

Like good stewards
of the manifold grace of God,
serve one another
with whatever gift
each of you has received.

—*Peter, in 1 Peter 4:10*

Pioneer Pastor

EMMA SOMMERS RICHARDS

Eᴍᴍᴀ Rɪᴄʜᴀʀᴅs carries the distinction of being the first Mennonite woman to be ordained into pastoral ministry in the Mennonite Church of North America. She was installed as copastor of Lombard Mennonite Church in October 1972, and ordained to the Christian ministry by Illinois Mennonite Conference in June 1973.

For twenty years Emma pastored the Lombard congregation with her husband, Joe, and also served with Joe for two years as Illinois conference ministers. In June 1998, she was honored for twenty-five years of pastoral ministry.

During earlier years, Emma taught various levels of school. She and Joe served as missionaries in Japan with Mennonite Board of Missions in 1954-66. Emma has been a member of the Mennonite Church General Board and its Executive Committee; has chaired the Mennonite Church's Council for Faith, Life, and Strategy; and has served as president of Illinois Mennonite Conference. For six years she also chaired the churchwide Women in Leadership Ministries Committee.

Emma earned a B.A. from Goshen College, a B.D. from Goshen Biblical Seminary, and a Master of Education degree from St. Francis College, Fort Wayne.

She continues to teach Sunday school, preach occasionally, and is currently preparing a paper for the 150-year historical celebration of her home church—Howard-Miami Mennonite near Kokomo, Indiana. Emma was honored as Pastor Emerita of Lombard Mennonite Church in 1991, and chosen Alumna of the Year at Goshen College in 1994.

The Richards have three children, Evan, Kathryn, and Lois; and nine grandchildren. Emma's special interests include Japanese cooking, flower arranging, and reading historical novels, biographies, and devotional materials.

WHEN I WAS a little girl, I was quite shy. I had to be encouraged to take something to a neighbor or to attend a birthday party. My older sister, Elaine, would take me by the hand after promising, "Yes, I'll do all the talking." I also recall hearing my mother say to my grandmother, "Emma is timid, but she'll grow out of it." Yes and no: my mother was partly correct.

For instance, in a group of persons discussing recent gardening experiences, I'd be too timid to share mine. But when an issue is on the floor that has far-reaching consequences, I can confront.

During my teaching years, I was on a curriculum committee to help select a new language arts series for the school district. The assistant superintendent (persuaded by a cutesy, flattering saleswoman) was ready to recommend what, in my opinion, was the least-desirable series. I spoke up. With the support of the other committee members, another series was selected.

How Did I Become a Pioneer Female Pastor?

In recent years, I have served on church boards, committees, and programs, which may have given me the reputation of speaking out and confronting. So my mother was partly correct. Over the years I have grown out of some of my timidity. Yet how did I ever get into the pioneer situation of female pastoral ministry?

On some levels, I'm not sure I have it all figured out. As I moved through various stages of ministry, I was confident that I was on the inside of God's will for me. That was important, and it gave me calm confidence.

In 1971 the Lombard Mennonite Church began processing my role in pastoral ministry. By then, I had college and seminary degrees and had served for twelve years as a missionary under Mennonite Board of Missions in Japan. I had experience in teaching, marriage, parenting, and two years of supplying the pulpit in a Presbyterian church with my husband, Joe.

This may look like a fair amount of experience, but I was really a novice. How was I to survive? How do pioneers survive? I concluded that pioneers survive by being prepared and keeping their eyes on the next step, thus avoiding ruts or snakes in the grass. They lift their gaze to the winding far-off trail, confident of the overarching sky of God's providence.

Early Decisions

As a way of being prepared, I made some basic decisions early in my ministry. When the going got tough, these decisions turned out to be quite helpful for me, and I trust others may find some of them helpful also. I recognize that time keeps changing, so some of my approaches may seem out of step to readers today. However, this was my experience. My notes, letters, sermons, and journals show the following nine decisions repeatedly emerging:

1. I purposed to keep up-to-date my inner resources and my devotional and listening life. I could not let the well run dry. For years I arose between four and five each morning to read, pray, write, think, and commune with God. Friends, books, my husband, continued studies, and retreats were also good resources. So were Bible reading, prayer, and meditation. These resources helped me greatly in my purpose to live a holy life, loving and doing good.

2. I determined to interpret the agenda before me in terms of the congregation rather than focusing on myself. I view pastors as shepherds and priests, bridge builders between the people and God. I purposed to love the congregation, its people, and its mission, and to show that in words and actions. I led with this approach.

3. I tried to be positive and forward-looking. Joe was quite helpful to me in this. At times, it would have been so easy to complain and blame, but that would have destroyed me and my role.

4. I promised my family and the congregation that they would not find themselves as illustrations in my preaching and teaching. I stuck to that, and it was freeing for everyone. However, I lost some excellent sermon material! Along with that, Joe and I set a climate of family involvement in church but did not promote our children as performers in services. They were active teenagers in the church, but at the initiative of the youth leaders or someone else in the congregation. Today our children thank us for that.

5. I tried to act and dress to fit my role as a pastor in the Mennonite Church. How? Some cues I carried along from being a speech teacher: "Never dress or wear anything that takes the attention of your audience away from what you want them to hear."

After preaching at a Mennonite General Assembly, I was accused in a church paper of wearing dangling earrings (another reason why we shouldn't have women pastors). I have never worn dangling earrings. This was in my pre-bifocal days, when I wore a chain on my glasses—what this writer saw. I could have worn a ribbon attached to my glasses, but some might have seen "covering strings" and been critical. We can't win them all!

6. I purposed to stay in the local congregation rather than accept invitations to preach and lead studies on the role of women. By staying and keeping my focus there, I could do more to show that the fears of having a woman pastor were unfounded. These fears included dire predictions that attendance would decline, men wouldn't come to worship or go to a female pastor for help, and so on. By staying in the local congregation where my support was high, I could allay those fears. All of those projections proved untrue.

7. I tried to preach well-prepared, mostly expository sermons, keeping Jesus central in sermons and worship. This included—

• Preaching Old Testament sermons in light of Jesus and the new covenant.

• Using inclusive, nonsexist language, following guidelines of the National Council of Teachers of English, to avoid the awkward and ridiculous church language prevalent in the 1970s.

• Using biblical women in illustrations as a teaching device, such as the woman Sheerah of 1 Chronicles 7:24, who built three cities. I cited her in a sermon on the rock-and-sand builders of Matthew 7. With such illustrations, I usually gave the biblical references so listeners could check it out for themselves.

• Following the old seminary acronym ACTS for public prayer: Adoration, Confession, Thanksgiving, and Supplication. I always thanked God for Jesus and acknowledged the guiding presence of the Holy Spirit, thus avoiding a prayer that could pass as Jewish or Buddhist.

8. I purposed to be an Anabaptist-Mennonite pastor through teaching, supporting, and living. This meant supporting and promoting the Illinois Mennonite Conference, our church schools, missions, publications, and faith positions like peace, discipleship, and believers baptism.

9. Most of all, I purposed that people would see Jesus through my life and ministry. What would Jesus do? What did Jesus teach? Answers aren't always easy to find. Jesus was both loving and stern, accepting and rejecting, gentle and forceful. One needs great wisdom and Holy Spirit guidance to say what Jesus would do in current situations. Yet we remember that Jesus died for us!

In keeping Jesus central, I found it easier to avoid faddish emphases that whirled around society and the church. During the years I preached, some of these emphases included—

• Do your own thing, women's lib, and the civil rights movement.
• Strong charismatic emphasis affecting music and worship styles.
• Liberation theology and activist forms of justice.
• Spirituality which may or may not be Christian.
• Entertainment worship and the feel-good syndrome.

I tried to keep Jesus and the good news central. That way, the church and the preacher can be rescued from being captive to psychology and cultural trends rather than to Christ and the gospel.

During a devotional at a Mennonite Church General Board meeting, I heard Ruth Lesher share an experience. They were visiting friends on the Western plains. In that great expanse, a fence surrounded the house. "Why," Ruth asked, "with all this lovely space, did you put up a fence? What are you keeping in or out?"

"No," the friend replied, "it is to give our children freedom. Now they know how far they can run and play without getting lost. The fence gives them freedom."

How true! I am glad for fences, for boundaries. They have set me free!

Many Blessings

Looking back from this vantage point, I am grateful for many blessings that put the negative in the shade. First, I am thankful that the Lombard congregation and Illinois Mennonite Conference went through the proper Mennonite Church channels for my ordination, even though it took two years of study and debate.

I am thankful for the many people who encouraged me to use my gifts. Only God knows how much my husband did and is responsible for. Also, our children helped in practical ways, and the Lombard congregation seemed to be confident in the bold step it took.

I am grateful to my parents and the congregation (Howard-Miami Mennonite) that nurtured me in my growing-up years. I am grateful for our church schools I attended. I am grateful for women who have taken on the work of pastoral and leadership ministries with integrity and skill. I am grateful for church leaders who trusted me in my role.

I am thankful that I was an advocate for abused women and that I believed them before it was a thing to talk about. This also gave me insights into ways to protect myself from possible accusations or harassment.

Finally, I am deeply grateful for the confidence I have that Jesus has been near me and that the Holy Spirit has guided me. I did not experience doubts in what I was doing. I have been free. I am so grateful for the overarching grace and mercy of God, who came to me in Jesus Christ!

The High Step

There are so many stories; here's one. As I was coming down from a platform after preaching to a large group, a man found himself caught in front of me, with no escape. He said, "Nice sermon. I suppose your husband prepared it for you."

Meekly, I replied, "No, I did it." But in my reflections, I have answered that man many more times!

A Japanese expression *shikii ga takai* means "the threshold is high." It refers to the entrance of a Japanese home, where you remove your shoes and take a high step up to the main level. For me, the threshold was high, but upheld by God's grace and mercy through Jesus. I took the high step. To God be the glory through Jesus Christ. *Amen!*

Emma E. Richards

By the Grace of God

GRACE BRUNNER

GRACE BRUNNER and her husband, Paul, are interim pastors at Blooming Glen (Pa.) Mennonite Church in the Franconia Conference. Together they have completed other interim pastoral assignments: Zurich (Ont.) Mennonite Church; codirecting the pastoral ministries program at Hesston College; Trinity Mennonite, Hillsboro, Kansas; Trinity Mennonite, Phoenix, Arizona; and Tabor Mennonite, Newton, Kansas.

As a member of the Mennonite Church's Board of Education, Grace is working on the interim joint projects committee with three members from her board and three from the Higher Education Commission of the General Conference Mennonite Church. They represent and develop higher education projects, anticipating integration of the two denominations.

Grace earned an Associate degree at Eastern Mennonite College and a B.S. in Education at Goshen College. She spent eight years as president of Women's Missionary and Service Commission. She was a member of the Mennonite Church General Board for some years, and was also on the nominating committee for the MCGB.

The Brunners served in long-term pastorates at Wooster (Ohio) Mennonite Church; Zion Mennonite, Hubbard, Oregon; Whitestone Mennonite, Hesston, Kansas; and Beech Mennonite, Louisville, Ohio. Grace was ordained at the Beech Mennonite Church in 1989.

Grace and Paul have two children, Beverly and Jon Scott, and five grandchildren.

T HE STORY I am telling is mine, and yet I do not own it. The story belongs to God, a God who loves to give gifts, who loves to impart grace.

Grace is the name my parents gave me—the fifth child in a family of seven. Along with my siblings and parents, our family consisted of my mother's parents and a woman who worked part-time for us. Our house was full and busy and mostly a happy place. In Kitchener, Ontario, we lived a few blocks from the large, thriving First Mennonite Church—a church that was part of my family as well, because my father was the pastor.

Growing Up a Preacher's Kid

While growing up as a preacher's kid, I was not subjected to many of the restrictions in the Mennonite Church at that time. However, I could not wear slacks, I had long hair, and I faithfully wore my covering following my baptism. Dad believed in reaching people for Jesus Christ more than he did in making them follow the rules.

The workings of the church were carried out by the men in the congregation. Dad had a deacon, who helped him in worship and visitation. Our chorister was also a man. When the church council came into being, they were mostly men.

There was one departure from this norm. My father ordained a deaconess, who helped him in visiting and counseling women. The women of the church basically used their gifts in Sunday school, Bible school, and preparing those wonderful meals for which Mennonite women are famous. I found myself sharing my gifts within those parameters.

I had a tremendous drive to experience life, but that drive was also tempered by a deep spirituality. Early in life, I came to realize that my calling would involve my total lifework. I was not sure what that would be, but I knew the depth of the involvement.

In my freshman year of high school, I left the city high school and transferred to Rockway Mennonite. This school setting was a large farmhouse, and the forty students had great times of study and fun as we worked, ate, and played together.

In my junior year, I transferred to Eastern Mennonite High School (EMHS) in Harrisonburg, Virginia, and for that opportunity I am forever grateful to my parents. No high school student in our area had done such a thing, but I was given the freedom to go.

My years at EMHS introduced me to a whole new aspect of spirituality that included rules and regulations about dress and conduct. Because I wanted to be there, I conformed. The experience was mostly good for me. I believe the only negative was that I found myself becoming a bit judgmental of others who did not conform to the "proper standards."

Following graduation from high school, I entered Eastern Mennonite College (EMC), also at Harrisonburg. Instead of going back to Canada that summer, I spent those months in voluntary service. The next summer I also remained in the U.S., working at the Mennonite Publishing House in Scottdale, Pennsylvania. Those experiences gave me new insights into the workings of the Mennonite Church. They also enlarged my concept of service.

During my years at EMC, there was a strong emphasis on service and evangelism. I found myself taking part in many outreach activities. We didn't spend a lot of time deciding who would do what as we prepared to go out to serve. We knew the women would tell the children's story and help with the singing. The men would read Scripture and preach. At that time there was a clear understanding of what women did and what men did. Since we didn't have any other model, we followed protocol.

Those years also nurtured me spiritually and deepened within me a sense of the calling on my life. At college I became aware that I was to be a pastor's wife. I didn't have any idea whom I would marry, but I knew my life would continue to be in the pastoral setting.

My father was a positive role model for me as he ministered through the years. Along with my mother, he made the pastoral setting such an enjoyable experience that I found myself challenged and excited about continuing that journey.

After two years at EMC, I went home, planning to work in our local hospital. During that year of work, I began to feel that this was not what I was to continue doing and I should go back to college. That fall I went to Goshen (Indiana) College to complete my degree in secondary education.

In my senior year there, Paul Brunner came to the seminary to prepare for ministry. We began dating and by spring were engaged. We married in the summer of 1954. That fall I began teaching school while Paul finished seminary studies.

Women Can't Even Count Ballots

Our first pastorate was in Wooster, Ohio. I remember those as learning years. Two children came to us and kept me busy. I also did quite a bit of substitute teaching as well as teaching in the Sunday school and Bible school.

During those years, the whole idea of small groups surfaced. I remember writing a letter to my mother about the small group we were forming. She wrote back and cautioned me about such things. She just wasn't sure it was a good idea for women to be sharing so intimately.

Our church continued to be led by men. The elders were all men, and most of the church council as well. The worship leaders and the choristers were also men. At that point in my life, it was okay.

As women, we seemed to find our fulfillment in leadership with the WMSC (Women's Missionary and Service Commission) and other organizations for women. We didn't spend much time thinking of taking leadership in areas that were "for the men." We certainly didn't think of being pastors.

Our second pastorate was at Zion Mennonite Church in Hubbard, Oregon. What a wonderful part of God's earth! We built our first and only new home and settled into the ministry there. Again, I found myself doing what I enjoyed most—teaching, forming small groups for Bible study, entertaining, and substituting in our children's local school.

Soon after arriving in Oregon in 1966, something began to happen within me. I noticed that women in our church were not being used to their potential because they were women. Women were not permitted to teach in mixed-class settings, and not allowed to be commission chairs. These women had gifts to be leaders. At the same time, I saw less-capable men being put into those positions. I had some strong feelings about that.

It all came to a head one day during a business meeting. They called for several people to count the ballots—and they were all men. Something popped inside me. I remember muttering to the woman next to me, "We can't even count ballots!"

Will There Ever Be a Day When My Gifts Will Be Used in a Church Setting?

During this Oregon pastorate, I was asked to serve on the commission on family life for the Pacific Coast Conference. James Lapp chaired that commission, and he had a way of making people feel valued. He listened as I shared, and he encouraged me. I would go home from those meetings feeling invigorated and challenged. I worked with that commission for several years. It birthed some new directions for my life.

One of these new directions was to serve on the conference WMSC. Through this position, I traveled, led meetings and workshops, and grew in ability to take leadership. All of that leadership, however, continued to be outside the local church setting.

Paul was deeply involved in a number of churchwide and college boards. He would fly to some meeting about once a month. I would pack his bags, make sure he got to the airport on time, and take care of things at home while he was away.

I especially remember one day when I was getting his things ready. All of a sudden I stopped and said to him, "I wonder if there will ever be a day when I will fly away to some meeting. Will there ever be a time when my gifts will be used in a churchwide setting?" As I sit and write about that now, it brings tears to my eyes. I remember the longing in my heart to serve in new ways.

After nine years in Oregon, we moved to Hesston, Kansas, where Paul pastored the Whitestone Mennonite Church. While there, I became the church secretary and edited the church paper. Those in leadership positions in the church were still mostly men.

I wanted to do more and to use my abilities in new areas. In retrospect, I realize that I was bound because I still held rather strongly to the conviction that women were not to take leadership when men were there to do it. Even in the early years at Whitestone (1975-77), I did not teach any classes when men were a part of the class.

It took some years for me to rethink my position—years, and hours of discussions with friends. I began to take a new look at the place of women in the church and how they might be called to use their gifts.

Nurtured by WMSC

In the latter years at Whitestone (1979-80), I began to teach integrated Sunday school classes. During our years at Hesston, I was asked to become the WMSC president for our denomination. The decision to accept that position was another life-changing one for me. On the WMSC board, I was mostly working with women who were professionals. The experience gave me new avenues to express myself and a new acceptance of my gifts.

I traveled around the country, leading WMSC meetings, seminars, and retreats for women—and I loved it! Because of my position, I even found myself bringing the morning message in several churches.

Following our years in Hesston, we spent a refreshing semester at Associated Mennonite Biblical Seminary (AMBS, Elkhart, Ind.) before going on to our next assignment. I saw the seminary modeling the use of men and women according to their gifts, not their gender!

At that time the broader church was in a struggle over the issue of women in leadership. Opinions were strong, and I found myself caught somewhere between camps. I was sorry that there was so much hurt involved and that the issue could not be solved in a less-stressful way.

People must recognize the place of WMSC in nurturing leadership skills of women across the church. WMSC called forth women and empowered them to serve and use their gifts in ways not yet possible in other church settings. WMSC helped prepare many of the women who are now in leadership positions in the Mennonite Church.

Women were the ones who dialogued with me about leadership and talked honestly about issues. They helped me move off center and cheered me on as doors opened for me.

From the seminary, we moved to Ohio to pastor the Beech Mennonite Church. The Ohio Conference was quite open to the use of women in leadership. Several women had already been called as pastors for churches in our area. The Beech church was also open to women's gifts and wanted their pastor's wife to actively participate. At my request, they drew up a job description for me and empowered me to do some of the things I really enjoyed doing.

A Pact with God

Coming into the Ohio Conference was like having someone tell me, "Grace, whoever you are, come out of the box." People were called because of their gifts, and I experienced a new sense of freedom to be who I am.

I became a part of the conference leadership commission and found myself preaching in a number of congregations. I remember telling the conference minister, Wilmer Hartman, that since I was not a minister, perhaps I should not be preaching. He affirmed my gifts and told me he thought I was already using the gifts of a pastor and should be recognized as such. In many ways, Wilmer became an advocate for me, as well as for other women in the conference.

In our Ohio experience, my longings "to fly away" and experience working on churchwide committees came to fruition. I was asked by the conference to be their representative on the Mennonite Church General Board, and I also served on the nominating committee.

As my job with WMSC drew to a close, I began to wonder just what I would do with my extra time. I contemplated a job, perhaps teaching again. One day, as I walked down Schmucker Drive between high rows of corn, I began to pray about my future. As I strolled, I clearly heard a word from God: I was to become a pastor.

I could not believe the message and began to cry. I found myself saying to God, "That will never happen!" On that walk, I made a pact with God—something I do not do lightly. I told God that if I was to become a pastor along with my husband, it would be the doing of God and not me. I would not tell the people around me, not even my husband, of that calling.

Later, one of the elders of the church came to me and said, "Since you are already doing the work of a pastor, would you consider being licensed?"

I put her off by saying that I didn't think something like that could happen. Then another elder and his wife came to me and said the same thing. I told them that it was up to the elders to discern the direction.

They took it upon themselves to pursue this. When Paul's evaluation came up, they asked each person how they would feel about licensing me as associate pastor with Paul. The response was very positive.

After congregational discussions with the conference minister, plans were put in place. Within a year of my calling on Schmucker Drive, I was licensed in a wonderful service at Beech Mennonite Church in 1987. Two years later I was ordained.

The Marvel of God's Timing

My husband's response to my calling was and is a profound gift to me. For him, it meant moving over and giving up some ministerial duties he had held for many years. Not all men would do that willingly.

As we began to think about how we could minister together, Paul would say, "Well, I can see you doing this well." Then about a month or so later, he would say, "You know, I think this is a good job for you." I never felt that I needed to push my way onto the team.

One day, Paul and I were sitting on the front steps of the parsonage and looking out over the neighbor's cornfields. I was feeling a deep sense of peace and fulfillment. I knew then that if the church had not recognized my ministry, and if Paul would have been unwilling to share his space, something within me would have died.

Instead, we have pastored as a team for a number of years and are comfortable as we work together, each using our own gifts.

When I think of my life and ministry, I realize that the struggle many women have (and continue to experience) was not mine. My reality was that most of my moves came as a surprise—a joyful surprise! As a teenager, I felt God's call. But because avenues of service were so limited, I never thought in broad terms about how this might be realized in my life.

What deeply impresses me is the gentle way God has led me through people, places, and circumstances. Some things were as small as serving on a committee, and some as big as becoming a pastor. There were years of growing and waiting for God's timing, and of changing my own thought patterns and beliefs. The doors opened at just the right time. God led in the whole process!

This is my story thus far—a testimony to the acts of God in the life of a pastor's daughter named Grace. By the grace of God and the confidence of the people who enabled her, she grew up to be a pastor herself. What else can I do but "proclaim the mighty acts of God."

Rooted, So I Could Sway in the Wind

DOROTHY NICKEL FRIESEN

Howard Zehr

DOROTHY NICKEL FRIESEN is pastor of the First Mennonite Church, Bluffton, Ohio. From 1990-95, she was assistant dean at Associated Mennonite Biblical Seminary, Elkhart, Indiana. She has pastored two congregations in Kansas.

Dorothy has served on the Commission on Home Ministries of the General Conference Mennonite Church (GCMC) and the steering committee of the Pastorate Project (GCMC and Mennonite Church). She is currently serving on the Integration Committee for the (new) Mennonite Church.

Over the past twenty-five years, her writings have appeared in Mennonite publications such as *forum, The Mennonite, Gospel Herald, MCC Women's Concerns Report, The Mennonite Quarterly Review* (Oct. 1995), and a sermon in *Weaving Wisdom* (ed. D. Y. Nyce; 1983).

Dorothy is a graduate of Bethel College, North Newton, Kansas (B.A., English); University of Kansas (M.A., religion and education); and St. Paul School of Theology (M.Div.). She is married to Richard Friesen, and they have two daughters, Melissa, and Joanna.

Dorothy's special interests include murder mysteries and chocolate.

I GREW UP on a farm in southwestern Minnesota, surrounded by tall cottonwood trees to the west and north. Every school morning, I would peer out the window, looking for the orange bus. When the leaves had disappeared (and many had by early September), the view through the trees gave me a glimpse of at least a mile. There was plenty of time to walk to the end of the lane and meet the bus—on time.

Those sturdy, shimmering large trees protected our house against the wild winds of winter and drifts of snow blowing our way. The grove with its supply of fallen branches gave us endless hours of climbing play.

I remember being told that the roots of the cottonwood go deep and wide, able to tap deep water sources. "Those roots keep them upright when the winds come," my dad would say. The winds did come. And the cottonwoods stood.

Rooted in Faith, Fed by Adventure

There have been several "trees" in my life that have given me roots. I remember many fine and committed Sunday school teachers, and I certainly was raised in a Mennonite Christian home with Christian parents. Meanwhile, there was my Aunt Kate.

Aunt Kate stood at the chalkboard with her hands behind her back, rocking back and forth on her platform shoes, wearing the same navy dress with white collar that she wore each Sunday. She explained Mennonite history to this seventh grader.

We sat in our wooden chairs from the old library and tried to follow her finger on the map of Europe (or was it Russia?) as she pointed out spot after spot of great historical consequence. Somehow I caught on that I was connected to another continent through my blood and my faith. Of course, we were a polite but fairly unenthusiastic audience of girls, all restless with hormones and overactive imaginations.

My Aunt Kate was my junior high Sunday school teacher, and she loved history. Known as a "crackerjack of a teacher" in the community in years past, she now taught in church as a volunteer. She had taught my own parents in country school, and now a second generation sat under her tutelage.

Aunt Kate made the stories of the Anabaptists come alive. Every Sunday she told us the religious history that ran through our veins. Sunday after Sunday, I got hooked on the story of a people who stood up for what they believed, got kicked out of a few places, but somehow survived. Thus my congregation, the Bethel Mennonite Church in Mountain Lake, became a living testimony to those early Mennonites.

Perhaps it was then that I became certain I would be a teacher someday. I loved her class, even if it was Sunday school. I didn't know it was supposed to be boring! All I knew was that history, faith, and my life were somehow connected. At a tender junior-high age, I was catching on to the fact that my life made a difference to God.

I became rooted in the faith of a people through my home, my church, and its day-to-day activities. I was nourished by examples more than by explicit teaching: "Our lives are to count for something." I was fed with a sense of adventure in the church.

Maybe my imagination worked overtime. Maybe my avid reading of novels got mixed up with Bible stories. But in my young faith, I truly thought that I was chosen to be part of a grand plan, as was everyone else. Now the adventure began. What part would I play in this unfolding drama?

The Winds Blew

While I was still in high school, my roots took hold and the wind started blowing. I was naively open to change and possibility. After all, my pastor, Albert Gaeddert, was speaking clearly about civil rights, fairness, and Christian responsibility. I listened.

I learned that Mennonite men of social conscience, mostly pastors, had gone to Mississippi to help with voter registration. Unsure of what that really meant, I soon caught on that blacks in the South were not treated fairly. Somehow, whites in Minnesota could do something about it.

My early teaching about connections between continents and generations suddenly became a living object lesson. It was clear that we, in a tiny village, could show a Christian response to this discrimination. So the winds of change were blowing up north, too.

Could our congregation hire a black associate pastor? After all, our church was looking for more staff. A few of us (how could I have known about the wind?) decided to present a proposal to the church council. We suggested that Bethel set an example and offer a job to a qualified black pastor.

Coming on the heels of a youth retreat with a black Chicago pastor as resource person, this was my immersion into church politics. I was on fire for Jesus! The retreat had talked of the Holy Spirit descending on us like fire. And Jesus called us to love others! It was too logical. It was altogether faithful.

Our proposal was received and then politely ignored. I remember telling my parents that one deacon had dozed through the meeting. How could he? I can still feel the indignation that was deep within me. A passion for the less-fortunate was finding its home, deeply rooted in a faithful tradition. I was swaying in the winds of change, holding on for dear life. I was disappointed.

I was sure that it was in the church that real change happened. After all, Jesus was on the side of truth and love. Certainly our country's laws needed to be respected, no matter the color of skin. It all seemed so clear to me. It was also clear to me that some Christians lacked moral will and could hurt one another. I grew up—but not bitter. My roots deepened, and the winds died down.

Bending in the Wind

My rather casual decision to attend Bethel College marks the watering of roots in a flood of education, ideas, personalities, and church history that has nourished me. Since my closest friends were going to Bethel, I went too.

I wanted to be a teacher, and my high school counselor had recommended Mankato State Teachers College, only fifty miles away. Choosing to go five hundred miles south to a Kansas college, however, wasn't outside of the acceptable. I had two aunts who lived in Hillsboro and Whitewater, and many from our congregation went to Bethel.

I packed new towels, an iron, a new Remington typewriter, plus a green trunk full of sweaters and winter clothes, and headed to college. I never looked back, thinking this was another natural and wonderful adventure. At Bethel, my faith life and my commitment to the church became wedded.

In college, I found opportunities to develop my intellect and leadership abilities. It never occurred to me that there would be limits. This was the age of possibilities and expanding horizons in space, in education, in careers. My decision to teach was never questioned. My dreams of teaching led me.

I loved student teaching—where outstanding grade-eleven students (like Patty Shelly) studied under my budding identity. The church college had given me confidence and assurance that following a call to teach was connected to following Jesus Christ.

However, the sixties were tumultuous, and Vietnam hammered at our conscience. I protested, I marched, I fasted, I signed petitions. I dated a young man of conscience who was classified 1-O, and alternative service became the next step for us as a married couple.

For me, the seventies were a mixture of love and hate of the Mennonite church. I was in Mennonite Voluntary Service, but assigned an "earning" role so the men could do the "service." I hated that sexist system. However, I became the first secretary in the office of Urban Ministry for the Denver-area Mennonites. I typed, filed, and answered phones. I set up an office and learned about organization from an outstanding community Mennonite leader interested in urban development.

I thrived in the urban environment, attended lectures, and began reading secular feminist books. It dawned on me that my faith (my Christian Mennonite faith) had a more wholistic and nonviolent answer than confrontational politics. My roots sank deeper as I drank at the wells of feminism, protest, and the nurturing context of a Mennonite congregation. The winds were definitely blowing and I was bending.

Not Serving in the Pulpit

In seminary classes at Elkhart, a new resolve began to dawn on me: it would be good to stay in the church, but *not in the pulpit.* Later, several professors discouraged me from completing my degree at Associated Mennonite Biblical Seminary (AMBS) and encouraged me to go back to teaching. Christian teachers were desperately needed. So I left seminary, fully intending to teach and not work in the church.

This narrow view of leadership seemed antiquated and restrictive. Didn't the church know that 50 percent of its membership was women? Did the church realize that this was a treasure?

Our journey took us back to the city, this time for a full decade. My country farm roots were so deep that I felt right at home in an inner-city neighborhood. People there were living close to relatives and had been there for generations. There was an expected code of behavior and a simple neighborly hospitality that felt comfortable.

Raising two daughters seemed possible when surrounded by caring neighbors, friends, and a progressive congregation. I cringed every time we sang the old gospel hymns because I missed the rich harmony and musical diversity from seminary. Yet I began to love the people with all my heart.

The winds came. Violence and poverty were pervasive. Neighbors had fistfights, and gangs were walking our streets. Children had no playgrounds, and medical care was expensive. Where was Jesus? Where was the church?

I found that at least one congregation was plugging away at these issues. We intentionally lived among the poor, building the community from the base of the congregation. In high school I had assumed that the church offered the answer for whole living; that belief seemed to be confirmed again.

I taught English to street kids. I settled one knife fight (thank you, Jesus, for protection). I hired poor kids (who smoked) to babysit my kids. I risked things that now, in retrospect, seem foolish. But I was not afraid. The winds were blowing, and I was bending. But the roots were going deeper into the streams of healing waters.

The first thirty-five years of my life were a rich tapestry of rural and urban, education and career, children and teaching, adventure and hard work. These early decisions, some made so casually and naturally, were shaping me in a way that has given me strength.

Roots for Serving in a Pulpit

I now serve in a pulpit, another story of miracle in my life. It never occurred to me as a child or young adult that pastoring a large congregation might be a career option. I simply let the wind blow, hoping the roots would hold as I said yes to God's call through a congregation.

Those cottonwood trees have been uprooted on my farm home in Minnesota and replaced with a new grove of trees. That rural house has been destroyed by an electrical fire and replaced with a modern home. But my roots are sunk deep into that soil of geography and spirituality.

Teach your children well. Move beyond the boundaries of family. Trust the Holy Spirit to guide and direct. Improve your mind. Study. Pray. Sink those roots as deep as you can because the winds will blow and you will bend.

Dorothy Nickel Friesen

God's Smile

BRENDA ISAACS

BRENDA ISAACS serves as
executive director of Church
Community Services (CCS)
in Elkhart, Indiana. CCS is
an agency funded by several
dozen churches of various
denominations in Elkhart. The
mission of CCS is to provide
crisis assistance to those in the
community who need help
with food, clothing, medicine,
rent, utilities, emergency housing, transportation, and other
necessities.

Brenda earned a B.A. in Language Education at Fisk University, Nashville. She complet-
ed a second B.A. in Biblical Studies at University of Biblical Studies,
Bethany, Oklahoma; and an M.Div. and a D.Min. from Friends International Christian University, Merced, California. Brenda also has an M.A.
in Library Science from the University of Southern California in Los Angeles. She received a scholarship from Southwest Mennonite Conference
to study at the Fuller Institute of Evangelism and Church Development in
Pasadena, California.

Brenda was licensed as a missions pastor in 1990 by the Southwest
Mennonite Conference, comprised of Arizona and Southern California
(now the Pacific Southwest Mennonite Conference). She was ordained
by that same conference in May 1992.

Prior to formally entering the ministry, Brenda served as a teacher in public and private schools, media specialist, vice-principal, and finally principal of a Mennonite elementary school in California.

After moving to Indiana, Brenda has served the Sunnyside Mennonite Church twice as interim pastor. Since 1996, she has also been a monthly columnist with *The Elkhart Truth.*

Brenda and her husband, James (also a Mennonite pastor), have three children: Kevin, Tiffany, and Johannah.

FOR ME, the distinction of being a "woman of the cloth" has had as many challenges as rewards. We are supposedly living in an age of enlightenment, but there is still a lot of prejudice against women in ministry.

The African-Methodist Episcopal Church Never Barred Women from Ministry

I came to Christ as a young adult in the African-Methodist Episcopal (AME) church in the late 1960s. This branch of the Methodist church, the oldest black denomination in the United States, was founded by Richard Allen in 1787. Allen was ordained as an elder and then as a bishop by Bishop Asbury of Philadelphia. He became the first black bishop in America.

Before Allen founded the AME church, the blacks in Philadelphia attended St. George's Methodist church. But they were not allowed to sit up front or take communion. Eventually they grew tired of that arrangement and sensed a need to form their own church.

"Mother Bethel" in Philadelphia became the first AME church established by Richard Allen. Charles Wesley, the great Methodist preacher and theologian of England, wrote a book about this church pioneer: *Richard Allen, Apostle of Freedom.*

The AME church has never barred women from the ministry. The first woman preacher I ever heard was an AME—and she was dynamic! Over the years, this church has produced female preachers, pastors, and even bishops. It thus is a pioneer in affirming the ministry of women.

"Before You Came, We Didn't Know We Were Supposed to Do Anything in the Church"

In my ministerial career with the Mennonite Church, I have been associated with three congregations. The first of these was a Belizean church in Los Angeles, where I first began to preach publicly. The people there loved the gospel so much that they accepted anyone preaching it.

My husband was free in allowing me to preach when the situation called for it or when the people requested it. When we left that church after serving a four-year term, the women said to me in a public service, "Before you came, we didn't know we were supposed to do anything in church." That was a strong affirmation for my early ministry, something that made me smile.

After a year on sabbatical, we were called to an African-American Mennonite Church in Inglewood, California. It was also a pleasure to minister there; the people were welcoming and accepting. During that time, I wrote a weekly column for a Christian newspaper. Once a young preacher came up to me and responded to an article I'd written: "I've never seen a woman who can deal with the Scriptures the way you do—most women are too shallow."

I did not know whether to smile or frown. I didn't know if this was a compliment to me or an insult to women in general. It likely was both!

Ordained in the Mennonite Church

In 1990, I was licensed as a gospel minister in the Southwest Mennonite Conference (now the Pacific Southwest Mennonite Conference) and ordained by that same conference in 1992.

In August of 1994, our family moved to Elkhart County, Indiana. Early in 1995, my husband, James, and I were called as a team to be interim pastors of Sunnyside Mennonite Church in Elkhart, Indiana, while the pastor, Gerald Good, was on sabbatical. When we moved to Indiana, we never even dreamed that we would be called to a "white" church, but we were. It turned out to be one of our most valuable experiences in ministry.

The Sunnyside congregation was definitely welcoming to our family at a time when we really needed acceptance and affirmation.

Most of the members there are either professional people (teachers, professors, nurses, and the like) or highly skilled people in the building trades. They warmed up to us and loved us as Christians should—regardless of race, sex, or any other variable.

The greatest criticism we had during that whole period was from the Baptist minister of the church across the street. He asked Gerald Good, "Why did you have to call them? Couldn't you find some white people?"

Gerald told him, "Well, they're Christians—and that's all that matters to us."

I'm still smiling and even laughing about that exchange.

Two years after the Sunnyside experience, they called me a second time to be interim pastor (alone this time) while they were waiting for a new pastor from Kansas. Again, it was a rich experience.

Preaching Is a Lot Like Delivering a Baby

I love the Word of God. I love to study, meditate, observe, and prepare messages. I'm always a little squeamish when it comes time to deliver the message, sometimes even asking myself, "Why did I get involved in this?" But once I get started, the Spirit generally flows. It's a lot like delivering a baby. Once you're in the delivery room, the baby's going to come whether you want it to or not.

I have often been blessed by my own messages because I realize that they come through me, not from me. For example, I never heard a message on biblical aspects of sexuality until I preached it myself in the early 1990s, when I was past forty years old. I preached from Leviticus 18, which has all the safe-sex guidelines that any generation will ever need.

The people were spellbound; they didn't know that kind of information was in the Bible. They referred to this message time and again over the next several years.

Three Areas of Ministry

Three areas of ministry have stood out in my journey. First, ministering to my own children has always been a priority. During their growing-up years, we had regular Bible studies at home, and I prayed with them every night. I still pray with my one remaining child at home, my fifteen-year-old daughter, Johannah.

I told myself, "How can I be out ministering to others if I neglect those who are right in the home with me, those especially assigned to me by God?" God has always honored that.

My second area of commitment is preaching the unadulterated Word of God. Sometimes I get into trouble for that because some people don't want to hear it. But I still preach it anyway. I like to preach and teach the full gospel; I like to hear the full gospel. I don't like to hear apologies for the Word. I believe people should "tell it like it is." I further believe that people should do what the Word says.

Finally, I love to minister to the poor. I live for that. In Los Angeles, I had ministries on skid row, in hospitals, in nursing homes. Nobody paid me specifically for these ministries. But God called me to them, and God paid me—handsomely!

I clearly remember an experience I had on skid row in Los Angeles. One evening my husband and I had gone to conduct a service at one of the local missions. We had also brought food to serve after the ministry.

When we walked into the mission, I laid my beautiful, black velvet coat down in the lobby, then proceeded to take some trays into the fellowship area. A few minutes later, I came back to the lobby to collect my coat, but it was gone. Nobody had seen it, they said.

I was a little perturbed, but then I consoled myself, "Well, somebody here needed the coat more than I did." Several weeks later I received a postcard in the mail saying I'd won a fur coat and that I could schedule an appointment to pick it up at a certain location. That was a complete surprise to me because I had not entered any contests, raffles, or anything of the sort

We decided to check it out. Sure enough, I received a beautiful, black fur coat that was much more luxurious than the one I'd lost at the mission a few weeks before. I summed it up as God's never-failing providence. The Lord always provides for those earnestly seeking to serve him.

Many times I've had similar experiences. Though we should not primarily be seeking the world's goods, these things are created for our use. Certainly God wants his own children to have the best of things.

God's Smile

The most important role model in my ministerial life has been Mother Teresa of Calcutta, the most awesome saint of our time. It doesn't matter how long her church filibusters about making her a saint—she was and is one. She lived as a saint, she ministered as a saint, and she died as a saint.

Mother really loved Jesus with her whole heart, and she served God with her entire being. I read something in one of her books that has become the daily motto for my ministry and my life:

> At the end of life we will not be judged by
> how many diplomas we have received,
> how much money we have made,
> how many great things we have done.
>
> We will be judged by
> "I was hungry and you gave me to eat,
> I was naked and you clothed me,
> I was homeless and you took me in. . . ."

I constantly meditate on the powerful little nun's exhortation, letting it shape my character. And I pray that when my work is evaluated, God will smile.

Brenda Isaacs

Ode to Joy

CHARLOTTE HOLSOPPLE GLICK

CHARLOTTE SERVES as a conference minister for Indiana-Michigan Mennonite Conference, providing oversight for thirty-seven congregations and their pastors. She and her husband, Del, were pastors at the Waterford Mennonite Church in Goshen, Indiana, from 1980 to 1990. During 1990-92, they were in the People's Republic of China, teaching English with China Educational Exchange.

She earned a B.A. in Elementary Education from Eastern Mennonite College (1969), an M.A. in Counseling Education from Millersville State University (1978), and an M.Div. from Associated Mennonite Biblical Seminary (1993).

During 1969-73 Charlotte taught grades 7 and 8 at Johnstown Mennonite School. She was Director of Housing and a teacher at Lancaster Mennonite High School in 1973-78. She also served as coordinator of the Mennonite Youth Convention at Waterloo, Ontario, in 1979, and was cochair of the Worship Committee and coleader of worship at Mennonite General Assembly at Purdue 87.

Later Charlotte served as chair of Mennonite Board of Congregational Ministries. During 1982-89 she was an adjunct Professor and Convener of the Women-Men in Ministry Colloquium for Associated Mennonite Biblical Seminary.

Charlotte and Del have one daughter, Reneé. Charlotte enjoys collecting recipes, creating scrapbooks, and traveling with her family.

IT WAS A SPRING Sunday morning in my senior year of high school. I was the song leader for the worship service in my small rural Mennonite congregation in western Pennsylvania. As usual, my uncle was preaching the sermon. I sat on the third bench from the front, near the center aisle, as I always did when I led the singing.

However, something besides the sermon was being spoken that morning. I have no idea now what the theme or the scriptural text was for the morning. I was not even thinking about the sermon during that service. Usually I listened intently so I could choose a suitable ending song. On that particular morning, my inner soul was hearing another voice.

That voice seemed to come directly from the mouth of Jesus, out of the picture hanging for years behind the pulpit—Jesus praying in the garden of Gethsemane. I heard, "These things I have spoken to you, that my joy may be in you and that your joy may be wholly mature."

Other words followed: "You will be a leader. You will speak and teach. Accept every opportunity with courage and confidence. You will be asked to preach." I didn't know then and I don't know now if that preaching line came with the other clear declaratives, or if it was my own dream-voice. I do recall it all as part of the same "inner voice."

The thoughts lingered throughout the service. At the close, I led number 51 from the old *Church Hymnal*, "The Lord My Shepherd Is," to which I always resorted when nothing else came to mind. I was preoccupied with my own thinking and more than a little perplexed. So I avoided as much conversation as I could on my way to the family car in the parking lot.

In the auto parked next to us was a former youth sponsor, also my Sunday school teacher, friend, and advocate. We had often talked of my plans for the future, and he dreamed with and for me. He saw possibilities on the horizon and was free to share them.

Ironically, not knowing my thoughts, he told me, "You did well this morning, as usual. You'll be a leader wherever you go."

I wondered if Dorsey had heard the same sermon. At that moment it felt like something new leaped within me. I was certain it wasn't a baby (as for Elizabeth, Luke 1:41), but I shivered with joy.

The Journey Begins

It was difficult to leave my home environment and head for college. This Mennonite community of eight hundred, tucked away in the Allegheny mountains, had provided safety and much affirmation for who I was. My parents lived and encouraged values of creativity, initiative, and relationships. My extended family, with three preacher uncles, introduced me to ways of giving and receiving counsel and critique.

Nevertheless, even my community and my church were not exempt from hurts, brokenness, conflict, and suffering. I learned about grief and loss as I cried with my father when his brother was crushed to death in a local coal-mine accident. Yet in and through and beneath all my encounters lay a joy far beyond happiness.

In that Mennonite community, I questioned the tradition and practice of wearing the prayer veiling. I doubted if only men could be pastors when I discovered Scriptures appearing just as valid as the specific passages used to explain "the accepted rules."

My pastor uncle and I often stood at the church basement door, where we both parked our cars, to continue a discussion from prayer meeting or youth group. We both held strong opinions about how to do church and be church. We both wanted to make sure the other knew our point of view, and we both tried to listen.

In those debates, I began to understand some of the unspoken dynamics of the church. Uncle Harry respected me. I respected Uncle Harry. He wanted me to turn out "good." He was delighted when I told him of my interest in voluntary service assignments and when I was asked to serve on the district youth leadership cabinet.

The Growing Nudge

The inmates of the Harrisonburg, Virginia, city jail became my "congregation" during those four years of college. I sang with the mixed quartet and led Bible studies. My faith was confronted with more acute pain and brokenness than I thought imaginable. In that context I planned worship and even preached several sermons.

I also visited women in their homes when they were out on parole, took them to employers for job possibilities, and heard their fears, anger, and occasional successes. In my junior and senior years, I was secretary of the jail program and did most of the planning and administration. Before this, only male students had ever held this major public leadership position for the jail ministry.

The college environment and the three summers of voluntary service between those years of study were enriching. They provided space for articulating questions I had begun to formulate years earlier with my parents, youth leaders, teachers, and my uncle Harry. I wondered why I as a woman was affirmed for my leadership. I pondered why I was asked to take many responsibilities and why certain leadership roles were "out of the picture."

Why could I as a woman not be the voluntary service leader unless I was married? Why did people seem to feel uncomfortable when I was "too" assertive? Why were such questions passed off by others as rhetoric? Amid these wonderings, I continued to serve as a leader on the conference youth cabinet and as camp director and voluntary service project organizer.

The Seminary "Ah-ha"

Then I enrolled in a class at Associated Mennonite Biblical Seminary (AMBS). It was the summer of 1976, after four years of teaching junior high and three years of being dorm "mom" at Lancaster Mennonite High School. The course subject was discipleship. Del, my husband, was already on a pastoral ministry track, and I registered for personal enrichment.

Professor David Schroeder was an exegete of the Gospels. In his gentle, prophetic manner, he explained that all persons, women and men alike, are responsible for their own call to follow Jesus. He declared that women could be affirmed for congregational pastoral leadership just as women ministered to and were disciples of Jesus in his earthly ministry.

Once again, something leaped within me. Like Elizabeth, I was filled with joy and delight.

A Congregation Willing to Take a Risk

A God-surprise came when, at the end of my husband's M.Div. training at AMBS, we received calls from four congregations inviting us to serve as co-pastors. This time the inner feeling of joy turned to fear. What were these search committees asking? Didn't they know how risky it would be to invite a woman to be on the pastoral team?

The conversation buzzed around the dinner table in the home of an elder in the Waterford Mennonite Church (Goshen, Indiana). The male elders present convinced me that they were serious. Were they unrealistic? Perhaps. But if they were committed to helping interpret the gifts within me that they sensed were needed in the congregation, the question became mine. Was I ready to take the risk?

If I were to accept this call, I would be a pioneer. I would be an oddity. I would need to explain my role. Where were the models? There was only one woman in pastoral ministry in Indiana-Michigan Mennonite Conference. Who was I to think I could start something new in the church? I wasn't out to rock the boat.

Yet pastoring brought together all the things I loved to do—be with people in various situations, teach, organize, plan worship, and discern how to reach out to those who don't know Jesus.

I engaged in soul-searching, study of the Scripture, and my usual pattern of gathering a discernment group together for making difficult decisions. Finally, I accepted the call of the Waterford Mennonite Church, and so did Del.

In my Pennsylvania Dutch-speaking home, my parents would say, "Mir mache en Breddicher heit (we're making a minister today)," when a pastor was licensed, ordained, or installed. The Waterford congregation "made me" a pastor-preacher.

They asked hard questions: What will this do to our congregational life? How will we deal with the fact that we've never had a woman as a pastor before? Can we listen to a woman in the pulpit? I received a range of comments from "every congregation should have a female as a pastor" to "my Bible says that women should not preach."

A Brave Conference

I was surprised by the invitation to serve a local congregation as a pastor. I was even more surprised when the reality of serving as a conference minister dawned on my consciousness. The conference leadership opportunity came a year after our family had returned from two years of teaching in the People's Republic of China with China Educational Exchange.

The Indiana-Michigan Mennonite Conference invited me to serve as one of three regional conference ministers. Imagine my astonishment when I was first referred to as "the bishop." Now the issue changed from debating the biblical position on women being ordained ministers in the church to the appropriateness of a woman ordaining other women and, yes, ordaining men.

The Joy of Call

There have been significant moments since my high school days when I was seriously questioned about my "inner call" to pastoral ministry. Why couldn't I accept being a pastor's wife and working alongside my husband, as many other faithful women have done? How could I be hearing the voice of God correctly when the Bible was so clear that women were to be silent in church, according to some folks?

These questions made me doubt. They drove me back to the Scriptures to re-examine the texts. They sent me to friends who held opposing positions, so I could clarify my own view.

I recall one short drive from the Waterford meetinghouse to the Greencroft Nursing Center, to visit an elderly member. I just ended a conversation at the office with another member who doubted my call. I prayed aloud in desperation: "How long, how often, O God, will I have to explain my position?"

Peaceful assurance fell over me like a warm blanket with the words from Isaiah (43:1): "I have called you by name, you are mine." The visit was delightful. My eighty-two-year-old friend, who had openly opposed my coming to Waterford to pastor, affirmed me as I closed her apartment door. "Thanks for coming. I love when you stop by to visit, and I love your prayers." My desperation turned to joy.

The Joy of Commitment

There have been moments in the last three decades when I wished I had committed my life to being a public school administrator or a business executive. In those times, my thoughts rush quickly to the revival meetings held spring and fall in my home community. I remember traveling evangelists who challenged all young people to commit their lives to Jesus Christ and to service.

I heard options mentioned: missionary, church worker, Sunday school teacher, and occasionally "pastor." On one of those occasions, I told God, "I don't know what you're leading me to, but let it be something within the church."

That commitment solidified as I chose my career of teaching and counseling, and then found myself at seminary. I gave little attention to vocations and employment outside church ministry leadership, even in Mennonite church circles. I'm fully aware that my commitment to "church work" didn't qualify me for the kingdom any more than other vocations I could have chosen. But having made the commitment, the "bumps" in the journey were more bearable. Joy came in knowing I was where I was called to be.

I was overwhelmed by the commitment of congregational members and pastors to affirm the giftedness of all persons, women and men alike. They worked at discerning together the voice of God on this issue. Respect and words of encouragement, inclusion, and trust came frequently in my responsibilities. Mutual commitment has graced my pastoring with joy.

The Joy of Challenge

The word *challenging* describes periods in the early 1980s in the Mennonite Church and in the seminary communities. Intense debates and extremely opposing views on women in pastoral ministry abounded. Some women and men were exhilarated that women finally were permitted to share their giftedness in preaching, leading worship, baptizing, and sharing communion.

Some believed the women's liberation movement accounted for women wanting to be pastors. They were devastated and alarmed that the Mennonite Church was following the mandate of the society around us. Harmful but perhaps necessary anger, frustration, and rejection filled letters to the *Gospel Herald* and *The Mennonite*.

As a living example in the controversy, I could not escape the questions, concerns, and dialogue. Particularly difficult in the early years was critique from other women also interested and involved in pastoral ministry. They said I had sold out to the system by promising the congregation I would not preach until they were ready for me to do so. Equally painful were comments that I became a pastor only because I was married to one.

In my present role as a woman conference minister, people tend to expect that I should be able to place all women candidates in some excellent congregational setting. My level of anxiety has increased with this expectation. I am committed to discerning the best match possible.

Occasionally, persons in the congregation wanted to talk to Del rather than me because they considered only him the pastor. Perhaps they thought of me as the secretary, pastor's wife, or assistant to the pastor. Sometimes pastors have called one of the male overseers in the conference for advice and pastoral wisdom, even if I had just attended a seminar on the subject of their interest.

I am not a stranger to debate. Even so, I found conversations with Rachel Fisher from the Mennonite Church and Phyllis Carter from the Church of the Brethren to be life-giving and energy-producing. They helped me meet challenges that came my way. I continue to find courage in networking with women pastors. I deeply appreciate acceptance from scores of men, even when I am often the only woman in the group.

The Joy of Change

On some days of these last two decades, my bones cried out in frustration and desire for openness to change, so God's kingdom work could continue. In the midst of one of those cries, I made a hospital call to a member.

In my pastoral candidating process, she had declared that her Bible said, "Women should be silent in the church." That day she introduced me to her roommate as "my pastor." My heart was warmed with joy!

The Joy of Community

During many moments in the last twenty years, I have dreamed of not needing to think about whether a person is male or female when being considered for pastoral ministry. I have longed for the time when the issue of women in pastoral ministry would cause no debate, justification, rationalization, or separation.

I have prayed that all of us will respect each other as we struggle with this important issue. I have even pleaded with God for this issue to go away completely. However, I have come to accept that such will not happen in my generation.

I have been blessed with love and acceptance, challenge and rejection. I live with great hope and confidence in God's faith community. I dream for my daughter and all those daughters now being born into the church. I believe their gifts will be freely recognized, along with the giftedness of their spiritual brothers.

In *The God Who Comes,** Carlo Carretto may say best what fits my journey within the church:

> How baffling you are, oh church,
>   and yet how I love you!
> How you have made me suffer,
>   and yet how much I owe you!
> I should like to see you destroyed,
>   and yet I need your presence.
> You have given me so much scandal,
>   and yet you have made me understand sanctity.
> I have seen nothing in the world
>   more devoted to obscurity,
>   more compromised, more false,
> and I have touched nothing more pure,
>   more generous, more beautiful.
> How often I have wanted to shut
>   the doors of my soul in your face,
> and how often I have prayed to die
>   in the safety of your arms.
> No, I cannot free myself from you,
>   because I am you, although not completely.
> And, where should I go?

Joy has emerged in surprising and unusual places and in the steady influence and support of my spouse, daughter, parents, siblings, pastors, congregational members, and friends. I have felt joy leaping within me as new realities were conceived. I have come to know the joy Jesus prayed for through the love and encouragement of the church community.

---

*Maryknoll, N.Y.: Orbis Books, 1974; used by permission.

Since Christmas of 1996, we as a family have been living and coping with the devastating diagnosis of cancer, first on my tongue, a year later in my neck, and in the fall of 1998 in my back and lung. The journey has been rugged, painful, and uncertain. It has included surgeries on my tongue, neck, and back, as well as extensive radiation and chemotherapy.

We have considered healing and hope as special gifts nurtured by the supportive prayers and care of God's people. Yet at times healing and hope seem to be distant realities.

Most precious is the joy I know in relationship with my God, the source of all my joy. I am convinced that together we can go on with joy.*

Ode to joy!

Charlotte Dalrymple Glick

---

*On February 8, 1999, Charlotte, age 51, passed on to be forever with her Source of Joy.

Proceed with Much Prayer

RUTH BUNDY NAYLOR

Ruth Bundy Naylor, a spiritual director and writer, lives at Bluffton, Ohio. She serves as a deacon at First Mennonite Church in Bluffton, where she was ordained in 1987 and was on the pastoral staff for twelve years.

Ruth grew up in a Quaker community near Adena, Ohio, and graduated from Olney Friends Boarding School at Barnesville before attending Bluffton College. She earned a master's degree from Bowling Green State University while teaching at Bluffton High School and then did additional graduate work at Associated Mennonite Biblical Seminary in Elkhart, Indiana.

She is a graduate of the Shalem Program in Spiritual Guidance. Just before her retirement in the fall of 1996, she served an eighteen-month stint as interim Conference Minister in the Central District of the General Conference Mennonite Church.

In the past, Ruth has served as chairperson of the General Conference Program Committee, as a member of the Joint Integration Exploration Committee, President and board member of the Central District Conference, and many other planning committees for church conferences.

Ruth's poetry and articles have appeared in a wide variety of publications over the past thirty years. She and her husband, Stan, are the parents of Kimberly Anne and Geoffrey, and the grandparents of seven.

WE WERE TAKING a break in our 1975 General Conference program committee meetings when Heinz Janzen, general secretary of the conference, approached me. "Ruth," he said with a smile, "when are you going to go to seminary and become a minister? That devotional was most appropriate this morning."

I sidestepped his compliment and quipped, "Heinz, you forget that I already am a minister."

He remembered that I had been raised a Quaker, and he knew how Quakers teach that all Christians are ministers, including women.

"I consider my home, church, conference, and English classroom to be important fields of ministry," I added.

From Quaker to Mennonite

I first met Mennonites when I wrote to Bluffton College for information in 1952. The way I became a student there still mystifies me and reminds me of God's willingness to direct and provide.

Being the youngest of three children raised in a broken home, I had no money and no encouragement to pursue a college education. In the silence of a midweek meeting for worship, I finally told God that my own exploration had netted nothing. If I was to obtain further schooling, the Lord was going to have to show me how and where.

God spoke. The inaudible voice in my mind was clear: "Look at the little brown bulletin." I knew immediately which little brown bulletin, and I could hardly wait to check it out. Within two weeks, Paul R. Shelly, head of the Bible department, was at my door. He was working as admissions counselor during the summer.

Our visit was brief. He asked why I had applied to Bluffton, and I told him. As he left, he said, "Ruth, there's no question about your eligibility for a scholarship, but the employment you'll need is not so easy to guarantee. All campus jobs were assigned last week. But I'll see if there's anything I can do."

Then came the letter stating that I was to be Dr. Shelly's secretary, working every afternoon after classes—even helping with correspondence for his conference committee. On Saturdays I was to type and mimeograph the bulletin for First Mennonite Church in town. Just a few weeks later, my brother drove me and my trunk of belongings to a part of the state where I'd never been, and to a campus I'd never seen.

Two years later, I was engaged to marry one of those Mennonites who was graduating from Bluffton College. Mennonite Central Committee (MCC) had arranged an alternative service position for Stan as business manager for Brooklane Farm in Maryland. Then Stan's Indiana draft board informed him that they needed him in Indiana and were not willing to honor an out-of-state placement.

Thus we began our married life working at Methodist Hospital in Indianapolis, Stan as a payroll clerk and I as secretary in the superintendent's office. The administrative assistant to whom I was directly responsible was well-known throughout the hospital as a difficult and demanding woman.

At the end of our two years there, the assistant superintendent drew me aside and said, "Mrs. Naylor, I need to make a confession to you. I have never had much respect for conscientious objectors. I've always figured these 1-W boys claim conscience as a way to save their own necks. But as I've watched you constantly finding ways to get along with Miss ____, I've decided that you people are serious about wanting to make peace in the world."

Church Planting

Two or three years later, while living and working in Fort Wayne, we were amazed to discover that the Evangelical Mennonite church we were attending was not teaching pacifism. So we were quite interested when representatives of First Mennonite Church in Berne approached us about helping them plant a new Central District church.

The first meeting of what is now the Maplewood Mennonite Church was held in our living room.* I laugh now as I look back at pictures of the Berne Church extension committee with the Maplewood planning committee, and of the 1961 groundbreaking ceremony. It was clearly a man's world. We women weren't questioning that.

One day Stan called from work to say that Harry Yoder, assistant

---

*The Maplewood Church story is recounted in *Maplewood Roots: Growing in Faith*, ed. David L. Habegger, published by Maplewood Mennonite Church, Fort Wayne, Ind., 1994.

to the president of Bluffton College, had stopped and asked if we might consider moving back to Bluffton so Stan could work in financial aid. With a sense of God's direction in our lives, we sold our brand-new home and moved. Our children transferred to the Bluffton schools, and I grabbed the chance to pick up my studies at the college.

I would be lying if I said that all went smoothly. However, the time to write that story has not yet come. God never promised us a rose garden. This was a time when my faith was tested. I wanted to doubt the rightness of our move, yet I cannot. I graduated and taught high school English for thirteen years, enjoying the students and also the synchronized off-work time with our two children.

New Leadership Roles

First Mennonite, where Stan and I had been married, was again our church of choice in Bluffton. I taught a college-age Sunday school class. Then a future-minded nominating committee asked if I'd be willing to let my name go on the ballot for congregational chair.

They laughed as they said, "Maybe we could call the position chairperson instead of chairman."

We all laughed. It sounded so strange! Never before had there been a woman on the ballot for that position. Besides, a strong male candidate's name was also on the ballot. I felt sure I wouldn't be elected, so why not let my name stand?

However, on January 10, 1974, I was elected congregational chair by a two-vote majority. When our chairman announced the election results, he paused—then announced dramatically, "Well, friends, we have just entered the twentieth century." I knew then what was ahead for me.

Many people seemed excited about this new step in our church's life and showered me with congratulations. I was scared—but not about to let people know it. That night as I crawled into bed beside Stan, I remember thinking how much I hoped this wouldn't change our relationship. I felt much in need of his continuing love and support.

That was the beginning of new leadership roles for me at First Mennonite. Before that, however, I had served on the Central District program committee, and then was elected to the General Conference program committee in 1971. I eventually chaired that committee and served the maximum of two six-year terms.

In retrospect, the years run together. As a representative of First Mennonite Church on the Mennonite Memorial Home board, I was eventually elected to serve as its first female chairperson. When I was elected to the pastoral search committee at First Mennonite, I pleaded that I was too busy to chair it, but I was conscripted. I simply didn't know how to say no and make it stick.

Proceeding with Much Prayer

I was working hard in the church and growing restless at school. By this time, our children were both married and I was a grandmother. My devotional life in the spring of 1984 led me to believe that I was in for a big change. The company for which Stan was working had been bought out by a large corporation, and management was being systematically let go. I figured God was preparing us for another move.

One morning, my devotional magazine had only one statement on the page. It was advice from John Wesley to Ellen Gretton in 1782: "Proceed with much prayer, and your way will be made plain." I felt that the words were being spoken directly to me.

Conference headquarters at Newton had contacted me about two job openings they wanted me to consider. I confidentially told my small prayer group that I was going to resign my tenured teaching position as soon as school was out for the summer, but that I had no idea what I was going to do after that.

Mark Weidner, conference minister and a member of our group, said, "Ruth, you ought to apply for the associate position at the church."

How preposterous, I thought! I wouldn't dream of it.

However, I did resign, and within the next two weeks I received three different invitations to apply for positions in our area which would not involve relocation. This was confusing! Stan, feeling that his own job security was tenuous, encouraged me to explore openings wherever I thought God might be calling me.

I have to admit that I had begun noticing a number of voices that were wittingly and unwittingly inviting me to consider First Mennonite. The congregational chairperson was almost twisting my arm. Perhaps God knew that gentle shoves wouldn't do it for me this time.

The hardest part was knowing that First Mennonite's constitution required all full-time pastors to be hired by vote of the whole congregation. Never before had we voted on a woman as pastor. The previous assistant pastor had been employed part-time, without a vote.

There would be no comforting second name on the ballot. I was afraid of being rejected outright, with no way of knowing whether it was because I was a woman, because they felt unready to add another full-time pastor, or because they simply knew me too well to want me in that position.

I was also afraid of the immensity of the assignment and my lack of preparation for it. Still, there was God's promise to Moses, "I will be with you." Wilderness or mountaintop ahead, I felt that same promise from God. That promise gave me the courage I needed. God knew I wasn't seeking the position. There was no way I'd want to be where I wasn't wanted—whatever the reason.

I was affirmed and licensed by the congregation, then ordained in 1987, and I served on the pastoral staff for twelve years.

"You're Going to Be All Right"

Soon after being hired by the church, I was invited to tell my faith story at the 1984 Dialogue on Faith, in Wisconsin. Women in leadership was one of the controversial issues certain to come up.

I knew a nearby pastor was one of the scheduled speakers—and I knew that he believed the ordination of women to be unbiblical. But being unaccustomed to driving long distances alone, I telephoned to ask him if we might ride together.

He politely declined, saying he needed the time alone to prepare his mind. I was surprised but tried not to feel rejected, reminding myself that I also needed solitude sometimes.

Kenneth Bauman, pastor of the Berne church, was also on the program at the Dialogue on Faith. I was fairly sure he would question the appropriateness of ordaining women. I felt a deep love and appreciation for the Berne congregation and the wonderful way they had helped to establish the Maplewood church in Fort Wayne. So I hated to think of "going against" his or their views regarding the place of women in leadership.

Before supper that first evening, I made it a point to speak to Pastor Bauman. I confessed my lack of ability to debate in a scholarly way and said I had simply been asked to tell my faith story.

Clearly, we read each other's heart. After my presentation, he came to where I was sitting, put his arm around me, and bent over to whisper, "You're going to be all right." Then he patted my shoulder and repeated, "You're going to be all right."

Introduced as Church "Secretary"

During the time I was serving as associate pastor, the eldest granddaughter of a Mennonite bishop from a neighboring state, went through our catechism program and requested baptism. Pastor Schmidt asked me to call the bishop and invite him to take part in the service.

I knew this distinguished bishop by sight and reputation, but we had never met. On the phone I explained that I was the associate pastor at First Mennonite Church in Bluffton and that we were inviting him to read Scripture at his granddaughter's baptism.

He was pleased, and we finalized details.

The bishop and his wife arrived early on the designated morning. When I saw them sitting nearly alone in the sanctuary, I went in to greet them. "Hello," I said, extending my hand, "I'm Ruth Naylor. It's good to have you here."

Recognizing that I was the one who had spoken with him on the phone, the good bishop turned thoughtfully to his wife and said, "This is the church secretary."

Moving Toward More Conference Leadership

During these years my lead pastor, Mel Schmidt, put my name in nomination for vice president of the General Conference Mennonite Church. The nominating committee was looking for two women, one Canadian and one from the United States. This was a logical way to see that a woman was elected to that high office.

I would have been happy to serve with Kenneth Bauman, the president. But at the Saskatoon triennial sessions, Florence Driedger was elected by an eighteen-vote margin. That night, at the Bluffton College alumni gathering, Ken hugged me and said, "I really thought you would be elected. I was looking forward to working with you."

A year or two later, when Pastor Bauman died, all I could do was thank God that I had not been elected. Florence was the better person to take over his awesome responsibility. Stan and I traveled from Bluffton to attend his funeral service. The huge Berne church was filled that day with folks from far and wide.

As we approached the door, an usher shook Stan's hand, greeted us warmly, and admitted that he couldn't remember our names. "Stan and Ruth Naylor," Stan said.

"Oh yes. . . ." The usher was searching Stan's face for more complete recall. "Are you a pastor, Stan?"

"No," replied Stan.

As the usher led us to a seat in the middle of the sanctuary, he explained, "I just wanted to make sure. You see, we're inviting all the pastors to sit together up front." He pointed to a nearly full row of dark-suited men.

It never occurred to him that *I* might be a pastor. Anyhow, I didn't feel like making a point of it. It was more important that I felt Ken would have welcomed me there.

When the Central District nominating committee asked to put my name on the ballot along with Jim Schrag's for president-elect, I felt safe enough to allow it. Although Jim was new to our district, his gifts were well-known.

I was truly surprised to be elected, and I'll never forget Jim's gracious comment: "I couldn't be happier. It's time we get some women into these positions."

I knew he meant it.

Four years later, Rachel Fisher and I chaired the joint meeting of Central District Conference and Indiana-Michigan Conference in Fort Wayne. Rachel was vice moderator of the I-M Conference. The sessions were relaxed and productive.

During the final discussion time, Harold Bauman expressed his amazement at how far the two conferences had progressed while he was on sabbatical in England. His warm comments about having women in leadership brought enthusiastic applause from the delegates.

Conference Minister—the Unexpected Pulpit

While serving as president of the district, I was named to the integration exploration committee—a committee where gender balance was intentionally and thoughtfully planned. Little did I know that before I retired, I'd be asked to fill an eighteen-month interim as conference minister.

At my first meeting of the northern Indiana pastor-peer group, Howard Habegger welcomed me with the news that Silverwood would soon be ordaining Steve Slagel. He emphasized that they'd be expecting me to officiate. Steve was gracious too, and all went well.

It was not as easy for another young pastor who had graduated from Dallas Seminary to accept the fact that a woman might license him for ministry. He made an appointment to see me in my office and asked his lead pastor (who had similar views about ordained women) to join us. I prayed sincerely for ability to listen and deal fairly with his concern.

In the end I said, "I understand that for you it would be a sin to have me officiate at your licensing. I'll see what we can work out."

When he came for his licensing interview with the ministerial committee, he was feeling more at ease with the possibility. He said he thought he could allow me to serve him.

However, later he phoned to say that he and his lead pastor had discussed it again. They felt it would raise too many questions in their church.

So I arranged for Pastor Willard Roth, chair of the ministerial committee, to do the licensing.

On the other hand, I served many Central District pastors and churches without any questions being raised. Yet I didn't know what would happen when it was time for the Berne church to install John Freed as their new minister of pastoral care. As it turned out, Pastor Craig Maven handled the situation diplomatically.

I was invited to bring greetings from the Central District. Pastor Maven read the questions regarding installation since the position was being drafted specifically to fit Berne's needs. And I, along with the deacons, participated in the prayer and laying on of hands.

In my public comments that day, I recalled the time when the Berne congregation was working with Stan and me at Maplewood. I acknowledged I could never have believed that someday I'd be standing in their pulpit, bringing them greetings from the Central District. It was a good day.

These are good times for all of us to be serving God together.

Ruth Naylor

God's Mysterious Doors

PAULINE GRAYBILL KENNEL

PAULINE KENNEL is pastor of Christ Community Mennonite Church, Schaumburg, Illinois, where her husband, LeRoy, is Minister of the Word. Since 1990 they have been copastors in this congregation.

Pauline earned degrees at Goshen College (B.A., Music, 1953), West Virginia University (M.Music, 1969), Bethany Theological Seminary (M.A., Theology, 1971; and M.Div., 1978), and Northwestern University (Ph.D., Music, 1980).

She has taught piano and public school music, music education, and Christian education. She has been a minister of music, a director of Christian education, and an administrator and director of development.

Pauline serves as a board member of Illinois Mennonite Federal Credit Union, and as president of the board of Mennonite Housing Aid, for Chicago Area Mennonite Ministries.

The Kennels are the parents of Jon, Rita, Janice, and Jay, and they enjoy seven grandchildren. Pauline's special interests include going to concerts and drama, as well as home decorating.

I WAS CONFRONTED with a reality I have never forgotten while a student at Bethany Theological Seminary in a course on the "Theology of God." In 1970, this class was taught by Warren Groff, dean of the seminary and soon to become president. I was thoroughly enjoying my studies, even though I was the only female in most of my classes for the program, master of arts in theology.

"I Wrote It Myself"

Our assignment was to write a paper presenting our personal theology of God. Class members took turns reading and critiquing each other's papers. When my turn came, I experienced the usual scrutiny and challenges one anticipates in such a setting. It was a good and stimulating time until I heard from Jimmy, an older student who had been a pastor and now was back at seminary: "A good paper, Pauline! LeRoy did an impressive job for you."

Suppose Jimmy had said, "Pauline, I don't feel that women have any business going to seminary, nor that it's right for them to be in ministry, because I don't believe that the Bible is clear about this." I could have accepted that as his way of thinking. But I was not prepared for his comment, which implied my inferiority to men, be they fellow seminarians or my husband, who was a professor at Bethany.

I was too shocked and meek to express my dismay, disappointment, and anger. I could only assert that, in fact, I wrote that paper myself.

Coordinator of Chicago Area Mennonites

Twelve years later I was presented by the Chicago Area Mennonites (CAM) Council and the Illinois Mennonite Conference minister to be the candidate for the position of coordinator of CAM. This is an organization of eighteen area Hispanic, black, and white congregations.

Responsibilities included relating with CAM churches, from Rehoboth, south of Chicago and near Kankakee, to Maple Avenue, near Milwaukee. I would assist them with church life, preparing annual budgets, pastoral searches, and dealing with church conflict as needed.

A woman present raised her concern that a woman would not be adequate for the position. The coordinator would have to drive to congregations in all parts of the city, including the ghettos, and relate to them. She likely wasn't aware that I had already traveled into most of those districts in my seminary commutes. She didn't know that I had related closely with some of those very congregations as a summer volunteer long ago and as an interim pastor's wife.

She also wasn't aware that I, LeRoy, and our children had dear friends among other races and cultures in these communities. She didn't know that in the 1960s we had "laid our lives on the line" to rent an apartment we owned to the first black family in the village limits of Lombard, a western suburb of Chicago.

A male pastor raised the concern that there might be pastors who would be unwilling or unable to relate to a female overseer. He stated that he personally would not have a problem—and he truly didn't, as our relationship during the seven years of my position proved. "But would others?" he wondered. No one raised another objection. I was installed as coordinator.

I was energized by the challenges of this CAM position. My many years of serving as pastor's wife, more than three years of seminary studies, and ministry in two large Presbyterian churches had given me good preparation.

I was invited to attend the annual meetings and retreats of the denomination's conference ministers, where I felt treated with respect and collegiality by the others, all male.

Hearing God's Call

I did not grow up feeling I was inferior or incapable because I was female. I was raised on a farm in rural Freeport, Illinois, the oldest of three children. I worked with my father in the fields and in the barn, milking cows.

My parents, Paul and Ruth Yoder Graybill, were good parents, encouraging and instilling self-esteem. They had each attended a year of college, received elementary teacher's certificates, and taught several years. My mother stopped teaching to get married, move to Illinois, and raise her family. Later she taught as a substitute teacher and served as the Women's Missionary and Service Commission (WMSC) churchwide treasurer for many years. My father left teaching to farm.

As a teen, I felt affirmed within my church and community. At age thirteen, I started giving piano lessons to area children. Various times I was asked to speak on a Sunday evening "topic," lead congregational singing, teach in summer Bible school, and provide leadership in the youth group.

I was led to a music education degree at Goshen College in 1953. There I was inspired by two strong and gifted faculty persons with whom I was blessed to work as student assistant: Mary Oyer, teaching music and fine arts; and Lois Winey, of the commerce department. They were loving, challenging, stimulating, encouraging, deeply committed Christians who expected good things from their students.

Never once did I consider pastoral ministry as my calling. My goal was to become a music teacher. The sense of call to pastoral ministry did not come until the school year of 1976-77, when I was forty-five years old and taking courses at Garrett Theological Seminary. My concentration was Christian education. Here professors and students named my pastoral gifts.

I realized then that I wanted to be prepared not only for music ministry and Christian education, but also for pastoral ministry. I took courses to complete a master of divinity degree.

Did I have a thick skull? Why did I sense this call so late in life? I didn't know female ministers earlier, so pastoring didn't seem to be an option. Yet I believe all of this was in God's providence. My call, coming in my youth, was to follow Christ and to serve wherever God would lead me.

I had eagerly accepted all leadership roles the church presented to me. I found my guiding light in two Scripture texts:

I appeal to you therefore, brothers and sisters, by the mercies of God, to present your bodies as a living sacrifice, holy and acceptable to God, which is your spiritual worship. Do not be conformed to this world, but be transformed by the renewing of your minds, so that you may discern what is the will of God—what is good and acceptable and perfect. (Romans 12:1-2)

Strive first for the kingdom of God and his righteousness, and all these things will be given to you as well. (Matthew 6:33)

I opened myself to be in close communion with God and to follow the Holy Spirit's leading in my life. Although I received this call to pastoral ministry at the age of forty-five, its fulfillment was not realized until some years later.

Church Planting

I married LeRoy, a seminary graduate, in 1953. Prior to my pastoral call, I participated with him in ministry at Metamora, Illinois. He was called in 1954 to plant a new Mennonite church in Lombard, Illinois, and he served as its pastor for over twelve years.

One of the significant developments for me at Lombard would have far-reaching effects. During the first year, the leadership of our little group engaged in discussion about effective ways to plant a new Mennonite church in an urban-suburban setting. We implemented many methods still employed in church planting: door-to-door community calling, hospitality evangelism, and printed brochures for distribution.

We took seriously the words of J. D. Graber, then executive secretary of the Mennonite Board of Missions and Charities. At LeRoy's installation, he asked us to trust the Holy Spirit, leading us to be an indigenous church, self-developing, self-propagating, and self-policy making.

Our group was concerned that most people in the area knew nothing about Mennonites and that first impressions would be crucial. We raised questions about the white head covering worn by female members of the Mennonite Church and by the members of our congregation in worship.

LeRoy suggested that the congregation do a serious and prayerful study of 1 Corinthians 11. In preparation, he shared the plans and questions for this study with a member of the Illinois Mennonite Conference executive committee.

Prayer Covering Issue

After this study and prayer for direction, the congregation decided to inform all participating women of the stand on this issue taken by the denomination and the Illinois Conference. However, the congregation wanted to be a truly successful church plant. We had a strong sense that the key text (1 Cor. 11:1-16) was given for a particular culture and time. We discerned God leading us to decide that women would not be required to wear the covering in our church.

We made it clear that we were not advocating this stance for anyone else—only in our Lombard setting. Women were free to either wear or not wear the covering. They could make their decision according to how they sensed God's Spirit leading them.

We did not know what the women members would do. When we gathered for worship the first time after this decision, only one woman wore the traditional prescribed covering. Some wore hats; others wore nothing on their heads.

The leadership of the Illinois Conference saw this as a heretical stance. They called the congregation to a hearing before the executive committee and then before conference delegates.

Conference decided that this new church plant at Lombard would be permitted to deviate from standard practice. However, they insisted that the pastor's wife should always wear the white head covering at worship.

It would have been so much easier for everyone, and especially for LeRoy, if I had agreed to this stipulation. But I could not. Such a double standard made no sense to me. I told conference that as a group we had felt God leading us in this decision. Either our sense of leading was wrong, or we would be wrong to require some (one) to wear the covering and not the rest.

Furthermore, as pastor's wife, I had a strong call to the leadership role this entailed as I related to people in the community and visitors to our church who were not yet Mennonite. I felt that if only I wore the covering, we would imply a lack of integrity and unity, something I highly valued.

Immediately Illinois Conference requested the Mennonite Board of Missions to stop the monthly subsidy they were providing to our church. They demanded the destruction of the five thousand brochures about our new church printed by the Illinois Mission Board.

To our small group, this was a big blow. It also meant that LeRoy needed to find an additional job so we could continue.

Nevertheless, God blessed the congregation. At a financially perilous moment, LeRoy was given a teaching contract at Hinsdale High School. For nine years he taught there, at Morton Junior College, and at Illinois State Teachers College.

The conference action also meant the termination of our membership on conference committees for several years. Nevertheless, we praise God that the congregation has become a strong and significant church, a blessing to many both inside and outside the denomination.

On to Ph.D. and Director
of Christian Education

Throughout the Lombard years, I was busy with mothering (our four children were born during this time), teaching piano, and some part-time public school music, and church work. Yet it became even busier in ensuing years as I kept responding to God's leading.

After the Lombard years, this leading included extensive educational preparation. I received a master of music degree from West Virginia University in 1969. When LeRoy was appointed to teach at Bethany Seminary that year, I thought I would find a music teaching position, but none was available.

I have discovered that when there is a closed door, I need only to ask, "Okay, God. So what do you have for me next?" I am convinced that the exciting journey of my life has been made possible or even directed by the closed doors. Otherwise, I believe I would still be teaching music. God works in mysterious ways.

Through LeRoy's encouragement in 1969, I began my first pursuit of a theological degree. At Bethany Theological Seminary, I entered the program for a master of arts in theology. I desired a good theological undergirding for my work in church music. In 1971 I completed this degree.

I was also serving as Bethany's director of music and organist during 1969-75. Since I felt increasingly stimulated and challenged, I applied for and (in 1970) was accepted into a Ph.D. program in music education at Northwestern University. Not till 1980 did I complete my dissertation and receive the degree.

This doctoral program was stretched out because during this same time I also sensed a call for more seminary study in Christian education. So I took the classes at Garrett Seminary, where others named gifts for me that challenged me to get an M.Div. Yet even after completing the M.Div. degree in 1978, I sought out positions in music. Again, I found closed doors!

Almost immediately I received a call from nearby Yorkfield Presbyterian Church to interview for a position. I was hired as director of Christian education because "the congregation isn't ready for a female assistant pastor." Nevertheless, people were soon introducing me as their assistant pastor. I stayed for four good years, working with an excellent young pastor in a fine team relationship.

The High Cost of Leadership

Why did my journey include the intense work and cost of the Ph.D. in music? I never did go back to music teaching afterward, except in church ministry settings and interim appointments at area schools.

I know without a doubt that the Ph.D. program developed much self-confidence, self-awareness, and courage within me. This training gave me courage to be open to and able to embrace situations I would never have imagined.

These opportunities included the position of CAM coordinator; part-time or adjunct seminary teaching at Bethany, Northern Baptist, North Park, and Associated Mennonite Biblical Seminary; and administration and development positions at Chicago Mennonite Learning Center.

My appointment in 1990 as copastor of our Schaumburg congregation, Christ Community Mennonite Church, was not without problems. We had begun this church in 1988, after a study by Chicago Area Mennonites had targeted the northwest region of the area as a good location for a church plant.

Our church was composed mostly of persons without earlier Mennonite experience. Many had their own ideas of what a church should be like.

When LeRoy made a proposal that I be named copastor, there was a congregational decision to proceed. However, two vocal men refused to accept biblical interpretation that women could be in leadership roles. They and their families withdrew from the church. Those eleven people were a big loss, but the congregation remained firm in its commitment to call forth all the gifts within the body, regardless of gender.

Christ Community Mennonite Church stands as a wonderful model of the kingdom of God. Women, men, children, African-Americans, Hispanics, Asians, and Caucasians are living, worshiping, learning, and working together. We are serving God's reign in this town of over seventy-five thousand people—and still growing.

What a privilege it is to be called to help create the kingdom of God!

Pauline Graybill Kennel

I Never Intended to Be a Pastor

JOYCE SHUTT

JOYCE SHUTT was the second woman to be ordained as a minister in the General Conference Mennonite Church. She was ordained in 1980 and since then has been pastor of the Fairfield Mennonite Church in Adams County, Pennsylvania.

Adams County, with the historical Gettysburg Battlefield, and the orchards of apples, cherries, and peaches, has been the geographic center of her life and ministry. While pastoring, she worked as a part-time chaplain for Adams County Green Acres Nursing Home from 1986-91.

Joyce earned a B.A. at Bluffton College and an M.A. in Religion at Gettysburg Theological Seminary. During 1959-61, she and her husband, Earl, worked with Mennonite Central Committee in Austria, Germany, and France. From 1962 to 1989, they were fruit farmers in rural Adams County.

Joyce served on the literature committee of Women in Mission (General Conference Mennonite Church) and was one of the first women members of the Commission on Home Ministries.

With her family's permission, Joyce wrote the book *Steps to Hope* (1990), to share with others the help that is available in twelve-step programs. In 1991 the book received an Award of Merit at the annual Angel Award ceremonies.

Her hobbies are reading, gardening, and quilting. Joyce and her husband, Earl, are the parents of Kris, Gretchen, John, and Tim, and they have four grandchildren.

WHATEVER MY PASTORAL GIFTS and passions, they flow from my efforts to make lemonade out of the lemons of life, from the paradoxical promise of the death-resurrection motif that has kept me going over the years. In spite of all that's happened, my many emotional and spiritual deaths, God has been very good to me.

I've had my share of tragedy and pain, but so much goodness has come my way. So much goodness! Such is the mystery of God. He loves us in spite of ourselves. Even when we are most tempted to give up on ourselves, God never does.

My Father's Legacy

I never intended to be a pastor. Never in a million years! I graduated from Bluffton College in 1958 with a degree in dramatic literature and a longing to try my hand at theater. But being a "good little Mennonite girl," I never did.

However, one thing is sure: I never considered pastoral ministry as an option. After all, Timothy says a pastor must be "the husband of one wife" and "a person of impeccable character." I am neither.

Yet here I am, pastor of the Fairfield Church and the second woman ordained as a minister in the General Conference Mennonite Church! How in the world did that ever happen? Some stories are stranger than fiction. Sometimes I feel that way about my life.

I grew up in the Fairfield Mennonite Church, a gentle congregation that gave its members permission to grapple with the big questions of life and faith. "God is bigger than anything we will ever know or understand," my father used to tell me. "Never be afraid of your pain or doubts. God can handle whatever you have to give him! Above all, be honest and question everything, for when you stop questioning, you might as well be dead."

Question I did, and still do. That questioning spirit, my father's precious legacy, has been both my curse and blessing. Today my faith is deeply grounded, streaming forth from life's paradox of joy and pain.

I met Earl at Bluffton College. Earl and I are an interesting married pair, well-matched in many ways, terribly mismatched in others. My passion, nonconformity, and intellectual emotionalism counterbalances his quiet conformity, reserve, stability, and orderliness.

Ours has been a stormy and yet committed relationship. Not a day goes by that I do not thank God for this quiet man, or give thanks that we hung in there long enough to reap the benefits of the love we share today.

From 1959 to 1961, we worked in Europe with Mennonite Central Committee (MCC). Earl was doing his alternative service. I worked as housekeeper in the various units where he served. Those were wonderful years, formative in so many ways.

My dad taught me to question. Bluffton College taught me that God is far greater than any idea or accomplishment of humanity, so I need never fear science, knowledge, or education.

Mennonite Central Committee introduced me to a big world, cross-cultural experiences, and an understanding of church that completely changed my perception of life and faith.

Gettysburg Lutheran Seminary and the General Conference taught me about grace.

Finding a New Mold

From the beginning, I did not fit into the traditional box of family and home. But I tried. My mother didn't fit that mold either, though she never admitted it. I left MCC pregnant and did not return to teaching. When I became restless, we had a second child. Within five years we took in thirteen foster children and adopted two biracial boys.

During that same period, I began reading Betty Friedan and other early feminists. Their writings touched something deep within me, even though I'd convinced myself I was completely happy being a housewife and mother.

Then Earl's health began to fail because of rheumatoid arthritis.

He told me he couldn't handle all those children and my frenetic activity. He said he was attracted to another who was calmer and more centered than I was.

I "cracked up." Angry and depressed, feeling betrayed by God and the church, as well as my husband, I contemplated suicide, and went into therapy.

Then wonder of wonders, in 1968 I was appointed to the literature committee for the General Conference Women in Mission. Those writing assignments and trips to Newton, Kansas, opened up a whole new set of options and responses for me. They challenged me to use my anger for constructive change.

I was one of the first women appointed to serve on the Commission on Home Ministries (CHM) and the General Conference ministerial committee. I met people who looked past my anger and bitterness, my tears and emotional outbursts, and saw gifts and abilities that I never saw in myself.

Several significant memories stand out from those years. There was the time I was sitting in the back row as an observer at a CHM meeting. At that time, the commission was made up of only ordained men. They were trying to decide who to send to a special evangelism consultation.

Suddenly I heard a voice: "You men make me sick. You act as if there's only one kind of person in the world, ordained men. Well, I've got news for you. Over half of the world's population is made up of women, and the rest are men who are not ordained!"

I became aware that it was my voice. To make matters worse, I ran weeping from the room. Imagine my amazement when one of those same ordained men I'd attacked came looking for me.

He gently said, "What you just did was beautiful and prophetic. You were absolutely right in what you said. We want you to join us at the table as our spokesperson for women's issues."

The Pieces of My Faith Puzzle

In the fall of 1969, I was sitting in my therapist's office and telling him how I was dying emotionally and intellectually. I wanted to go back to school.

He said, "But you have a responsibility to look after your family. Perhaps when Tim is ten. . . ."

Black rage I kept stuffed deep within erupted once again. I kicked a hole in his newly paneled wall with my high-heeled shoe and said in deadly calm, "If I wait that long, I'll be dead."

Several weeks later, I enrolled as a part-time student at Gettysburg Lutheran Seminary. On my application form, I wrote, "For years I've had a love-hate relationship with God. I've got to resolve it one way or the other, to fall in love with God or get him off my back. Maybe this will help."

I fell in love. But I never intended to go into the ministry.

Except for my father, no one in my family understood my compulsion to go back to school. Earl felt threatened. My in-laws thought I was neglecting the children. My mother interpreted my struggles as a bad reflection on her as a parent. Our four children complained vociferously, pushing my already-overactive guilt buttons to overload.

I planned to take only one or two courses per semester. When it came time to register for that first winter term, Earl and I had a horrendous fight. In despair, I ran into the orchards behind our house, screaming at God: "Why is it that every time I find something that gives my life meaning, you take it away?" I sobbed uncontrollably until all fight and tears were gone.

Then came a still small voice of unbelievable love and compassion. "Every time your wants and needs get in the way of what is best for you and those you love, I will take them away."

I went back to the house. "I've decided to drop out of seminary," I said.

Several months later, Earl gathered me in his arms. "Go back to school, with my blessing. I now understand that this is something you truly need to do. You are a better wife and mother when you are doing what you love."

I truly loved seminary. I loved the flow of words, the ideas, the intellectual challenge. I loved the way studying in a Lutheran school helped me rethink my Mennonite heritage and thought. I loved tangling with other students and professors. I loved being an apologist for adult baptism, pacifism, and other Anabaptist concepts.

As a result of my experience at Gettysburg Lutheran Seminary, I became a convinced Anabaptist. But my exposure to Lutheran and Pauline thought spoke to something deep inside of me, supplying a missing piece of my faith puzzle. The blending of my experiences with Lutheran theology convinced me that without a solid foundation of grace, our focus on discipleship and service turns into a tyrannical form of legalism.

Yet as much as I loved doing theology, preaching, and leading worship, I never intended to go into the ministry.

Called to My Home Church

During the eight years I was in seminary, the combination of going to class and serving on the various committees and commissions of General Conference gave me more than enough outlets for my restless energy.

I served on numerous committees. I helped resource workshops. I worked on women's issues. I went to consultations on the role of women, war taxes, and voluntary service. I wrote for *The Mennonite, Builder, Gospel Herald,* and other magazines. I served as worship leader and often preached at my home church in Fairfield, Pennsylvania. I was happy, energized, and busy.

Gettysburg Lutheran's M.Div. program has always taken four years: three years of class work, a summer of clinical pastoral education, and two semesters in a church internship. I did my internship at Fairfield Mennonite, my home church, in fall 1978 and spring 1979.

Gradually the unthinkable became thinkable. Could a hometown girl who seemed to have the gift for pastoral ministry be a candidate for our empty pulpit? We tested that idea with my professors and with persons I worked with in Newton and elsewhere. Receiving affirmation and support everywhere we turned, the congregation and I requested ordination.

The Eastern District ministerial committee decided they could not approve our request for ordination because I was a woman. So we appealed to the ministerial committee of the General Conference.

Several years earlier, the General Conference Mennonite Church had passed a resolution that ordination should be determined by gifts and call, not gender. Since then, they had ordained Marilyn Miller in 1976.

Because of the refusal of Eastern District and the resolution of GCMC, Central District ordained me the same weekend I graduated from seminary, in May of 1980. It was an incredibly beautiful experience!

Fish to Catch and Sheep to Feed

The years that followed were both challenging and stormy. Things at Fairfield Mennonite flowed smoothly. Things with the district did not.

Year after year in Eastern District, resolutions were submitted, calling for sanctioning Fairfield Mennonite and removing my credentials. We endured study conferences and discussions. We tried to be gracious and accepting of those who interpreted the Bible in a way different from our understanding. But in time, each discussion or resolution became more and more painful.

When our daughter ran away and my father was killed in an automobile accident, I was torn by grief, family trauma, and the ever-difficult challenge of juggling church and family. I was ready to resign and play by the accepted rules. And then I had a dream.

I dreamed I was attending a consultation on the role of women held at Zion Mennonite in Souderton, Pennsylvania. At this meeting, the women were forced to sit at the back of the church. Only the men were allowed to speak.

After hours of intense debate, I grabbed the microphone and said, "Gentlemen, while you are debating how many angels can dance on the head of a pin, I have sheep to feed and fish to catch." I then walked out of the meeting.

Several weeks later I shared my dream with our conference minister. I told him that I would not be attending our spring conference. Instead, I would go to Harrisonburg, Virginia, for a conference on women in ministries. Whatever they decided about my credentials was fine with me.

In the end, it was their problem, not mine. Whatever the unresolved issues about women in ministry, God had placed me in a position where I had fish to catch and sheep to feed.

I have been fishing and feeding ever since. Yet things have not always gone smoothly. Our two adopted sons struggled with addictions, wandering in and out of drug rehabs and the juvenile court system. Our daughter was diagnosed with depression and panic and anxiety disorder.

I questioned whether I could continue pastoring when our family life was such a shamble.

My father's death devastated our children and left my mother heartbroken and dependent. Earl's rheumatoid arthritis intensified, with one surgery following another. Side effects from his medications led to other complications, hospitalizations, a near-death experience, and heart bypass surgery.

The summer of 1989, I had a hysterectomy that didn't turn out to be routine. Before the nightmare was over, I had had three major surgeries and lived through two code blues in the span of only six weeks!

During my recovery, with my family's permission, I wrote the book *Steps to Hope.* Our experience with drug addiction made us keenly aware that other good Christian families struggled with emotional illness and drug and alcohol addictions, but were afraid to let anyone know.

We were convinced that pain should never be wasted, but used to help others. So we decided to share our story and the help we'd found in twelve-step programs.

I Never Intended to Be a Pastor, . . . But God Intended for Me

Through it all, Fairfield Mennonite stood with us, held us up, prayed with and for us, refused my resignation, and challenged me to use our experiences as a springboard for helping others. In time, I began to see how God was leading me through the valleys of deepest darkness to make me more sensitive to the needs of his people.

My years in therapy and the near collapse of our marriage made me sensitive to those who were hurting and made me a more caring counselor. The insights I gained participating in twelve-step meetings deepened my faith and taught me how to give others permission to follow the God of their understanding. There, too, I learned how to detach with love, a skill any pastor needs for working with those who are troubled, hurting, sick, or dying.

Our years with MCC led to our congregation holding a yearly consignment sale for Self-Help Crafts, now Ten Thousand Villages.

My experience with sexual discrimination sensitized me to prejudice and various isms that hurt and maim. That suffering made me painfully aware of what it feels like to be excluded from the body of Christ for reasons beyond one's control.

I also developed compassion for the elderly through the many years I worked as a part-time chaplain at our county's nursing home.

I am doing jail ministries, and I serve on the board of a local drug and alcohol agency. I am convinced that the church must be a place for healing and new beginnings. Hence, I have gathered in the lost and the broken, the separated, divorced, abused, recovering addicts, homosexuals—all with congregational support.

In the process, our little congregation has been blessed by some incredibly gifted and deeply motivated individuals who have inspired and enriched all of us.

I have attempted to get other congregations and denominations involved in gathering in the lost and broken. This ministry has sensitized me to ecumenical issues. As our Ten Thousand Villages sales grew, we turned to the larger community for help. And help they do!

I devoted much energy into reorganizing the Fairfield Ministerium. Just as attending a Lutheran Seminary made me a more committed Anabaptist, so participating in the flowering of our local ministerial group has made me appreciate the larger church.

How rich my spiritual life has become as a result of these ecumenical experiences! It has confirmed my belief that if we are to be faithful to Christ, then we dare not waste our pain and varied experiences.

Likewise, we need not fear different ways of seeing, doing, and "phrasing" church. God is faithful, and the Spirit is ever vigilant and present on our behalf.

Looking back over almost twenty years of pastoral ministry, I have few regrets and many praises. Like Paul, I am learning to be content in whatever situation I find myself.

I ponder all the things I have tried to do in my ministry and life, all the people I have met and loved, and all the ways I have tried to live out my Anabaptist understandings of discipleship and peacemaking. But I am most awed that two of my closest companions in Christ are a Catholic priest and a Franciscan sister.

It is so easy to question whether this or that is God's will. The ups and downs of life have taught me that discerning God's will is not as much about what we do as it is about *whose* we are. When we are in relationship with God, we find ourselves doing many unpredictable things and sailing in uncharted waters—like my being an ordained pastor.

I never intended to go into the ministry. Yet it appears that God did intend that ministry for me. And in the end, that's all that really matters.

By God's Providence

RUTH BRUNK STOLTZFUS

RUTH BRUNK STOLTZFUS is the first woman to be ordained by Virginia Mennonite Conference. She was ordained at the age of seventy-four in recognition of her ministry in the wider church and at the Shalom Mennonite Congregation, started in 1986 and meeting on the campus of Eastern Mennonite University. Ruth has served as interim pastor twice in Ohio, and once as co-pastor in Richmond, Virginia.

Ruth has been an entrepreneur. She founded the Heart to Heart broadcast for mothers, carried by thirty-two radio stations, and was the speaker on it for eight years. She also is founder of Concord Associates Family Life Series for newspapers.

Ruth and her husband, Grant, have spoken in many churches and conference sessions, promoting Christian values in family life. Grant, a professor of church history at Eastern Mennonite College, died in 1974.

In 1989 Ruth received the Eastern Mennonite College Distinguished Service Award in recognition of forty years of speaking at hundreds of church functions, writing newspaper ads and radio spots on family life themes, and doing counseling work. Ruth has also served on the Council of Faith, Life, and Strategy and has been a respected stateswoman in the Mennonite Church for many years.

Articles by Ruth have appeared in the *Church Advocate, Daughters of Sarah, Family Digest, Gospel Herald, Purpose, WMSC Voice, Workman Quarterly* (of the Church of God), and *The Mennonite*. Her poster

"Mother's Pledge," translated into Russian and Spanish, has been distributed widely. Moody Press published *Her Heart and Home* (1959), a collection of Ruth's radio messages to mothers.

At age eighty-four, Ruth Brunk Stoltzfus is hoping to finish her books, *Blueberries and Briers: A Woman's Journey;* and *Heart to Heart: Day by Day,* a book of 365 daily meditations.

Ruth and Grant have five children: Allen Grant, Eugene, Ruth Stoltzfus Jost, Kathryn Stoltzfus Fairfield, and Helen Greenberg Stoltzfus. They have twelve grandchildren and three great-grandchildren.

I WAS THE EIGHTH of nine children, the fifth daughter of George R. and Katie Wenger Brunk, Newport News, Virginia. Ours was a rich, secure, and happy home, where we had everything but money.

Mama, loving, efficient, and busy, was so pleasant that she could hardly look cross even when she had to correct us! Papa was a busy bishop. But our home life still had a balance of love, labor, fun, and faith. We enjoyed Bible nurture, work on our farm, recreation, and more.

Papa took us to historical celebrations at Jamestown, Yorktown, and Williamsburg. After we heard an Indian chief speak at Williamsburg, Papa went up front and told him, "The Mennonites never fought the Indians." A man yelled out, "You never fought the Germans either!" This brought me, an eight-year-old, a new awareness of our Mennonite worldview as conscientious objectors.

Our Souls in Thy Service

Papa's table prayer often included, "Bless this food to its intended use and our souls in thy service." *Our souls in thy service.* The words were riveted into my being.

My first taste of public speaking was as a child at our Sunday evening church meetings. Typically, a child recited a Bible verse, an older child read a paper (likely written by a parent), a young person gave a talk, a grown woman often spoke, and the final speaker was a man.

Beginning in my teens, I was active in church as Sunday school song leader, teacher, and summer Bible school teacher. At age six-

teen, I was elected president of our young people's week-night Mennonite Literary Society. Papa helped me with my inaugural address:
"I thank you for the confidence you have shown in electing me. . . ."

More than once I was asked to give readings by memory. Papa
helped me select them, and I rehearsed them before him, receiving
suggestions for voice variations and gestures. In one, as I held a goblet of "wine" to impersonate a woman speaking against drinking,
he had me drop the goblet at a certain point and let it crash on the
floor.

Until I was twenty-two, he also helped me with speeches and debates while I was at home and when I was two hundred miles away
at Eastern Mennonite High School and College.

More than once Papa's letters said, "Ruth, . . . service in the
church, . . . service in the church." Could my service in the church
be a speaking ministry? While Papa did not believe in the ordination of women, I felt that he did groom me for a speaking ministry.

Once minister Ray Shenk asked him, "What shall we do with
those Bible verses about the silence of women in the church?"

He answered, "Men can't latch onto one or two verses in the
Bible about silence just to please our own egos."

Heart to Heart

In God's providence, it was possible for me to be a wife, mother
of five children, and still engage in a part-time speaking ministry.
My husband, Grant M. Stoltzfus, shared parenting duties though he
was busy over the years as an editor, writer, teacher, and active
church layman. I kept an open-door office in our home, for access
to and from the family. If we had been missionaries on foreign soil,
we would have had help with home duties. We were missionaries on
home soil and had part-time assistance with housework.

During seventeen years, while Grant taught at Eastern Mennonite
College (EMC), he and I conducted weekend family life conferences
in many churches. Sometimes we took the children along in our station wagon, which he said was to haul "babies, books, and bag-
gage."

Time and again in 1950, I felt God leading me to start a broadcast for mothers. Grant respected this and went with me to a radio
station, to see about such a venture. We were leaving the station

with a negative answer from the assistant manager when the manager walked in and invited us back to his desk. Yes, there was available time, and I would go on the air "this Friday at 11:00 a.m."

After the children were in bed that evening, we talked of a name for the newborn broadcast. "What do you want to do on the broadcast?" Grant asked.

I mentioned some ideas and said, "I just want to talk heart to heart."

"That's your name," he said. "Heart to Heart."

The Mennonite community of Christian businesses, church groups, and individuals put the program on thirty-two stations. This brought invitations for me to speak in hundreds of pulpits over the church. It led to my weekly illustrated Family Life Series for newspapers and to Minute Messages for radio. Eventually requests came for me to serve as interim pastor twice in Ohio, and once as copastor in Richmond, Virginia.

There were also times of frustration. One weekend, Grant and I traveled to a congregation to speak on family topics. Each of us had sent a separate list of topics on which we would be prepared to speak.

On short notice, the topic requested for the Sunday morning message was "The Home and Discipline." That was my topic. Yet because it was Sunday morning, I as a woman could not give it, so Grant was asked to speak on the topic. (Oh! how I still miss him!) He struggled through my scribbled notes and abbreviations as well as he could while I sat on the bench, bursting with things I had prepared to say.

Moving into Public Ministry

I continued to receive many invitations to do public ministry. I believed in the power of the Spirit to nurture, change, and equip us through God's Word. I valued the opportunity to share personal responses with each other. After giving a message, I often felt led to invite those in the audience to accept slips of paper from ushers and finish the sentence, "I feel God is calling me to . . ."

Persons could choose whether or not to participate, sign their name, share their writing verbally, or hand in the paper. The hundreds of responses were evidence of God's Spirit at work in this speaking ministry, as shown in these samples:

I feel God is calling me to—

- rededicate my life to Christ—to leave behind the luster of worldly things.
- give of my resources for distribution to the needy.
- consider a term of service with Mennonite Central Committee.
- help with Bible study at Boys' Correctional Center.
- forgive someone special in my life who has deeply hurt me.
- pray more fervently for our family to come to the Lord—those who are Christians-to-be. [What faith! We paused right there to pray for them.]
- be more affirming with my children and spouse.
- be a loving husband, father, to be actively involved in this fellowship and outreach.
- be an intercessor in prayer. Thank you, God, for allowing me to attend this meeting.
- be a person of reconciliation within our fellowship.

At times I felt led to invite audiences to stand for an object lesson on forgiveness based on Ephesians 4:32: "Forgiving one another, as God in Christ has forgiven you." First we looked up to God with outstretched hands, while breathing in God's forgiveness. Then we looked around to breathe out and spread forgiveness to others.

Women in Ministry

I experienced affirmations and put-downs in the church. Yet the positives far outnumber and outrank the negatives.

In 1972, EMC president Myron Augsburger said, "I want you to know your work does not go unnoticed. I'm thinking you ought to be commissioned and put on the road more. Maybe EMC can do this if Virginia Conference does not."

At the Mennonite Assembly 1973 in Harrisonburg, Virginia, during the discussion on women's role, I felt moved to speak. Among the many affirming comments afterward, a young woman told me, "Now I feel more like staying in the Mennonite Church."

During our 1981 Mennonite Assembly at Bowling Green, Ohio, opportunity was given for discussion after presentation of the study report on Leadership and Authority. I was a member of the Council on Faith, Life, and Strategy, which had been asked to be a listening committee at the Assembly. I sat near the front, close to a floor mike, in case I felt moved to speak.

After some men and women spoke on women's role in the church, I begged the Lord to guide my words and went to a microphone. This is part of what I shared:

> It is interesting that the verse "And, ye fathers, provoke not your children to wrath: but bring them up in the nurture and admonition of the Lord" [Eph. 6:4, KJV], is interpreted to exclude men from home duties, and Romans 12 and 1 Corinthians 12 are interpreted to exclude women from the use of their gifts in the church. . . . A heresy begins when a doctrine is based on one or two Bible verse—a doctrine that violates the teaching of the verses on women using their gifts in the church. . . .

Other men and women spoke. Then a motion was passed that the General Board appoint a committee to study and facilitate the process of bringing women into full participation in leadership ministries of the church.

By the final session in that 1981 Assembly, 87 people (45 men, 42 women) came to me with affirming comments. My critics did not approach me. Later I learned of some of their attitudes.

A phone call brought me the disturbing news that my talk at Bowling Green might not be on the tape recording. "Someone kicked out the cord of the recorder. Outage was for five minutes," the caller said. I wrote out the talk as well as I could and sent it to the *Voice* editor, Vel Shearer, as she had requested.

A Bowling Green observer wrote to *Gospel Herald*, "It reminded me more of a group of rebels bulldozing their way through, than saints in search of God's will."

At first I thought I would not dignify the remarks by replying. But hadn't five sisters stood before Moses, the priest, the leaders, and the vast assembly to request fair treatment (Num. 27:1-7)? And hadn't God told Moses they were right?

I wrote to the *Gospel Herald* "Readers Say" column:

> Judging by the many spiritually minded men who strongly affirmed my comments at Bowling Green 81, I believe they have been embarrassed for men in their treatment of women, as I have

been for whites in their treatment of blacks. . . . Let us listen honestly to each other and pay better attention to the gifts and the call of God's strong Spirit to women and men. Then, with courage, caution and charity, let us get on with necessary changes so that in the home and church, both crucial areas of ministry, male and female will share responsibilities as taught in the Word.

Later I wrote an article for the *Gospel Herald* on the use of women's gifts in the church. I received this stinging rebuke: "I picture you as counseling girls to have abortions, seeing no harm in divorce, and stomping down any man's authority you don't like."

In response to another *Gospel Herald* article, "Jesus and the Role of Women," I received twelve positive responses, and one insulting card simply signed, "A Woman." A daughter left a note of enthusiasm on my desk. A sister phoned humorous affirmation: "If anyone criticizes that article . . ." Of the other ten positive responses, six were from women in five states and Canada; four were from men in three states and Canada.

Under an assumed name, a Mennonite wrote a *Gospel Herald* article on the "woman question," including Bible verses calling women to be silent in the church.

In "Readers Say" of that paper, I responded that verses on silence for women should not be mentioned without references to women leaders in Old and New Testaments. I also noted Paul's instructions to men and women who pray or prophesy in the public assembly (1 Cor. 11:4-5).

This same writer must have had a change of heart. In another Mennonite publication, he later centered on God's words to Israel: "I sent Moses and Aaron and Miriam to lead you." He wrote, "God's Micah 6:3-4 for me goes as follows: 'I provided H. S. Bender, J. C. Wenger, and Ruth Brunk Stoltzfus to lead you, but you, donkey-like, resisted. For shame.'"

The dear brother! I thought.

I became convinced that no one should speak or write on the subject of women in public ministry until that person had made a thorough study of women leaders in Old and New Testaments. The study shows that we are not yet as up-to-date as these examples in Bible times.

Frederick Franson, the first missionary commissioned by D. L. Moody's church, once listed every Bible reference to speaking ministries or responsible positions of women, totaling a hundred. He found it strange that a doctrine of silence for women is built on two passages that appear to be against women's spiritual ministry. Such a teaching violates all the other ninety-eight Bible references. He warned that this is how heresies begin.

While speaking on the subject in meetings, I sometimes illustrated at the board the hundred Bible references by making twenty dashes in each of five columns. Then I drew a circle around two dashes to show that we cannot form on two verses a doctrine that violates the teaching of all the other ninety-eight verses.

The apostle Paul illustrates this point. In 1 Corinthians 11:4-5, he gives instructions to men and women who pray and prophesy in the public assembly. Then in 1 Corinthians 14:34, Paul, the same man in the same letter, says women should be silent in the church.

Bible commentators have asked, "What local circumstance caused Paul to forbid what he had allowed? In what way had women not been quiet enough?"

John M. Lederach asked me to speak on "Freeing Daughters to Prophesy" for the November 12, 1987, Philhaven teleconference luncheon series for clergy and church workers. At age seventy-two, I felt I had waited decades to give this message, but I also felt thanks for persons like John who came on the scene before I move off the scene.

Seated with Eastern Mennonite Seminary people in Harrisonburg, Virginia, I spoke by phone connection to noontime groups at Lansdale, Pennsylvania; Ephrata, Pennsylvania; Neffsville, Pennsylvania; Salunga, Pennsylvania (Eastern Mennonite Board of Missions); Mt. Gretna, Pennsylvania (Philhaven Hospital); Manchester, Indiana; Elkhart, Indiana (Mennonite Board of Congregational Ministries). I spoke on four points:

- Prophetesses and Other Women Leaders in Bible Times
- Longstanding Myths About Women
- Jesus' Treatment of Women
- Suggestions for Freeing Women to Prophesy

Both negative and affirming responses continued. A church in Virginia canceled an appointment their pastor had made for me to speak on "Lasting Married Love" at their Sunday evening meeting before Valentine's Day. The pastor apologized and said objections came mostly from women in the church.

Later, following a Sunday morning message in another church, a high school principal wrote:

> Your sermon on discipleship—loving God first, not having other gods in my life—cut like a knife. . . . Then when you said what you did at the door, my faith was stirred that God still has something for me to do in spite of my sin (inability to discipline myself with money and finances).

A woman once wrote me twenty-four years after she had been in my audience:

> The message—the way you reached us—I remember thinking, "She should be an ordained minister of the gospel in the Mennonite Church." I believe God had ordained you, even if the church had not.

For years I had taken seriously the statement of Charles G. Finney: "No church acquainted with the Holy Ghost will object to the public ministry of women." I once told my friend, Willard Swartley, "Maybe women with gifts from the Spirit for public ministry should get together and ordain each other—similar to the early Anabaptists who baptized each other." He replied, "Oh, please let the men be present too."

I have collected some choice quotations, such as these:

> The main theme we tend to miss is that the subservience of women is related to the Fall, which Christ came to redeem. By continuing to assign a secondary status to women, we are perpetuating the Fall. This theological background needs to be understood. . . . (Paul M. Lederach, Franconia Mennonite Conference bishop)

> Our translations tend to cover up the extent to which women were leaders [in Bible times]. . . . We have a long way to go until

we give women the freedom to serve in our congregations that the New Testament allowed. (Marlin Miller, Goshen Biblical Seminary president)

I want to apologize to you for my brothers who have treated you unfairly by denying your gift and calling as a minister. (Angel Ocasio, two days after his ordination)

Ordination

I was seventy-two and an active member at Shalom Mennonite Congregation (Harrisonburg, Va.) when the pastor, Christopher Gill, visited me at the advice of overseer Paul T. Yoder. He said, "There's been talk of ordaining you to the ministry."

I soon consulted my nephew, George R. Brunk III, dean of Eastern Mennonite Seminary. He advised me to talk (one by one) with several Virginia Mennonite Conference leaders: Owen Burkholder, John R. Martin, and Samuel Weaver. I was to ask each, "Would your perception of the current situation in the conference lead you to encourage my consent to ordination?"

He also advised me to discuss with overseer Paul T. Yoder and Pastor Gill the wisdom of stating in writing the grounds for my ordination.

My bishop brother, Truman H. Brunk Sr., had said in the 1985 slide production celebrating the 150th anniversary of Virginia Conference, "I believe the time will come when Virginia Mennonite Conference will ordain women." Now in 1989, he commented on the pain of going against the wishes of some people: "Simply say, 'There is talk in the conference about ordaining me, and it's in the hands of the church leaders. I'm an obedient servant of the church.' "

When I phoned nephew Truman H. Brunk Jr. about talk of my ordination, he said, "Someone is needed with experience, seasoning, and careful words, to plow the way for other women. There is no one else to do it. I pledge to be in prayer for the next twenty-four hours."

My daughter Kathryn said, "Mother, for the sake of other women, you'll have to experience the pain of going against the wishes of some people."

Pastor Emma Richards wrote: "Please keep me informed on what might be happening concerning your ordination. I do so hope it is done by the church—recognizing what God did long ago!"

I was ordained on September 10, 1989, at Shalom Mennonite Church. Paul E. Groff chaired the meeting, Faye Yoder led the singing, nephew George R. Brunk III led devotions, John R. Martin gave the message, and overseer Paul T. Yoder gave the charge. He stated as grounds for ordination my ongoing preaching assistance at Shalom Mennonite, and my ministry in the wider church.

Next was my testimony, followed by responses from Doris Gascho, a friend; James A. Burkholder, co-worker in my family life newspaper series; daughter Kathryn Stoltzfus Fairfield; and nephew Truman H. Brunk Jr., who also led in closing prayer.

My brother George R. Brunk II and I love each other, but we do not agree on ordination for women. Soon after my ordination, he kissed me and said, "I love you anyhow." Sometimes he honked his horn as he drove by. Never before had I thanked God for a honking horn.

After my ordination, I was comforted and affirmed by church leaders, relatives, and friends who phoned, visited, and wrote words of affirmation and promises of prayer.

As I close this account of my journey, I bow my heart in thanksgiving for God's great grace and providential hand all along the way.

Ruth Brunk Stoltzfus

Educators

The gifts Christ gave were that
some would be . . . teachers,
to equip the saints
for the work of ministry.
—*Paul, in Ephesians 4:11-12*

The Holy Ghost over the Bent World Broods

MARY K. OYER

J. Tyler Klassen

MARY OYER has recently retired as professor of church music at Associated Mennonite Biblical Seminary. Earlier she spent forty years at Goshen College, Goshen, Indiana, as a professor teaching music and related arts.

She earned an M.Mus. in Music Literature (1947) and a Doctor of Musical Arts degree (1958) from the University of Michigan. She was the first string player to receive this musical performance degree at the University of Michigan.

Mary was the first woman to be on a Mennonite hymnal committee. She served as executive secretary for *The Mennonite Hymnal* (1969). Mary was also on the committee that developed *Hymnal: A Worship Book* (1992). Although Mary resigned before this project was completed, she edited the *Hymnal Sampler* (1989), a forerunner of the 1992 volume. Mary also wrote *Exploring the Mennonite Hymnal: Essays* (1980).

She has written numerous articles on hymnody and African music that have appeared in *Festival Quarterly, The Hymn, Gospel Herald,* and *The Builder.* In addition, Mary contributed the article on "Amish and Mennonite Music" to *The New Grove Dictionary of American Music.*

Since 1969 Mary has spent five years and many summers in various parts of Africa, studying African cultures through traditional and church music.

Mary has been an influential leader in church conferences and congregations worldwide over the past fifty years. In April 1998, Mary was honored by Associated Mennonite Biblical Seminary in a weekend Hymn Festival for the many ways in which she has helped Mennonites understand and appreciate hymns and their role in worship.

> In the beginning when God created the heavens and the earth, the earth was a formless void and darkness covered the face of the deep, while the Spirit of God moved over the face of the waters. Then God said, "Let there be light"; and there was light. (Gen. 1:1-3, KJV/NRSV)

WE HUMANS HAVE always struggled with order, chaos, and creativity.* Creativity can bring order to chaos; but order, in turn, can stifle creativity. Throughout our lives we move back and forth, seeking order, yet longing to create. Since the beginning of time, people have tried to reconcile their sense of unity with the gift of creativity. These struggles are not always easy; they are sometimes uncomfortable, and yet always rewarding.

---

*Mary's contribution here is from her 1994 commencement address at Eastern Mennonite College, Harrisonburg, Virginia, as adapted from *Christian Living,* June 1998, and used with permission.

During my lifetime, I have known this struggle, searched for order, and experienced repeated surprise at the creative work of the Holy Spirit. In my case, the arts—especially music—have been an important part of living with the tension of order and discovery, of creativity and faith.

Longing to Connect Music and Faith

I remember longing in college for some orderly, rational scheme that would connect my interests in the arts with other aspects of my life. When I studied medieval history, I was struck with the sense of unity permeating that time. In the Middle Ages, people believed they could order their lives with a single intellectual model. Scholars produced encyclopedic works, studies that pulled all knowledge into a unified whole. All aspects of faith and life were interconnected.

The thirteenth-century "Hymn to the Sun" ("All Creatures of Our God and King"), by St. Francis of Assisi, for example, is an encyclopedia in miniature. St. Francis praises God for the four known elements—air, fire, water, and earth—that comprised the complete scientific handbook of his day. The hymn, in effect, praises God for the periodic table of the times.

The Gothic cathedral is another splendid encyclopedia of all of life on a grand scale. Its sculptures cover history from creation to judgment. Its walls, paintings, carvings, and floor plan illustrate Bible stories, literature, philosophy, and mathematics. Thousands of diverse elements are integrated into a system of symbols pointing from the physical world to the spiritual. All things ultimately pointed to Christ, whose figure as Ruler of the world was at the top of every window, and whose very Being created a watershed for the architecture, dividing the dark, north, Old Testament side from the light, south, New Testament.

At times I longed for the synthesis and integration of life that I saw in the medieval world. In that era, it seemed, theology, the arts, science, and literature were intimately related. They belong together.

Can We Embrace the Arts?

However, back in my world, teaching at a Mennonite college, I had to search long and hard for a place for the arts in education. In the 1950s, the arts were not especially welcome in the curriculum.

Selected arts were present, with uneasy acceptance, but they were not embraced in freedom and joy and pleasure.

The arts might be suitable for children, but adults soon moved on to more-important jobs in the "service fields." There was a great fear that one could not be a disciple of Christ and move seriously into the arts.

Early in my teaching career, I vividly remember a gathering of church musicians. One church leader stood up and declared, "I don't understand how Mary Oyer can play a cello and be a Christian."

I wish I had laughed and said he didn't know what he was missing. But we were terribly serious about such issues. I could not have known then how much both he and I would change in years to come.

Perhaps it was the renewed interest in our spiritual ancestors that brought on our hesitation. The Anabaptists, our teachers told us, had other priorities than music-making or painting. Yet a group of Anabaptists themselves gave us an interesting example of openness to the arts.

In the 1530s, men and women imprisoned for their faith in the dungeons of Passau on the Danube produced many hymns. Some were ballads about martyred friends; others were songs of sheer praise. The prisoners borrowed new tunes from the Lutherans, as well as older music from Catholic and folk sources. And they sang!

They did this in spite of teaching against music by church leaders like Ulrich Zwingli and Conrad Grebel. Even after the Anabaptist leader Peter Riedemann issued a severe warning against the carnal nature of music for Christians, other Anabaptists published these prison hymns.

I believe that the Holy Spirit was moving over the face of the earth, freeing the hymn writers and singers to create, to lament, and to praise. But in the 1950s, we did not hear the voices of these hymn-singing ancestors. We listened instead to those who warned. We feared that embracing the arts might be wrong.

The Holy Spirit Had Always Been There

My release from this fear came gradually—at first through rational calculation. I decided to work on a doctorate in cello. I wanted to focus on instrumental music because it was so maligned in the church and I was convinced there was something wrong with that position.

During my study, I discovered the struggles of Christian painters and poets throughout history. I realized that Mennonite concerns with the arts had been difficult issues that Christians had faced since the days of the early church. With considerable relief, I recognized that I was not alone.

The other aspect of my study centered on actually playing the cello. This was so different from the logical and analytical aspects of music history and theory. It was difficult to move back and forth from one area of study to the other. I could discipline myself within each, but I found it hard to cope with the gap between rational and intuitive modes of knowing.

The content of cello playing, I eventually discovered, couldn't be described in words. It simply had to be caught. I realized that I could not use argument to convince my Mennonite community of its value.

Then I found a remarkable sonnet by Gerard Manley Hopkins* that spoke to me. I even memorized it—something I rarely did as an adult.

God's Grandeur
The world is charged with the grandeur of God.
  It will flame out, like shining from shook foil;
  It gathers to a greatness like the ooze of oil
Crushed. Why do men then now not reck his rod?
Generations have trod, have trod, have trod;
  And all is seared with trade; bleared, smeared with toil;
  And wears man's smudge and shares man's smell; the soil
Is bare now, nor can foot feel, being shod.

And for all this, nature is never spent;
  There lives the dearest freshness deep down things;
And though the last lights off the black West went
  Oh, morning, at the brown brink eastward, springs—
Because the Holy Ghost over the bent
  World broods with warm breast and with ah! bright wings.

---

*In *Poems*, 1918.

"The Holy Ghost over the bent world broods"—*that was it!* The Holy Ghost had always been there, through all the deadening arguments and dull nagging fears that it might be wrong to play the cello. The creative Spirit was there, affirming life and empowering me to live.

I Changed My Opinion on What Was "Good"

Since then I've had many experiences which verified the creative activity of the Spirit. In the 1960s, I joined the committee that produced *The Mennonite Hymnal.* I still remember my motivation. I believed I knew what was good. I expected to weed out hymns of poor taste. For me, that meant gospel songs. I had been taught—and I bought the idea—that such songs were cheap and tawdry.

However, during the years that we worked on the *Hymnal,* I began to appreciate gospel songs. I had not intended to change my opinion on what was "good," but it happened. The result was a freedom to discover events and experiences that are truly important in congregational singing. I found the support and unity we feel as the song emerges, or moments when a sudden and surprising insight flashes across our consciousness.

There they are: the bright wings of the Holy Ghost brooding over the bent world.

Learning Music Without Notes

In the early 1970s, I spent a sabbatical year recording traditional music in East Africa. I had received a doctorate in cello more than a decade earlier, and I went with a fair amount of confidence as a musician and educator. But when in Uganda I heard a man named Yonny play enchanting music on a simple instrument of ten keys made from bicycle spokes, I knew that I had been missing something important in the field of music.

I also knew I wanted to learn to play this kind of music and not simply to record it. It was difficult to find a teacher. Ugandans learn by hearing the music from childhood and then experimenting with other musicians. There was no formal training and certainly no printed notes to follow. I finally found a teacher who was acquainted with Westerners and could tolerate strange questions, ignorance of oral tradition, and the primitive sense of rhythm that I brought to the lessons.

It was humbling. I learned to fall back on a sense of humor to cope with the laughter of children who stood around, amused by this foreign-born, middle-aged woman who learned so slowly. But the rewards were enormous. Friendships with local musicians emerged.

I developed a healthy respect for oral tradition and learning, not just the written word on which I depended. This nondancing Mennonite learned that the whole body is needed for music-making. In the indigenous churches, I saw rhythmic movement that allowed the whole person to express faith. I began to notice those anthropological aspects of music my classical education had bypassed. Again, the Spirit was hovering over the face of the earth to enlighten and bridge the chasms we human beings create.

Able to Discover, Create, and Change

As I reflect on my life's journey, I realize I have moved in directions that, at one time, I could not have dreamed possible or even desirable. New situations, new promptings of the Spirit, have confronted me and invited me to change direction—to move into unexpected areas of experience. I have found both order and creativity at work in surprising ways in my life.

Today I no longer look for a single intellectual scheme to draw fragmentation and chaos into a comforting whole. Instead, I believe the Holy Spirit hovers over each of us, with power that frees us to discover and create and change.

Mary K. Oyer

Go and Teach
Christian Education

BERTHA FAST HARDER

BERTHA HARDER is a Docent at the Kauffman Museum, North Newton, Kansas, guiding school groups who come to learn. She helps with the Fall Festival at Bethel College, directing the Low-German program. She is a free-lance speaker and storyteller, a resource person for Christian education workshops and leadership training, and a Sunday school teacher of children.

Bertha was an Instructor in Christian Education at Associated Mennonite Biblical Seminary, 1958-83. She has served the church as a member of the General Conference Mennonite Church Commission on Education for eighteen years, as well as the Board of Christian Service.

She was the first woman on a major General Conference Mennonite Church board, and the first director of Mennonite Voluntary Service. For five years, she was the Director of Christian Education for the First Presbyterian Church in Elkhart, Indiana. Bertha also assisted her husband, Leland, in pastoring the St. Louis Fellowship for three years.

Bertha wrote a teacher's guide for *Twelve Becoming* (1973). With Marlene Kropf and Linea Geiser, she coauthored *Upon These Doorposts: Leadership Training for Parents and Teachers* (1979). She published *Celebrate: Ideas for Intergenerational Celebration of Advent, Christmas and Lent/Easter* (1980). Bertha also wrote *Young or Old or In-Between: An*

Intergenerational Study on Aging (1986). These all were published by Faith & Life Press.

She was a member of the editorial council for the Foundation Series Sunday school curriculum, and writer for grades five and six in that series. She graduated from Bethel College in 1949, with high distinction, and in 1951 from Bethany Theological Seminary, summa cum laude. In 1986, Bertha received a distinguished achievement award from Bethel College as teacher, wife, mother, storyteller, Christian educator, author, teacher of teachers, and service worker.

Bertha and Leland are the parents of John and Tom, and they have four granddaughters.

> They feast on the abundance of your house,
>   and you give them drink from the river of your delights.
> (Ps. 36:8)

EVEN AS A YOUNG GIRL growing up on a farm, I liked my life. We had a fine farm with animals and growing things. I had two sets of grandparents, many uncles and aunts, and scores of cousins. Then there were my parents, whom we called Papa and Mama. I had an older sister, two younger sisters, and finally a baby brother. And there was the town of Mountain Lake, Minnesota, with our Mennonite church at its center.

Life Centered Around the Church

At our house, Sunday was a special day. The strong sense of Sunday began the moment we woke up. We had freshly baked zwiebach for breakfast. Smoothly ironed dresses were lying on our beds. In summer, Papa backed the newly washed car out of the garage and parked it at the front gate. We girls sat in the car, happily waiting.

Our family sang all the way to church—German and English hymns. At church, best friends greeted us with welcoming smiles. The minister announced the first hymn, my favorite, "Hallelujah, schöner Morgen" (lovely morning). I sang with heart and soul, feeling the joy of that moment in our church.

During the week I learned to work hard—in the house, the garden, the barn, and out in the fields as I grew older. Our parents were strong disciplinarians; we knew right from wrong. But they were fair and fun to be with.

Mama told us stories of exciting events that happened even before I was born. She taught us medleys. She hung brightly colored curtains at the windows and fixed bouquets for the center of the table. All this stimulated my imagination. Papa took us fishing and introduced us to his Norwegian neighbor friends.

Then Papa decided to run for the state House of Representatives. He had held leadership positions in the church, the school district board, and the elevator association. He chaired the Rural Electrification Association. Now he wanted to fulfill another dream, one vehemently discouraged by his father. We three oldest girls were enlisted by him to sing trios at Lutheran churches in our county, where Papa gave campaign talks.

High school for me was four years of stimulating experiences with friends, music, drama, clubs, early dating, and some serious study. There were times of distressing adolescent turmoil, but there were always friends, parents, and grandparents as stabilizing supports. The house of my mother's parents was a second home to me: warm, accepting, welcoming.

One winter evening during my freshman year, our family drove to church on a sled to attend special revival meetings. The church was packed, with most of my fellow high school youth sitting in the balcony. The sermon by the visiting evangelist spoke to my need for salvation.

I remember standing up in the presence of my peers to accept Jesus Christ as my personal Savior. That spring I attended catechism class and was baptized. In retrospect, I would have to say that the ritual of catechism and baptism was somewhat of a disappointment.

God Intervenes

At a Minnesota state teachers' college, I readily moved into leadership roles in the Student Christian Association. This was an eye-opening experience for me, coming from a Mennonite community. I was invited to join the prestigious college drama club.

The teachers' placement office helped me secure a fine position as a first-grade teacher in a small-town public school, a job for which

I felt well trained. During those years, however, I had to learn to be less critical of certain other teachers whose educational methods seemed out-of-date and ineffective.

During my seven years of elementary school teaching, I attended mostly Methodist churches, singing in their choirs, making friends with the pastors and their wives, and enjoying new forms of worship. There were times when I neglected my nonconformist Mennonite faith.

The children in my first-grade classroom were a constant source of challenge and discovery. Alberta and Alvina were identical twins from an impoverished family. They came with skinny legs, pale faces, large blue eyes, and were never in the top learning group. They found it difficult to identify even the names *Dick* and *Jane* on the reading chart. However, when I played the *Wilhelm Tell Overture* on a record player, they felt free to skip and dance around the room with rhythm and abandon.

During my last three years of teaching, Josephine Kremer, a gifted teaching supervisor, came into my room to observe and counsel. She was always affirming and inspired me to develop further as a warm, creative, and effective teacher of children.

In my fourth year of teaching, I became engaged to be married. Those were troublesome days in our country and in my personal life. A dear courageous friend asked me a probing question about my plans to be married and saved me from a catastrophe. The marriage would have led to a reversal of the "mission" to which God had called me.

This incident should be enough to humble me for the rest of my life. It left me little doubt that sometimes God intervenes in my life, often through other persons.

Mennonite Central Committee Bonds

Through my younger sister's intuitive suggestion, I volunteered with Mennonite Central Committee (MCC) to work in refugee camps abroad. That decision in the spring of 1944 brought me to a crucial turning point and a new direction. First I served in Egypt, where Yugoslav refugees lived in tents out in the desert. We had been loaned to the United Nations Relief and Rehabilitation Administration (UNRRA), and we were partners with other workers from many UN member nations.

When refugees from Yugoslavia were repatriated at the end of the war, my beloved Aunt Marie Fast lost her life on the first return trip. Their ship hit a mine in the Mediterranean Sea. She had always been one of my loyal and loving supporters during my growing-up years and young adulthood. It was my task to inform our family about her sad and untimely death.

Then in the middle of 1945, I was transferred to a UNRRA camp being set up at the southern tip of the heel of Italy, on Cape Santa Maria di Leuca. This camp became a refuge for Jewish people right out of concentration camps in Belsen, Schwerin, and Auschwitz.

I worked with about eight hundred adults and forty children who had somehow stayed alive. We became a community and worked together to create a sense of order amidst the chaos of their recent experiences. Quite a number of the able refugees came to my office and asked, "How can we help?" One or two of these volunteers disappointed me, but most of them were trustworthy, talented, and hardworking leaders. Together we tried to make life as redeemable as possible for these survivors of the Holocaust.

Two Jewish sisters were volunteer cooks in the children's kitchen I set up. One Christmas morning, they came to my door to wish me "Fröhliche Weihnachten" (merry Christmas) and give me a precious gift. It was a small hand-painted wooden box they had saved for their younger sister, who perished in the gas chambers.

One day a Mr. Lebowitz came to our camp, asking, "Is there a Lili Lebowitz here?" Indeed, there was. I escorted him to House Number 34, where she resided. As I left him there, I heard the loud crying together of a brother and sister rejoicing in their surprise reunion after years of agonized separation. Lili had been left for dead on a pile of gassed corpses. Somehow she had managed to survive and escape.

There was also Meier Schacher, a Zionist leader from Israel, who told me, "I would not have believed that someone not a Jew could love my people like you!"

The last segment of my time with MCC was spent helping Waldensians in the Italian Alps, survivors of the Nazi occupation. They were poor and malnourished, but stout and fervent in their Christian faith, and so grateful for being found by MCC. We lived in their loving community for half a year.

There were some difficult times in my MCC experience. One had to do with occasional tensions with other Mennonite workers. One person in particular was not sympathetic with my style of fraternization. I felt free to accept invitations to parties and weddings in the camp, and to establish friendships—some of which crossed the gender barrier, a little too freely, she felt.

Maybe I should have been more reserved and circumspect in my relationships. But to this day, the MCC bonds established in postwar Europe are alive and well.

"Continue Working for Your Mennonite Church"

After returning from this life-changing assignment, I was blessed to be asked by a General Conference Mennonite commission to travel and speak for seven months. I was telling the stories and showing slides of my work with the refugees. I spoke in churches, colleges, and high schools in much of the United States and Canada. I sat in the kitchens of pastors, drinking coffee and talking, learning to know about their life and work, their difficulties and accomplishments.

Before this assignment was over, I was asked by Elmer Ediger, on behalf of the Christian Service Committee, to be the first director of General Conference Mennonite Voluntary Service. In many of the churches I was visiting, I could introduce the opportunity for young adults to do at least a summer term as volunteers in the mission churches of Chicago; the Youth Farm at Rosthern, Saskatchewan; or the Northern Cheyenne reservation of rural Montana.

Then came the unresolved question, "Where do I go from here?" I sought the counsel of my former teaching supervisor in Minnesota, who told me, "I'd love to have you back as a teacher, but I really feel you should continue working for your Mennonite Church."

As a result of counsel from her and others, I enrolled at Bethel College, North Newton, Kansas, to finish my B.A. degree. Then I attended the Mennonite Biblical Seminary in Chicago.

A Happy Surprise

What a happy surprise those two years at Bethel turned out to be. The Bible courses opened up a whole new field of study for me. As an older student, I had not expected to become involved in extracurricular activities. Nevertheless, I became a member of the student council, had a major role in the senior play, and developed many new friendships among students and faculty.

Then came the day when I boarded the train for the Mennonite Seminary, then affiliated with Bethany Biblical Seminary of the Church of the Brethren. What a whole new set of discoveries were made here! In this community, there was no problem with me being a single woman, even though most women my age were married. All the single Mennonite men and women lived in adjacent quarters, studying, worshiping, eating, and having fun times together.

Again there were opportunities to participate in leadership, first as a Mennonite representative on the Brethren Seminary student council. The two seminaries were geographically separated by many miles. When the council met, I stayed overnight in their student housing, eating with them, kneeling together in prayer at a worship center, and absorbing other new ways to pray from their uniquely Brethren spiritual life and discipline.

A Bethany professor, David Wieand, led the Mennonite Seminary community in a silent retreat, another spiritual discipline that I came to enjoy.

Support Role Turned to Leadership

At the seminary, I met Leland Harder, who has impacted the rest of my life's journey. We were married in 1951. After our graduation, Leland became the pastor of a General Conference Mennonite mission church in Chicago. We had to learn a new "language" to minister the gospel to nonethnic Mennonite people.

My role was to be Leland's support. But I soon began to give leadership in the Sunday school, vacation Bible school, and several women's groups. We truly became partners in the ministries of that church. We still receive regular correspondence from a few of those dear friends.

In 1953 our first son, John, was born. Since I was already thirty-eight years old, I had assumed that I would never have a chance to become a mother. So for me, this was a miracle. However, the new responsibility was awesome and frightening. "Will I ever be free to stroll down a street alone again, or meet friends in a cafe for lunch?" I did, of course. But life was never quite the same, just as a dear friend had predicted.

When I was forty-two, Tom was born. Our two boys have been special gifts of God to us. John is an industrial statistician, and Tom a musician and minister. They are our best friends and confidants, our most loyal supporters. They and their dear wives have given us the added gift of four granddaughters.

Leland and I have been partners for over forty-six years, including twenty-five years at the Associated Mennonite Biblical Seminary, Elkhart, Indiana. There I tried to balance the roles of mother, wife of a professor who still commuted to Chicago for graduate study several days a week, and part-time instructor in Christian education.

This juggling act was epitomized one day by our five-year-old son, John, who was ready to sit down for breakfast. As I was about to leave for class, I stopped at the table to pour his cereal. He casually said, "I'll put the sugar on; you go and teach Christian education."

"Dear Brethren and Bertha"

During my later years at the seminary, there were times when my gifts, my teaching style, and my role identities were tested by certain students. A strong feminist attitude emerged on the campus. I began to hear and feel a challenge to my identity as part-time seminary teacher.

My more traditional pattern of roles was involvement as wife, mother, part-time teacher, Sunday school teacher, and conference board member. This pattern was not acceptable to some strong advocates for gender equality emerging on the campus. But I persevered and went on with my life and teaching.

For four years, I worked alongside mostly men in planning the new Foundation Series Sunday school curriculum. I was the first woman elected to a major conference board. The mailings from the executive secretary began with "Dear Brethren and Bertha."

For eighteen years, the Commission on Education became like a second family for me. A humble executive secretary told me as he gave me a special gift of thanks, "You believed in me when I didn't believe in myself."

I could not doubt the vital role of women in church leadership when I worked with Cornelia Lehn, Herta Funk, Elizabeth Yoder, Marlene Kropf, Marian Franz, and numerous others in many areas of church work. I led workshops, spoke at retreats, and told stories at congregational and conference programs.

The Gift of Life in Abundance

I have continued to experience joy while teaching children in Sunday school. Boys and girls can give amazingly creative responses to Bible stories. One Sunday in a new city church, I told the exciting story of Joshua calling the people together to make a covenant.

Then as an aside I said, "Do you know that the adults of our fellowship are writing a covenant right now, saying what they believe about God, Jesus, and how he wants us to be peacemakers?"

Immediately hands went up as they proposed:

- Can we write our own covenant?
- We'll keep it a secret!
- We can tell what we believe about God and Jesus and war.

And so they did, according to the level of their understanding.

For Leland and me, the seminary was not only a place of employment. It became an extended family of support for us and our boys, and the center for many extracurricular activities. We had colleagues like Floyd and Sylvia Pannabecker, who were friends for John and Tom as well as for us. We could list so many—faculty, staff, and students. We continue to meet them at conferences, and many ring our doorbell.

Now, in our retirement in North Newton, Kansas, we give our home and family first priority. Two of our little granddaughters are here a lot, and I love to play "pretend" with them. I enjoy cooking and baking bread and zwieback. I try to be a gracious hostess, making our home warm and open to others. I feel strongly motivated to be a helpful wife and mother and grandmother.

I continue to love the church, even though we no longer sing "Hallelujah, schöner Morgen!" God's grace has been pervasive in my life. I will be forever grateful for the gift of life in abundance that has been given to me.

Bertha Fast Harder

Way Leads on to Way

MARLENE KROPF

MARLENE KROPF is Assistant Professor of Spiritual Formation and Worship at Associated Mennonite Biblical Seminary (AMBS), Elkhart, Indiana. She also works half-time as Minister of Worship and Spirituality for the Mennonite Board of Congregational Ministries (MBCM). Before 1983, Marlene taught high school English in Oregon and Jamaica.

Marlene is a graduate of Oregon College of Education, where she received a B.A. degree in humanities and secondary education in 1965, and an M.A. in teaching in 1968. She earned an M.Div. degree from Associated Mennonite Biblical Seminary in 1988, and a D.Min. degree in worship and spirituality from the Graduate Theological Foundation in 1997. She has also studied at the University of Notre Dame (Indiana) and at Oxford University (England).

In addition to churchwide responsibilities for MBCM, Marlene has served as secretary of literature for the Pacific Coast Conference Women's Missionary and Service Commission (WMSC). She was elected to the Mennonite Church's Council on Faith, Life, and Strategy, and she was a member of the Hymnal Council which produced *Hymnal: A Worship Book* in 1992. She and her family served for two years with Mennonite Central Committee in Kingston, Jamaica.

Marlene was ordained to Christian ministry in 1992. Today, in addition to teaching and serving as a spiritual director, she frequently leads seminars and retreats and also plans and leads worship for conferences and other events.

Her articles have appeared in *Builder, Christian Living, Gospel Herald, The Mennonite, MCC Women's Report,* and *Lectionary Homiletics.* She is co-author of *Praying with the Anabaptists: The Secret of Bearing Fruit* (1994), *Intergenerational Learning in the Church* (1982), and *Upon These Doorposts: How Children Grow in Faith* (1980).

Marlene and her husband, Stanley, are the parents of Jeremy and Heather. Marlene's special interests include growing perennials, home remodeling, traveling, reading fiction and poetry, and sailing with her husband.

A PRIZED POSSESSION on my shelf is a complete collection of Robert Frost's poems, given to me and signed by my students when I left high school teaching. In what may be Frost's most familiar poem, "The Road Not Taken," he writes of two roads diverging in a yellow wood—and how he chose one road and not the other. He ponders:

> Yet knowing how way leads on to way,
> I doubted if I should ever come back.

From Pigtails to Churchwide Ministry

Like many women, I am astonished when I look back over my life and ministry and see how "way leads on to way." When I recently traveled to Oregon for a family reunion, I took a side trip to Willamina, the small town of less than two thousand, in the foothills of the Coast Mountains, where I grew up.

As I drove through the streets, I wondered again, *How did the pigtailed little girl get from here to churchwide ministry?* Growing up where I did, I was expected to become a homemaker who stayed at home with my brood of children and lived a contented small-town life.

In this rough-and-tumble logging town, my classmates at Willamina Grade School were lucky even to graduate from high school. Few went to college. The congregation in which I grew up did not support higher education. I heard plenty of polemic against the dangers of education.

Even my parents were ambivalent. Though they were strongly supportive of Mennonite secondary education and made sure I attended a Mennonite high school, they did not consider it a priority for young women to attend college. I had to persuade them to let me go to Eastern Mennonite College (EMC) in Harrisonburg, Virginia, where I stayed for one year. Then I returned to Oregon to complete my college education at a state school.

Even now I find it hard to pinpoint precisely what pushed me out of the nest of comfortable expectations and on to a less-traveled way. What I do know is that I always wanted to become a teacher. What I didn't know was that such a vocation would call me away from my beloved valley and make me a leader in the church.

The Way Begins

In the forested, evergreen valley where I grew up, my first classroom was a makeshift arrangement in the bedroom I shared with my younger sister, Judi. In those days before *Sesame Street*, children didn't have ready opportunities to learn the alphabet and write numbers before they entered school. So each day when I came home from first grade, I proceeded to teach Judi everything I was learning. She must have been a whiz when she started school the next fall.

Another early classroom was the prayer room to the right of the pulpit, in the church of my childhood, Sheridan (Oregon) Mennonite. After my freshman year in high school, I was invited to teach a class of about twenty first-graders in the annual two-week vacation Bible school. I remember poring over the teacher's book, making detailed lesson plans, spending hours constructing elaborate and artistic bulletin boards, and being so excited I couldn't sleep before Bible school began.

That not-being-able-to-sleep habit hasn't changed in nearly four decades of teaching. I still get so excited before a new class begins that I barely sleep a wink the night before.

Since there were almost no models for teaching as a ministry of the church, I assumed that my call would take me into secular education. I followed my heart and prepared to teach literature and writing to high school students. After college, my first assignment took me to a wealthy suburban school district near Portland, Oregon.

Later, as part of an assignment with Mennonite Central Committee (MCC), I taught composition and English literature in Kingston, Jamaica. This was for a government secondary school in an impoverished inner-city neighborhood.

Both teaching experiences were immensely fulfilling. I loved few things more than seeing students' eyes light up when they discovered they really could understand Shakespeare's plays or were dazzled by the beauty of a line of poetry. I remember telling someone, "I don't think I could live without teaching poetry."

The Glass Ceiling

When we returned from our MCC assignment, I chose to do substitute teaching so I could be more available to our family. During those years, I became immersed in the educational ministry of Portland Mennonite Church, a progressive urban congregation composed mainly of young adults who had moved to the city because of 1-W assignments in Portland hospitals.

Many of us were geographically separated from parents and grandparents. So we looked to the church for guidance in raising our children in the city.

My first foray into teaching adults was a six-month course for parents of preschoolers that I team-taught with our pastor, Marcus Smucker. Later we taught a course for parents of school-age children, and another for parents of adolescents. That interest led to me serving several years as codirector of Christian education in the congregation.

What I discovered in those years was that teaching adults in the congregation was spiritually demanding. Though I knew well how to construct a syllabus and lead an energetic class discussion, something more was required in the church. As a teacher, I also became a spiritual guide—a role for which I was inadequately prepared. Because of that teaching ministry and an inner hunger of the heart, I began attending contemplative prayer retreats and taking courses in spirituality.

First a group of women and then a Sunday school class of both women and men asked me to take them on a contemplative prayer retreat. Soon other churches in our conference invited Marcus and me to lead them in weekend prayer retreats. Neither Marcus nor I dreamed that one day we would teach spirituality courses together at Associated Mennonite Biblical Seminary.

Though I couldn't see where these assignments were leading, I began to feel an inner pull toward ministry in the church. Again, the absence of models kept me from seeing any shape for such a ministry.

During those years, I became active in leadership roles beyond the congregation. I served as a member of a Pacific Coast Conference committee on family life and joined the conference WMSC executive committee as secretary of literature. About the same time, I was elected to the Mennonite Church's Council on Faith, Life, and Strategy. I wrote articles for various church publications and also coauthored two books on Christian education.

In these expanding opportunities for ministry, an obstacle appeared. My congregation was unwilling to deal with the issue of women in leadership. I had faced little resistance to my leadership roles in the educational ministry of the congregation and had been encouraged by my pastor and others. Yet a glass ceiling kept women from serving in the role of elder.

After Marcus Smucker resigned as pastor in 1979, several women's names—including mine—were submitted by members of the congregation as possible candidates for elder. I knew I had gifts and a call for such a role. I also knew that because the congregation had not faced this issue directly, it would be a hurtful process for women who were nominated.

In one of the most painful experiences of my life in the church, another woman and I took the initiative to meet with the elders. We told them of our fears and concerns. Our story was belittled and not understood. We left the meeting deeply hurt and angry, and we withdrew our names from the process. Although one of the elders later tried to make amends, the damage was done. In that conflict, I lost my innocence as a woman in the church.

Though I had been a feminist since my teen years, I had never before felt so directly and personally violated by patriarchy. I paid my dues as a feminist in the weeks and months that followed. I was struggling with the realization that even a nurturing church can fail its women members miserably.

The Road Taken

Had it not been for that disillusioning experience, however, I might never have awakened to the call to ministry that was being birthed in me. On Christmas Eve of 1982, I received a letter inviting me to apply for a half-time position in Christian education with the Mennonite Board of Congregational Ministries (MBCM), a denominational resource agency in Elkhart, Indiana. My Christmas was nearly ruined, for I couldn't bear the thought of leaving Oregon!

Even though there had been skirmishes with the congregation, a small group had begun offering alternative worship services on Sunday evening, with the elders' approval. These events were calling forth leadership gifts, including worship leading and preaching, gifts I had never used before. It was an exciting and fulfilling time. How could I leave?

Yet the possibility of moving to Elkhart meant that I could attend seminary. Though that dream was becoming more and more insistent, I certainly had no ambitions to work in a denominational office.

Like many Westerners, I harbored a healthy dose of skepticism toward any institution east of the Mississippi. When I admitted that prejudice to an old friend on the staff at Eastern Mennonite College, she replied, "You won't be any good working in a church office unless you *are* skeptical!"

After several months of discernment and prayer, I said no to the call. The timing didn't seem right. Leaving Oregon would be too painful.

Because the decision had been so long and painful in coming, my husband, Stanley, and I simply didn't talk about it again once we gave a negative answer. My heart, however, remained unsettled. A couple of months went by. Then one day Stanley came home from work and blurted out, "I think we made the wrong decision."

I replied, "Oh, no, I don't want to hear another word," and left the room in tears. What I recognized was that I too had been sensing that the decision was wrong, but I had no energy left to retrace my steps.

So we did nothing. A few weeks later Stanley received an invitation to apply for a new position in finance with the Mennonite Church General Board. The next morning I called Gordon Zook, executive secretary at MBCM, and asked, "Is the job still open that was offered to me?"

Gordon said, "Yes. And just last night I took a walk with my wife, Bonnie, and told her, 'I wish Marlene Kropf would call me in the morning and tell me she has changed her mind.'"

Two months later, I left Oregon with our two children, Jeremy (14) and Heather (11), and drove across the country to Indiana. I cried off and on most of the way to the state line. Five weeks later, Stanley joined us, after he sold our house and his business. He began a new job with the Mennonite Church General Board.

"I'm Not Surprised!"

In the fall of 1983, I began working half-time in Christian education at MBCM and studied half-time at Associated Mennonite Biblical Seminary. By the fall of 1984, I was invited to teach a course in Christian education at the seminary. From then on, I continued to teach education, spirituality, and worship courses part-time while I completed my studies.

I graduated with a master of divinity degree in May 1988, and went on to earn a doctor of ministry degree in worship and spirituality from the Graduate Theological Foundation (Indiana) in May 1997. That same year I was appointed Assistant Professor of Spiritual Formation and Worship at AMBS. I also continued to serve half-time as Minister of Worship and Spirituality at MBCM.

After our move to Indiana, what took me by surprise was how much I enjoyed my work in the wider denominational setting. I was soon given many opportunities for leading workshops or retreats and speaking in congregations and conference settings. Before long, I realized that this ministry was mainly a teaching ministry—writ large across the church.

Now, instead of teaching students how to read a poem, I was teaching people how to teach or pray or plan a worship service. After a while I discovered that poetry and stories could still be an important part of my work. The Mennonite Church was greatly in need of more right-brain emphasis!

The happiest confluence of my first and second careers occurred when I was invited to join the Hymnal Council that produced *Hymnal: A Worship Book* in 1992. Always a lover of the church's music, I found that my literary background was also useful for evaluating and writing worship resources. Later I cochaired the group that produced a new minister's manual for the denomination in 1998. Being able to serve the church's life of worship has indeed been satisfying.

I had come from a work environment in public secondary schools where women were as numerous as men. So I was startled at first to find myself the only woman in many administrative settings in the church. In such a context, I needed to think through role expectations, leadership style, and the implications of close working relationships with men.

I remember an important early meeting in which I chaired a committee of all men. Afterward, I telephoned my husband from the Pittsburgh airport to report that I had successfully survived the ordeal and was pleased with the outcomes. His comment, "I'm not surprised," was one he would frequently offer.

Though we never intended to stay in Indiana past my graduation from seminary, "way leads on to way," and our exile from my green valley has continued.

Reflections About the Less-Traveled Way

Earlier I noted that it is difficult to pinpoint precisely what sent me on the less-traveled way. I do have several clues, though, one of which is my childhood congregation. The Sheridan Mennonite Church, with its traditional expectations about women's and men's roles, did not intend for me to do what I did. Yet I believe that congregation unwittingly started me on the way.

While I was growing up, one of my best friends was Shirley Yoder Brubaker, now pastor of Park View Mennonite Church in Harrisonburg, Virginia. When she and I get together and reflect on where our paths have gone, we chuckle and say, "They did it all wrong at Sheridan if they didn't want us to end up where we are!"

Our congregation was truly Anabaptist in calling everyone to become a disciple, follow Christ, and serve as a functioning member of the Christian community. Shirley and I simply believed what we were told and acted on it. In addition, this congregation of more than three hundred did an unusually good job of nurturing the gifts of young people. Early on, we were assigned tasks that fit our gifts.

I've already mentioned that I was given sole responsibility for teaching a vacation Bible school class at age fifteen. In addition, youth led congregational singing, served on committees, and were expected to show up and participate at congregational business meetings from the time we were baptized. All young people—girls and boys—acquired experience in public speaking in the Sunday evening young people's meetings where we presented "topics" to the entire congregation.

An important turn of the way occurred after church one Sunday when I must have been nine or ten. Enos Schrock, the children's Sunday school superintendent, bent down and asked me in the hallway, "Marlene, what *are* you going to be when you grow up?"

Although no adult had ever asked me that question directly, I knew the answer: "I'm going to be a missionary nurse in Alaska!" I had been temporarily dissuaded from my earlier goal to be a teacher by a series of books I was reading about student nurses.

What matters about that question is not that my answer turned out to be wrong, but that someone in the church asked me, a girl child, to account for my goals. I was expected to become something!

Another formative influence was Western Mennonite High School. There I was nurtured by creative and faithful Christian teachers—both women and men who invested themselves personally in their students. Grace Herr, my favorite English teacher, inspired me with her love of words and good writing. She encouraged me to write, enter speech contests, and face the faith questions of adolescence. Another teacher, Merlin Aeschliman, opened wider doorways into the world of music.

Even in such a nurturing environment, however, I became aware of the potential for injustice in the church. In one amusing memory, I recall the chagrin of Marcus Lind, our Bible teacher, when he had to allow young women to present their biblical exposition papers in chapel. In our school tradition, the two best papers in the class would be presented as chapel addresses. Apparently, up until that year, it had always been young men who were awarded the honor.

In our class, my paper along with that of another young woman earned the highest marks. I still remember Marcus squirming and insisting that somehow this wasn't right. But he was a fair man. We gave the addresses.

Obviously there were many social and cultural influences that would have steered me toward conformity. This was, after all, before the women's movement days. However, Western offered ample territory for trying out leadership gifts.

Editing the school newspaper and yearbook, serving on committees, participating in speech contests and drama, representing the school in choir concerts and speaking engagements, singing in congregations as a member of the ladies' sextet—all these were helpful preparation for leadership in the wider church.

In examining my choices along the way, I cannot discount my own disposition. My high school yearbook describes me as "nonconformist." In part, I think I was infected by the free spirit of the West; in part I was also a typical high-achieving, leadership-prone first child. But beyond that, I had an earnest desire to serve Christ. I could not be satisfied if I could not fulfill the longings God had planted in me.

Gifts Along the Way

I am deeply grateful for abundant gifts along the way. My parents haven't always understood my choices. Seminary training and then ordination were particularly difficult pills for my mother to swallow. Yet they have always offered their love and support.

My husband and children have been loyal supporters as well. In recent years, as my travel schedule has escalated, my husband has chafed at this disruption to family life. I have struggled to keep ministry commitments within reasonable bounds. I especially appreciate the support of a faithful spiritual friend with whom I meet weekly. She keeps me honest and holds me accountable for making good decisions.

Many other people have believed in me and my gifts. An uncle and aunt have always made a point of offering encouragement. At one critical juncture, an older woman with whom I served in a conference assignment invited me to talk with her periodically about my life and faith. We each drove twenty-five miles to meet in a restaurant along the interstate highway. Though I didn't have a name then for what she offered me, I now know that she was my spiritual director.

After we served together on the Council on Faith, Life, and Strategy, Ruth Brunk Stoltzfus always found time to have lunch with me whenever I traveled to Harrisonburg, Virginia. Her wisdom, humor, and encouragement (as well as the latest news of her beloved children and grandchildren) were always welcome.

Other friends and ministry colleagues along the way have also been generous with love and support. On my study wall hangs a reminder I cherish from one of these friends: "Angels fly because they take themselves lightly."

As a young adult, my training in education was excellent preparation for ministry, though I didn't know this at the time. For one thing, it taught me how to plan and organize. It taught me to respond to the many ways people learn and process information. It has also made me keenly aware of the importance of communication.

As a teacher of high school students, I often faced unmotivated learners and needed to make learning exciting and accessible. Though the people I face in the church are usually motivated, I still care deeply about communicating in understandable, grace-filled ways. I know that "who" I am is just as important as "what" I teach people.

One of the incredible gifts along the way has been the opportunity to nurture and mentor young women in the church. Both in academic settings and in congregations, I have met remarkable women with extraordinary commitments to Christ and gifts for leadership. I remember a moment last year when I sat in a chapel service at AMBS led by students I had taught. Their worship design was creative, they led prayerfully, and they drew forth scriptural understandings I had never considered before.

I was compelled to worship God with my whole heart, body, soul, and mind. Afterward I realized (and told them) that they had surpassed their teacher. I could not have planned or led a service as well as they had done. It is the fulfillment every teacher hopes for.

I long for the day when God's way will lead me back to the beautiful valley from whence I came. In his poem, Frost doubts that he can return. I too wonder where the next bend in the road will take me. The Psalms, however, remind me that the road I travel is not just happenstance. God is my true and faithful guide:

> I show you the path to walk.
> As your teacher, I watch out for you. (Ps. 32:8*)

The God who has led me thus far along many delightful, surprising, and satisfying ways can surely be trusted for the future. May God be praised!

Marlene Y. Kropf

---

*From *The Psalter* (Chicago: Liturgy Training Pubns., 1994).

Two Stories on a Continuing Journey

SHIRLEY HERSHEY SHOWALTER

Sᴴɪʀʟᴇʏ H. Sʜᴏᴡᴀʟᴛᴇʀ
began serving as president
of Goshen College, Goshen,
Indiana, on January 1, 1997.
During 1976-96 she taught
in the English and history
departments, becoming a
full professor and English
department chair. In 1993-
94 Shirley took a leave from
Goshen College to be a
senior fellow for the Lilly
Fellows Program in Humanities and the Arts at Val-
paraiso (Indiana) University.
Shirley and her husband,
Stuart, a professor of communication and former chair
of this department at
Goshen College, led Study-
Service Terms (SST) to Haiti
and Côte d'Ivoire, West Africa.

Tom Strickland

In 1986-87 Shirley acted as the interim Vice President of the Consor-
tium for the Advancement of Private Higher Education in Washington,
D.C., while on sabbatical from Goshen College. In 1990, she won a
Sears Roebuck Foundation "Teaching Excellence and Campus Leadership Award."

Shirley earned a B.A. from Eastern Mennonite College, Harrisonburg,

Virginia; and an M.A. and Ph.D. from University of Texas at Austin. She is a frequent lecturer in higher education circles and has also served widely as a consultant.

She has been published by the University of Illinois Press, Herald Press, *The Heath Anthology of American Literature Newsletter, The Cresset, The Mennonite Quarterly Review, Leadership, Women's Studies Quarterly, Quaker History, The Washington Post, Gospel Herald, The Chronicle of Higher Education,* and *AAHE Bulletin.*

One of Shirley's greatest joys comes from making connections and bringing together diverse people, such as an alumna with a former boss, or a famous writer with an inner-city Mennonite church. Shirley says some of her greatest teachers have been her husband, Stuart; her children, Kate and Anthony; and her friends.

Shirley's interests include walking, reading, biking, tennis, and drawing. Her name means "from the bright meadow."

The Viewing

The day of death is better than the day of birth.
(Eccles. 7:1)

We shall not cease from exploration
And the end of all our exploring
Will be to arrive where we started
And know the place for the first time.
(T. S. Eliot, "Little Gidding")

WHEN MY FATHER was dying, he came to visit us in Goshen, Indiana.* At the time, no one knew he was dying, but we could tell he was slower—and colder—than he had ever been before.

He was fifty-four years old and looked even younger, except when he sat on the couch and shivered under the afghan his mother had made for me. To this day, my greatest regret of that visit, the last he would ever make, is that we kept our thermostat on its more-

---

* "The Viewing," first published in *Gospel Herald*, May 3, 1994, is adapted and used by permission.

with-less setting of sixty-eight degrees the whole time.

To me, even at the age of thirty-one, he was "Daddy." He had been my all-powerful god-figure in childhood and adolescence, capable of both anger and gentleness. As his body grew colder, his spirit seemed to warm. I can still see him standing in our kitchen, filling up all the space between the sink and the refrigerator. Afternoon light was shining on his black hair, highlighting the widow's peak of his broad forehead.

He was watching Anthony, our three-year-old son, playing on the swings in the backyard, which bordered on State Road 15. Daddy looked worried when he turned around to speak. "Watch out for that boy," he said. "The cars could kill him."

Six months later, in April 1980, a call from my Aunt Ann convinced me that I needed to go "home," to Lititz, Pennsylvania, to be with my father in what we all knew by then were his last days. My husband, Stuart, would come later, after he finished the course we were team-teaching at Goshen College. Little Anthony went with me. The 620-mile drive took us through plains and mountains to the familiar rolling farmland of Lancaster County.

Forsythia bushes were in bloom. Early morning sun illuminated one particular bush so that it shook out with flame in front of a brick ranch house. *This means something,* I thought as I sped past.

Here is the story of how I began to remember. Death, like birth, tends to suppress negative remembrance and enhance the positive. Hence, most of what I remembered on that long drive were Daddy's moments of gladness and sacrifice, even though he had been a strict father and I a strong-willed, oldest child. His dying had laid to rest our conflicts, but it did not change our history.

Three Decisions

On May 4, 1980, I helped my mother, three sisters—Sue, Doris, and Linda—and one brother, Henry, choose my father's casket. This was the first of three decisions we made to prepare for the viewing. For the sake of tradition, we chose a beautiful, burnished cherry casket, identical to the one in which my great-grandma Snyder had been buried more than a decade earlier.

Death had skipped a generation in the Hershey family, causing my elderly grandparents to shake their heads over the sadness of looking into their son's casket when they had been preparing to "go home" first.

Caskets are decorated, and so we made a second decision. This time we chose symbolical style rather than opting for family tradition. Instead of flowers, we picked wheat and corn to lie on top of the casket. Daddy's large hands, which had hoisted so many bales of straw and hay onto wagons and into the highest peaks of mows, lay still under emblems not only of his livelihood but of his identity. The newspaper had summed it up in one modest headline: "H. Richard Hershey, Farmer, Dies."

Our last decision was about place. We wanted the viewing to be held at the farmhouse instead of the funeral home. In doing so, we were honoring not only Daddy's long effort to be a good farmer but also five generations of other family members who had tilled the soil in the same place.

Our family had always been honored to live on the "home place," especially since the house was one of the oldest in the area. Count Zinzendorf, the Moravian missionary, had preached there in 1742 on his trip through the colonies. Among others, he converted one Jacob Hoober, who owned the house while it was still a tavern on the toll road from Philadelphia into the frontier. Mother and Daddy had framed the deed to the house, signed by the three sons of William Penn. It hung in the entry way over the pump organ, where we could be reminded as children that history carries responsibility.

"I Almost Died, Too"

My father's cousin, a mortician, had agreed to our strange viewing request of bringing the casket to the farmhouse. And so, the people came. We family members stood by Daddy's body in the living room and received the consolation of friends and relatives who made the same circle through the house that children always found when they came to play. The warm May evening passed, full of hankies, stories, and hushed tones.

My grandparents stood with us all evening and were among the last to leave. Just before she went out the door, Grandmother told me a fact I had never heard before. "I gave birth to Richard in this very room," she said, looking far away. "He almost died then. I almost died, too."

Instinctively, I found Anthony's hand. Grandma's words reached into one of my own deepest memories, touching me in a profoundly uncomfortable way. I too had endured an agonizing birth experience. My son had been doubly precious because he had been literally torn out of my body with the aid of forceps, five sets of hands, and all the technology available in the Goshen General Hospital in 1976. Now, in empathizing with my grandmother's grief in a new way—as another mother—I saw my son as an even greater gift. His perilous voyage into life had been so much like my father's.

The guests left. Only my mother, my husband, Stuart, and little Anthony remained in the house. The casket stood along the east wall in the living room. We went upstairs to bed. I slept in the very spot in my parents' bed and in the same room in which I had last seen my father alive in the house.

Three weeks earlier, I had been there when the disease that was thickening all my father's internal organs started to shut off his oxygen supply, turning his face blue. He had begged God to take him, but "Not this way! Not this way!" The paramedics had strapped him onto a gurney, speeding him out of the house of his birth, into the dark night. Now he had returned in his casket.

Beckoning Me Was Light

Sometime during the night, I was awakened. I felt nothing physical except a state of intense alertness. I heard nothing. Against my great desire to roll over and return to sleep came an inner command: "Go!"

I slipped out of bed carefully so as not to disturb Stuart. Since I had slept in the same room when I was growing up, I knew the terrain of the house by memory. When I reached the door and turned the corner into the hallway, I was enveloped in darkness. I had never before felt so oppressed by the absence of light.

I knew I had to walk through this dense blackness, my hand touching the wall to my left until it ended. Where the hallway became an L-shape and led to the second bedroom, I had to take a step of faith across pure space to the railing of the open staircase. Then once again I could touch something solid on my left side. My heart had taken over my whole body as I took that final step.

Gradually, the walk became less nightmarish as I turned the corner to the staircase and eased myself downward, one step at a time. Now it wasn't the darkness that haunted me; it was the thought of the body in the casket.

When I reached the last step and turned toward the living room, I let go of the banister and of my fear. Beckoning me was light, reflecting off the white satin onto the face of my father. I entered the living room, the room of the great Moravian preacher and of my grandmother's prodigious labor, and sat down in the chair by the coffin.

And Then I Saw the Sign

For a long time I did nothing. I cannot recall a single thought that drifted through my mind in those early morning hours. Feeling, not thought, lingers now. I felt as though I had entered the pages of the family Bible and had taken up residence inside them. Time was no more: I do not know if I sat there for one hour or five.

I do know that the sun rose gloriously that day across my favorite spot on the farm—the meadow. And I do know that as my old image of God was decaying in the flesh in front of me, a new one arose.

The pale yellow light pulled me toward the casket. I examined all six feet of my father's frame, touching the marble skin, amazed for the last time by the size of the huge hands. My eyes filled with tears, but they were not tears of grief. I felt more like I had three and a half years earlier as I came out of anesthesia and looked at my baby son for the first time. Wonder. Joy.

And then I saw the sign. How could it be that I had never seen it before? The marks were subtle, but there they were on both sides of his forehead—the scars from the forceps. I fingered them gently, with a mother's touch.

As if they were fresh.

The Call: A Sequel to "The Viewing"

Every woman needs a connection to other women before she can hear the voice of God calling her into Being.

Wisdom Is Her Name

By writing "The Viewing," I discovered that I was connected to my paternal grandmother, Sue Brubaker Snyder Hershey, in ways I had never imagined before. We shared a history of giving birth to sons, positions on opposite sides of my patriarchal father, and grief in his death. All these flattened the fifty years that separated us in time. Through her words to me at the viewing of my father, and through the awakening that happened as I touched the forceps scars on my father's forehead, I was invited into the infinite.

I was ready to reread Proverbs 8, as I did a few years later, and see for the first time that the Bible reserves one of the most powerful and creative roles of all for a woman. Wisdom is her name, and she tells us about her most creative moment:

> The Lord created me at the beginning of his works,
> before all else that he made, long ago.
> Alone, I was fashioned in times long past,
> at the beginning long before earth itself.
> When there was yet no ocean I was born,
> no springs brimming with water.
> Before the mountains were settled in their place,
> long before the hills I was born,
> when as yet he had made neither land nor lake
> nor the first clod of earth.
> When he set the heavens in their place I was there,
> when he girdled the ocean with the horizon,
> when he fixed the canopy of clouds overhead
> and set the springs of ocean firm in their place,
> when he prescribed its limits for the sea
> and knit together earth's foundations.
> Then I was at his side each day,
> his darling and delight,
> playing in his presence continually,
> playing on the earth, when he had finished it,
> while my delight was in the human race.
>
> (Prov. 8:22-31, NEB/NRSV)

Wisdom declares that she was there before time began. This is the source of her power. In the New Testament, Jesus will be described in the same way—as the firstborn of all creation (Col. 1:13-20).

Connecting to Wisdom

I believe women can catch glimpses of eternity and therefore touch Wisdom herself. Our relationship to Jesus connects us to Wisdom, and Wisdom connects us to Jesus. This is true power. When we are willing to give up everything else, sometimes we receive the gift of this kind of blessing. We get to play with God, as wisdom did. We touch the hem of God's garment and feel the electricity of power that has triumphed over death.

Our first connections with Wisdom are brief. They can come at any time in any age. They can happen often, once one has learned how to put oneself into Wisdom's way. Such epiphanies may or may not be connected with leadership roles. They are as likely to send one to solitude as they are to lead a community.

One can see both outcomes in the lives of outstanding women mystics from the Middle Ages to the sixteenth century. Teresa of Avila, for example, established seventeen Carmelite institutions, leading an active life even though she was drawn naturally to contemplation.

Often the woman leader who has touched Wisdom leads reluctantly at first. She would sometimes prefer to be alone or in the company of a few friends. Instead, her days are crowded with many appointments. She finds joy in her calling to lead, but her joy is tinged with great sadness.

Wisdom certainly will not prevent tragedy, pain, or depression. What contact with Wisdom brings us is the conviction that the separations in our lives, no matter how deep, can be healed. Wisdom teaches us to wait. Wisdom takes us to the love that surpasses understanding. Wisdom turns us into survivors because Wisdom has the power to negate our enemy, time. Wisdom also helps us within a time-bound world to see the things that will last.

Strength Women Give to Women

Connecting to Wisdom is different from finding role models and networking with them. Mentors are important and necessary, but the corporate leadership literature defines them far too narrowly as dispensers of helpful facts, especially information about power. Women of Wisdom seek a broader, wider, deeper definition of *mentor*. They operate from a spiritual base.

Marsha Sinetar has written extensively about the spiritual base of leadership and vocational choices. In *The Mentor's Spirit* she enlarges the definition. Our mentors do not need to be alive, for example. They can be writers and artists from another age. They can be books, films, pieces of music, nature, silence, historical and biographical figures, biblical characters, family, and friends. They can be people we have loved. They can be people we have never met. They can be people who love us, whether or not we have daily contact. Mentoring is a spiritual act.

First we must learn how to find mentors. Then we learn how to give the gift of mentoring to others. Sinetar calls mentors "artists of encouragement."

Women need to seek out spiritual mentors and not be restricted to people who actually hold titles for the type of job you might wish to have. Your mentor in gratitude might be the custodian. Your mentor in laughter might be the president. Your mentor in lament might be your student. Or vice versa.

Think bigger than any leadership box others might want to put you in. Pay special attention to the women in your life—mother, grandmother, great-grandmother, daughter, niece, cousin, aunt, friend, and sister.

What special strength can women give to women? We can pronounce each other good. We can share our life stories. We can in trust reveal our fears. We do not have to understand each other. Love is enough.

A Great-Grandmother First Named My Vocation

As I write, I am looking at a picture. My great-grandmother is in the center of a group of four others—her adult children, three women and a man. My paternal grandmother, the one who spoke to me at "the viewing," is on the left. How serious she looks and yet how compassionate and strong; she is a Mennonite *Mona Lisa*.

My great-grandmother is in the center, however. I have one vivid memory of her. I only remembered it by looking long and hard at her faraway gaze in this photo. When I was about twelve years old, I asked her to write in my autograph book, hoping for some witty aphorism.

She looked at the book, looked right into my soul, sat down, and

wrote, "Train up a child in the way he should go; and when he is old, he will not depart from it" (Prov. 22:6, KJV). At the time I was mortified. Now I see that she was giving me a powerful message about her high expectations for my personal moral behavior. She was also the first, probably without consciously knowing it, to name my vocation of education within the church.

This photo sits on my office at home. On the walls are the faces of many other women. One of them appears in a painting called *Journey Within a Journey*. She is sitting in a train, her feet propped up on the opposite seat, an open book in her lap. Coffee cups are in front of her, on the table. The landscape is Midwestern farmland, golden ripe wheat below a blue sky. Her auburn hair, long and abundant, is pinned neatly in a twist at the back of her head. She stands for all of us, so full of potential, so full of inarticulate, silent longing.

We are all on a journey. First we get on trains and venture outward into the world. Then something happens. If we are lucky, we will catch a vision of the beautiful, of pure and radiant love, and we will touch enough of it in this world to turn our faces toward eternity. From then on, our journey is inward. We will be ready to empty ourselves and listen, open to a call.

Two Phone Calls That Changed My Life

My own call to the presidency of Goshen College came in 1996, and it was surrounded by women. I had just spent a month in England. I recall the train trip from the Lake District to Leeds, where we were planning to visit one of my friends from college.

As we pulled out of the station in Lancaster, England, I thought about my own birth in Lancaster, Pennsylvania. On the train I wrote a poem about my mother. I was trying to imagine what was being born in her, as I also felt myself beginning to be born again. Something momentous was about to happen. But what?

In Leeds, something momentous did happen. The sky put on a fantastic display of color that lasted for several hours. It was cold and windy. The clouds streamed from left to right past the spire of the cathedral on top of the hill. And the colors! They poured out like paint, mostly pastels, but iridescent, glowing. I was transfixed.

Television reporters explained that we had witnessed a once-in-a-lifetime event called "Mother of Pearl clouds," formed by rare combinations of temperature and light.

A week later, I was back at Chapel Hill, North Carolina, our family's sabbatical-leave home. The phone rang. The search committee from Goshen College wished to speak to me.

That weekend, while my husband, Stuart, and I were visiting the Mennonite Publishing House in Scottdale, Pennsylvania, the phone rang again. This time it was a fire bell in the night. Our niece Alicia Showalter Reynolds, a graduate student at Johns Hopkins University and graduate of Goshen College, was missing.

She would not be found for more than six weeks, when her decaying body attracted buzzards to an isolated stretch of woods near where she disappeared.

Generations of Women Calling Me to Speak

In the weeks that followed, I felt generations of strong and yet often-silent women calling to speak with me. "Do it, Aunt Shirley," said the voice of Alicia from the grave. "Help to open possibilities for other young women, as I would have done had I lived longer."

"Go for it, Mom," said my daughter, Kate. There were, of course, many important men in my life involved in this decision, also. But today I thank and celebrate the women so that other women may have this story—and so that other desperately needed women leaders will be born.

In March of 1996, I was ready to read another biblical passage in a new way. When I was in Goshen, preparing to appear before the search committee for the first time, I was reading my daily selection from the book *Disciplines for the Inner Life.* The subject for the week was "guidance," and the biblical passage assigned for that day was 1 Samuel 16:1-13.

Samuel is looking for a king to replace Saul. The Lord sends him to Jesse, who shows him seven of his strong and handsome sons. As each appears, Samuel thinks he has found the king, but the Lord reminds him, "The Lord does not see as mortals see; they look on the outward appearance, but the Lord looks on the heart" (16:7).

After refusing the seven brothers, Samuel asks if Jesse has any other sons. "There is still the youngest, but he is looking after the sheep," replies Jesse.

When David appears, with ruddy cheeks and bright eyes, Samuel knows immediately that this is the one and anoints him in the presence of his brothers.

"Then . . . the spirit of the Lord came mightily upon David from that day forward" (16:13).

The Spirit of the Lord Spoke to Me, Too

When I read that passage, the Spirit of the Lord spoke to me, too. I had been mentored by a shepherd boy more than two thousand years ago. Even though the task ahead looked daunting, I felt courage. Later I discovered that the search committee had begun with a devotional reflection on that very same passage in Samuel.

During the days surrounding my father's death and my niece's death, God had been at work. I am no longer afraid of my own death, for these other deaths have helped prepare me for life, no matter how long or short.

These deaths, along with men and women of my past and present, have called me to leadership. When speaking to my community at Goshen College, I have uttered one promise, borrowed from Cardinal Joseph Bernadin upon his election to bishop:

I hope that before my name falls from the Eucharist prayer in the silence of death, you will know well who I am. You will know because we will work together and play together, fast and pray together, mourn and rejoice together, despair and hope together, dispute and be reconciled together. You will know me as a friend, fellow priest, and bishop. You will also know that I love you. For I am Joseph, your brother.

When I use these words in a speech, I add, "For I am Shirley, your sister." Fifty years ago I came "from a bright meadow." Someday I will belong again to eternity. In between lies the journey. The path is much less important than the journey itself—and the destination is home.

Shirley Hershey Showalter

It Just So Happened

JUNE ALLIMAN YODER

J. Tyler Klassen

JUNE ALLIMAN YODER is a teacher, preacher, conference speaker, and retreat leader. Since 1981, June has been Associate Professor of Communication and Preaching at Associated Mennonite Biblical Seminary, Elkhart, Indiana. Prior to that she served in various capacities at Goshen (Indiana) College, Coe College (Cedar Rapids, Iowa), and Morris Brown College (Atlanta, Georgia).

June is a graduate of Goshen College (B.A.), University of Iowa (M.A., theater arts), Associated Mennonite Biblical Seminary (M.Div.), and Bethany Theological Seminary (D.Min.). She was ordained as a Minister of the Word at (Goshen) College Mennonite Church in 1988. June was awarded the Staley Lectureship in 1986, 1988, and 1995; the C. Henry Smith Peace Lectureship in 1980; and the Marpeck Lectureship in 1998.

Several of June's sermons have been published: "The Untold Account" in *Weaving Wisdom: Sermons by Mennonite Women* (ed. D. Y. Nyce); ". . . And Peter" in *Lydia's Cloth* (Mar./Apr. 1992); and "Gospel Lite" in *Standing with the Poor* (ed. P. P. Parker; 1992). She has written other articles for *New Beginnings, Women's Concerns Report, Holy Moments with God, The AMBS Bulletin,* and *Medical Messenger.*

Over a period of twenty years, June has frequently spoken at church-wide Mennonite youth conventions.

June and her husband, John D. Yoder, have a daughter, Amanda.

I REMEMBER CLEARLY when I first became aware of the phrase "it just so happened." I was taking Hebrew in seminary, and we were painstakingly translating our way verse by verse through the book of Ruth. In Ruth 2:3, we translated, "It just so happened, she found herself working in a field belonging to Boaz." *It just so happened.* The phrase struck me as an important one.

Other translations read, "as it happened" or "by coincidence," all with reference to the quality of chance in the Ruth story. Yet these happenings seem to most of us now as divine intervention. It was by chance, apparently, that it was the season of the barley harvest when these two needy women arrived back in Bethlehem.

It seems to be pure chance that the field to which Ruth went to glean belonged to a relative and that Boaz was out in the field that day. It also seems like sheer chance that he happened to see Ruth and that he liked what he saw when his eyes fell on her. What appears on the human level to be chance, however, is to the eye of faith the hand of God designing the set, casting the roles, and helping each acting person play their part.

Not a Sidekick or Little Helper

I have seen a similar pattern of God's hand in my life. It just so happened that I was born into an egalitarian family. The fact that women and men received equal treatment in my family was due partly to necessity and partly to conscious choice. When I was born, my maternal grandfather was already deceased.

At an early age, I became keenly aware of how hard my widowed

Grandma (Anna) Richard worked to support the younger children still at home. But Grandma wasn't the only one who stretched to make ends meet. The children worked hard, too. Aunt Clysta and Uncle John tell of tossing bales of hay onto the wagon when their growing bodies were still much too young for such heavy work.

This same Aunt Clysta was a significant role model for me in another way as well. She went to Goshen College and then completed medical school and her residency in obstetrics and gynecology. That fact was indescribably important to me. As a woman, I saw another woman close to me whom I admired, one who was choosing a Mennonite College and a career path, and succeeding. That made me believe that I could do likewise.

However, my parents, Mae (Richard) and Gilbert Alliman, played the most important role in my development by always expecting as much from me as from my brother, Kirk. A prime example of this attitude is the way Mom and Dad mentored Kirk and me in relation to the lawn-mowing business we had before we were old enough to be hired for "real" jobs.

They let us know that the business was ours and not theirs. Both of us were to do the work to the customers' satisfaction. I was not Kirk's sidekick or little helper. The business was an equal partnership that we were both involved in and responsible for. They taught me confidence in my own abilities to take on responsibility and be an equal in any arena. It was a valuable lesson.

An even more significant story of the role my parents played in my life centers around yet another job I had. This time it was a paper route, when I was in the fifth grade. We were living in Kalona, Iowa, and the *Iowa City Press Citizen* divided Kalona into two routes. It just so happened that both of the routes were available at the same time. We decided that Kirk and I would each apply for a route. However, the *Press Citizen* had a policy that girls could not have paper routes.

This incident is the first time that I remember meeting discrimination, and I didn't like it. Kirk and my dad had the required meeting with the circulation manager to hear the policies and procedures, but Dad suggested that I "tag along and pay attention." I wondered why I should waste my time doing that. Both routes were combined into one, and Kirk got the whole thing. I was angry.

However, when we got home, Mother and Dad had a long talk with us and decided that Kirk and I would split the route. The paperwork would show the newly merged route under Kirk's name, but as far as the Alliman family was concerned, there would be two routes, one of them mine. This arrangement was one of the many ways my parents demonstrated to me that I had equal ability, worth, and expectation, even though equal opportunities were still lacking in most areas of the world.

Empowered by Trust

Again, it just so happened that during my high school years, we lived near Iowa Mennonite School (IMS). The years there were formative for me. At public school in those days, I felt different from other students. Though I helped plan the junior-high dances, I could not go to them. At IMS, I was involved in everything, and I saw my leadership skills being used and even welcomed. This was also a place where I was able to try new things and integrate school with faith. Indeed, IMS was a crucially important growing time and place for me.

Once more, it just so happened that the congregations we attended when I was young gave opportunities for young worshipers to grow and test their gifts. At Bethel Mennonite (Wayland, Iowa), we gave "topics" on Sunday evening. As a high school student at First Mennonite in Iowa City, I was allowed to help direct the choir, lead singing on Sunday evenings, assist with Bible school, and even teach a third-grade Sunday school class. Even today, churches may not realize how important it is to have ways of validating young people's gifts in the church setting.

At Goshen College I met many people and ideas that continued to shape and mold me. Just by chance, I happened into Miriam Sieber Lind's Sunday school class. Her study on the devotional classics opened a new body of literature for me and was life changing. She graciously hosted my almost weekly visits when I walked to her house, looking for counsel and encouragement. Instead, she gave me friendship and a listening ear. Her friendship during those years lingers as a model.

It also so happened that in the fall of my first year at Goshen College, the school play was *Letters to Lucerne*, the story of an international boarding school during World War II. I was just returning from a year as an exchange student in Germany, and the role of the German girl was the only one I wanted to play. Sure enough, Roy Umble cast me in that role. That was the somewhat serendipitous beginning of my desire to study drama.

I majored in speech communication, though I still joke about how I really majored in an extracurricular activity (drama), since Goshen College did not have a theater major at the time. I determined that I would go to graduate school and study further in the dramatic arts.

Eventually I called my parents at home in Iowa to tell them that I planned to apply to the University of Iowa for graduate study in acting and directing. I remember listening to the long silence at my parents' end of the phone line. Then they spoke: "We trust you" was all they said. That was an important, moving, and empowering day for me. I am grateful to them for that gift.

In the middle of the 1960s, I knew of no Mennonite who had gone to graduate school to study theater, and neither did my parents. It simply was not believed to be something that faithful Mennonites did. It was dangerous, but they trusted me. Now, almost every day in the classroom as I teach the art of preaching at Associated Mennonite Biblical Seminary, I use some element from that study time at the University of Iowa.

I met my husband, John D. Yoder, at Goshen College. His continual affirmation of my study and various roles in leadership and ministry has also been extremely empowering. I know I could not have taken jobs, explored areas, and dreamed like I have without his unwavering encouragement and support. His role will be understated in this account. But I truly believe that no married woman can achieve in this era without a supportive husband. It just so happened that I met and married a man who was able to support my life journey.

The First Woman I Ever Heard Preach

As it happened, one of the first jobs John and I had together was helping to plan the Mennonite Youth Fellowship convention in 1970. Since then, I have spoken at six conventions. I feel privileged and honored that I was asked to speak for these large gatherings of Mennonite young people. I have been most gratified to hear many young women saying I was the first woman they had ever heard preach. Their words of how important that was for them also empower me.

A few years later, when I was in my midtwenties, I was asked to represent young adults on the Mennonite Board of Missions (MBM) committee on student and young adult ministries. Coincidentally, the executive director of the committee, Virgil Brenneman, had officiated at my baptism over a decade earlier. Eventually, possibly in part because of his confidence in me and prior knowledge of me, I was named the chair of the committee—the first women to chair an MBM program committee.

From Director of Housing to Assistant Chaplain

At about the same time, Coe College (Cedar Rapids, Iowa) employed me as Director of Housing, with responsibility for all the dormitories and off-campus houses. As it happened, my office was beside the chaplain's office. One day I heard a woman crying in the hallway. Before long she sat down, but she continued to cry. Eventually I went out to ask if I could be of help.

"No," she said, "I'm looking for Chaplain Hay."

I knew that Chaplain Hay was not in his office, so I matter-of-factly told her that I was the assistant chaplain and would be glad to be of assistance. She declined my offer, smiled weakly, and left the building. Later I found out that she was Chaplain Hay's wife, and she knew there was no assistant chaplain.

The next morning, as it happened, Chaplain Hay came to my office door with a big smile on his face. "I hear you met my wife," he said. I was puzzled. He told me he was "going to make an honest woman of me," and let me know that his wife was the one I had reached out to the day before. Since I called myself the assistant chaplain, he would see to it that I truly was. The next year my contract read: "Director of Housing and Assistant Chaplain."

Chaplain Hay put me to work planning worship and retreats, counseling with women students, praying at the baccalaureate, and helping with Bible study groups. On a couple of occasions, he even asked me to fill the pulpit for some local Presbyterian congregations. This completely coincidental series of events was important in leading me to think of myself as a possible ministering person.

Inspired by a Need

Soon after all this, John and I received a call from Goshen College. As it happened, we were at a point in life where we were open to change. It just so happened that this was a shared position on the campus ministry team. The job was only an interim yearlong position. But it was another affirmation of my leadership that I see now as directing me toward leading roles in the Mennonite Church. I continued to work in various positions for Goshen College. During this time we had our child and made our church home with College Mennonite Church.

By coincidence, College Mennonite was a congregation with a woman on the ministry team. We decided to join partly because we wanted our daughter, Amanda, to observe women in leadership roles in the church. I am grateful to this congregation for being a role model for her, but also for the encouragement and opportunities it gave me.

As it turned out, one Sunday the sermon seemed like a mess. No matter how hard I tried to follow the message, my mind wandered.

At home after worship, I asked John, who had studied at the seminary, "What do they do over there at the seminary to teach people how to preach?"

"They teach mainly biblical interpretation and theology," he said.

I had long been concerned that though the biblical interpretation and the theological content of sermons were fairly strong, the style and delivery seemed weak.

Somewhere along the line, the glorious Word of God was getting gummed up. The important message was often lost in delivery. Sunday after Sunday I sat in church, a tortured communication person, wanting desperately to hear the gospel. Yet the sermon was presented in a lackluster way, often without enthusiasm or passion—barely dribbling over the edge of the pulpit.

They Took a Risk and Hired Me

At the urging of my husband, no doubt tired of my complaints only to him, I made an appointment to see Willard Swartley, dean of AMBS, to find out how they taught preaching. As it turned out, though there was genuine concern for the delivery component of preaching, one of the Bible professors usually taught preaching.

I learned that preaching is a blended discipline of biblical studies, theology, and communication; and that preaching has only recently been recognized as a discipline of its own. For years preaching was taught mostly by speech professors or by biblical studies experts who enjoyed preaching. Thus students received instruction in delivery *or* in content, but rarely in both. AMBS was no different except that for some years, preaching was not even taught at all!

At some point during our meeting, Swartley asked me if I had a résumé. I tried to explain that I had not come looking for a job, but simply as a concerned member of the Mennonite Church. Yet I was interested, so I quickly summarized my training and qualifications on paper.

After receiving my résumé, the dean proposed that I team-teach preaching with the Bible professor Erland Waltner. He thought this could blend together what might strengthen the delivery of our Mennonite pastors.

It just so happened that I made my way over to AMBS that day to see the dean. But the great "it just so happened" is that they hired me. I had no degree in theological studies. I had only a master's degree in dramatic arts. These really were not the credentials desired for new faculty in a theological graduate school. However, in the fall of 1981, I began my teaching at AMBS—tenuously at first, of course. I was hired to team-teach one course for one semester.

Empowering Mentors

Someone decided to take a risk and hire me. After a few years of team-teaching with Waltner, President Marlin Miller urged me to obtain theological training. With his encouragement, I began and finished the master of divinity degree in 1988. That fall I also began studying for the doctor of ministry degree at Bethany Theological Seminary (Oak Brook, Illinois).

These two men were empowering mentors for me. Waltner, whose personal style is quite different from my own, still welcomed me into his classroom. He shared his knowledge and authority with me, and he invited and valued my contribution. Waltner was in a position to make or break my first wobbly venture into the teaching of preaching, but he was always affirming.

Miller was a mentor in a different way. He counseled me with his high expectations for me and by pushing me to finish the next degree and to dream big. I appreciate the way he helped arrange a study leave for me, and how he applauded my academic milestones. Sometimes he seemed to believe in me more than I believed in myself. That always brought out the best in me.

I am grateful that Miller and Waltner just so happened to be at AMBS when I was starting my work there.

None of It "Just So Happened"

"As it happened," "by coincidence," "it just so happened"— There was a strong and loving family with high expectations. There were faithful and supportive friends who often saw in me more than I could see in myself. There were people willing to take risks. There were many able mentors. There were people who saw my possibilities and forgave my limitations.

Just as in the book of Ruth, all the activity appears to be by people alone. However, I stand in awe of what God has managed to do with coincidences in my life. In fact, it seems to me now that none of it "just so happened."

Administrators

If you keep silence
at such a time as this,
relief and deliverance
will rise for the Jews
from another quarter,
but you and your
father's family will perish.
Who knows?
Perhaps you have come
to royal dignity
for just such a time as this.
—*Mordecai, in Esther 4:14*

For Such a Time as This

MIRIAM F. BOOK

MIRIAM BOOK has been Associate General Secretary of the
Mennonite Church since 1989.
One of her assignments is to be
convention coordinator for General Assemblies and Churchwide
conventions.

She serves as executive staff
for the Mennonite Church Nomi-
nating Committee, the Inter-
Mennonite Confession of Faith
Committee (1989-95), and the
Council on Faith, Life, and Strat-
egy. Miriam is one of four staff
members on the Integration
Committee, and she is a member of the Mennonite World Conference
General Council.

Before 1989, Miriam was employed as coordinator of marketing for
Philhaven Hospital, Mt. Gretna, Pennsylvania. She also served in various
capacities for Eastern Mennonite Board of Missions (1974-84), in Salunga, Pennsylvania.

In August 1992, Miriam was ordained at Belmont Mennonite Church
for her churchwide ministries. She has been coordinator for the Business
and Professional Women under the General Women's Missionary and
Service Commission, 1983-89; adviser for the Business and Professional
Women Commission of Lancaster Conference, 1986-88; and chairperson of the Business and Professional Women Task Force, Lancaster Conference, 1984-85. She was also president of Women's Missionary and
Service Commission, Lancaster Conference, 1983-86.

Miriam received her B.A. from Eastern College, and has a diploma in pastoral studies from London Bible College, 1981. She participates in the Soul of the Executive Program of the Shalem Institute.

Miriam grew up in Lancaster County, Pennsylvania. Beyond her many church responsibilities, Miriam is energized by reading, journaling, walking, biking, gardening, and conversation.

MY LOVE FOR GOD and the Mennonite Church has been strongly shaped and influenced by people, places, and events—both in Lancaster Mennonite Conference during my early years and later in the broader Mennonite Church. Sensitive and godly men and women helped me discern God's call to ministry.

How Can This Be?

As a child I experienced God's presence and call through annual summer trips to northern Pennsylvania to teach outpost summer Bible school. My parents and I, along with others from the Paradise congregation, made these trips for eighteen years. Later I realized that these experiences sensitized me to God's voice and provided opportunities for ministry and leadership.

Singing "I have decided to follow Jesus, no turning back, no turning back" impressed on me the importance of lifetime commitment and discipleship. Teaching Bible school and building relationships with unchurched persons and persons from other than Mennonite backgrounds helped prepare me for my work today.

I attended Locust Grove Mennonite School and Lancaster Mennonite High School. Both nurtured additional awareness of God and the people of God. Teachers modeled their vision for expanding God's kingdom through their approachability and humility as leaders. At school, I was exposed to global missions by meeting missionaries and hearing stories of God's call and their faithfulness in responding.

Following high school, God's work in my life became more pronounced. My work in a printing corporation gave me new exposure to "the world." In the late 1960s, I attended a local interdenominational seminar on women's growth and self-esteem in relationship with self, others, and God.

During that weekend, I felt God's call to what I then labeled women's ministries. I envisioned myself leading, encouraging, and pointing others to Christ. I did not struggle with whether it was appropriate for me to lead because I had heard about men and women missionaries leading overseas. Also, in my home, my mother and father modeled shared leadership in parenting.

While I was growing up on a farm with many sisters and only one brother, I was quickly involved in farm work. There was no distinction between men's and women's roles. I also knew well the story of Queen Esther from the Old Testament, and how she was at the right place at a crucial time in the history of her people.

However, I did struggle with my own self-understanding. I was shy and withdrawn. As I felt God speaking to me during that weekend, I found myself repeating Mary's response to the angel who told her she would give birth to the child Jesus: "But how can this be?" I was not a public person or a leader.

After the seminar, I remember going to my bedroom and praying out loud to God, with questions about this call to ministry. I wrote the seminar leader to thank her for the impact she made on my life, but held back from naming my call. I went on to read anything I could put my hands on about women's ministries. But I never spoke to anyone about my call.

Opportunities to Speak

In 1973 I was invited to join the Eastern Mennonite Board of Missions (EMBM) staff in the overseas office, where I worked for eleven years. Here I grew rapidly—personally, professionally, and spiritually—as I traveled overseas, recruited missionaries, began the first pilot Youth Evangelism Service (YES) program, and provided pastoral care for missionaries.

When I was contacted by EMBM, I knew without a doubt that I was to go. Yet at the time I did not recognize the profound influence EMBM would provide in developing my gifts for ministry.

While at EMBM, I had tremendous opportunities for service in the Lancaster Mennonite Conference. The Women's Missionary and Service Commission (WMSC) asked me to lead junior girls activities, which helped me become better known in the conference. I was asked to speak on singleness and to lead retreats for women and youth.

As speaking opportunities came, I remember weeping and crying out to God, "I am not capable; I cannot do this." Then I remembered the call I received while attending the women's seminar and realized that this was beginning to fulfill God's call to church ministry.

Eventually I served as president of the Lancaster Conference WMSC and started the Business and Professional Women's organization. From Lancaster Conference, doors opened for me to serve on the churchwide WMSC board and later to chair the Nominating Committee for the Mennonite Church in North America.

In my work with EMBM, many persons believed in me and provided opportunities for ministry, leaders such as David Thomas, Paul Zehr, Don Jacobs, and others. Through respected churchman Mahlon Hess, I received invitations to speak and preach on missions in churches across Lancaster Conference. As I did so, I realized my heart was in the church, in opening God's Word, and in pointing others to Jesus Christ and greater faithfulness in following Christ.

In late 1970 I learned of the Evangelical Women's Caucus, a weeklong event in Pasadena, California, on "Women and the Ministries of Christ." I quickly made plans to attend, recognizing that to be obedient to God's call, I needed to learn all I could about women's gifts in the church.

At that time I first spoke with my parents about my call to ministry.

My mother said, "Well, Miriam, maybe someday you can take Dad's place in the church."

Dad (a pastor) was deeply moved. He responded with his characteristic expression at such times, "Well, well, well!"

My parents became advocates for me and nurtured my call by supplying information on women in the church. They gave me a safe place to talk about my call.

Learning About Leadership

At the 1970 "Women and the Ministries of Christ" gathering, I made new connections in my call to ministry. I met women pastors and heard about God's work in their lives. I also became aware of the Mennonite Women in Leadership Ministries group and started to attend those gatherings.

There I met Mennonite women leaders such as Ruth Brunk Stoltzfus and Emma Richards. While listening to their stories and calls, I identified and said, "Yes, this too is what I have experienced. Yes, in the church gifts may be used in leadership and preaching."

I recognized my need for additional training and resolved to work at completing my college degree in psychology and religion. I took a leave from my work at EMBM for a one-year pastoral studies program in London, England. There I again was greatly influenced by faculty men and women who opened the Scriptures.

In London, the Old Testament took on new meaning as I studied the characteristics of God through the eyes of the prophets. Studying with students from countries around the world brought new perspectives to the Scriptures, drawn from their rich cultural diversity. My understanding of God and the holiness of God grew during this time in England, expanding my relationship with the Lord to one of awe and reverence.

Before my travel to England, I had prayed earnestly to God to move things in my life that needed moving and to teach me new things I was blind to seeing. I felt more insecure and less in control in an academic setting. Also, since I knew no one, I found myself more open to God's presence in a way I had not quite known before. I was truly depending on God in yet another new way. Once again, I grew academically and spiritually.

In this culture, I learned more about servant leadership through the modeling of Anglican professor Peggy Knight. With her proper English manner beautifully blended with humility, she told me, "Miriam, my office door will always be open for you—for my colleagues and I are your servants in the Lord."

My eyes were opened to a greater awareness of key characteristics of a leader: being available to those the leader is called to be among and serve rather than isolating oneself, having humility integrated with a healthy self-esteem, and leading as one who serves.

God's Call Affirmed

During these years, many persons encouraged and nurtured me. They provided opportunities for testing my gifts, although most of them were not aware of God's call in my life to ministry. I often lacked the courage to talk about my call because sometimes when I did, it was misunderstood. Most of my experiences were positive and helpful in confirming God's earlier call on my life.

However, I also experienced several painful times where I risked telling my story regarding my desire to lead in the church. Several times I was told that church leadership could not be God's will for my life. However, open doors and informal mentors and role models along the way gave me courage and faith to believe that the God who called is faithful.

In 1989 I was invited to move from Lancaster, Pennsylvania, to Elkhart, Indiana, to work with the Mennonite Church General Board (MCGB) as the Associate General Secretary. At the time I did not fully understand the significance of being called to this particular part of the church. Today that is becoming much clearer.

In our Mennonite Church denominational office, I have the privilege of working in the heart of the church and partnering with Lancaster Conference as well as the twenty other conferences in the Mennonite Church. Here I have the opportunity for leadership through administration and management, preaching and teaching.

In this work, others across the church including my colleague, James Lapp, and my pastor, Duane Beck, have recognized my gifts. They encouraged my ordination to ministry and asked, "Are you open to being ordained?"

I said I did not seek ordination to ministry. However, I had clearly felt God's leading into ministry and therefore was open and excited by the church recognizing God's call and credentialing me for ministry.

Serving Christ Through Business Contacts

It has been my unique privilege to extend the work of the church into the business context. While my primary assignment with the MCGB is working with church leaders, a significant piece of my work includes churchwide convention planning. I work at choosing a convention site and negotiating prices for the convention center, hotels, meals, etc. All this involves building relationships with women and men in business and professions, similar to the church context and yet different from it.

Here I partner with people from a variety of faith traditions and sometimes with no faith commitment. In this context, as in the church, I aim to practice assertive, authentic leadership with integrity and humility. In the business context, just as in the church, I endeavor to model directness, vulnerability, and servant leadership.

One of the most exhilarating and humbling experiences I shall cherish for life happened as I planned one of these conventions. Along with other Mennonite staff and volunteers, I had worked with the key executive of a convention property for several years prior to the churchwide convention.

During negotiations, we dealt with misunderstandings and the usual ups and downs that go with planning any gathering for thousands of people. At times these experiences lead me to question my leadership style.

Did I push too hard in the negotiations? Was I too direct? Did I respect the perspective of the convention center employee? Did I represent the perspective of my church? How did I measure up as a Christian? Was it evident where my first loyalty is? Was I a carrier of God's presence in that setting? Did I recognize Jesus in the lives of those I negotiated with? Was I condescending in my leadership? Was Jesus thankful for my leadership on behalf of God's kingdom?

I ask similar questions about my leadership in the church. Yet in a convention setting, I am perhaps more in touch with the way my actions can invite a person to move toward or away from God.

Following the event, a convention center employee with whom I had worked for several years talked with me. I was exhilarated when she indicated her desire to connect with the Mennonite Church and return to the church and faith she had left some years ago.

She told us that she was called back to faith and the church by the servant leadership she experienced from us. She was awestruck by our approachability as leaders, the way we as leaders related to each other and to the people we were called to lead, as well as our relationship with her. She was attracted to Christ as she observed, amidst our humanness, our authenticity as followers of Jesus Christ.

Joining the Team for Such a Time as This

As I reflect on my years in church ministry, I am deeply moved by God's hand on my life. I am thankful for those persons who influ-

enced, nurtured, and paved the way for my ministry today. In looking back, I can more clearly see the finger of God writing on my life.
This gives me new insights and perspectives for the present and the
future. Looking back gives me new energy and courage for the future.

In ministry, I have experienced times of woundedness and disappointment. Invitations to participate in a conference setting have
been withdrawn because the conference did not want a woman
leader in the church. Weariness comes when the voice and vote of
men are considered stronger than the voice and vote of women. The
same happens when my voice is not received or respected in the
same way as my male colleagues.

Having a safe place to talk with trusted women and men brings
perspective to the present opportunity. Within the safety net of male
and female friends, I guard against isolating myself as a leader or
becoming a "one issue" or bitter person in ministry.

In the faith community of men and women, I have grown in being
more gentle with myself and with others. In the safety of the community, I "remember to remember" and marvel at God's creative
acts. In this community I begin to dance and sing as Miriam did
when she joined the team with her brothers, Moses and Aaron, in
leading the children of Israel.

I also solicit the prayers of my friends, as done by Esther of old.
These great models of faith give me courage in responding to God's
call to leadership for such a time as this.

Miriam F. Book

Birthing a New Denomination

DONELLA M. CLEMENS

Donella Clemens lives in Souderton, Pennsylvania, and attends Souderton Mennonite Church, where she has served as an elder for the past eight years. Donella is a graduate of Eastern Mennonite University, and the University of Pennsylvania, School of Social Work.

Donella's churchwide responsibilities have included serving as Secretary of Girls' Activities for Women's Missionary and Service Commission (WMSC) from 1981-89 and Moderator of the Mennonite Church from 1993-95. Currently she is Moderator of Franconia Conference and has just completed sixteen years as a member of the Board of Trustees of Christopher Dock Mennonite High School.

She is also a member of the Board of Directors of Mennonite Central Commitee (MCC) U.S. and binational as well as the Executive Committee for MCC binational.

Donella and her husband, Wayne, are the parents of Quentin, Kent, and Gwendolyn; and they have one grandson. In addition to Donella's many church responsibilities, she thrives on walking the beach, reading historical novels, and travel.

BEING A MENNONITE WOMAN in leadership has been a journey shaped by an intriguing mix of companions and events. At times I have suffered the agony of being lost on the path; other times I have taken the wrong road and suffered the consequences. But most times, it has been satisfying. The signposts along the way assure me that God is the ultimate designer of this journey.

Why Are Mennonites Different?

Faith in God and the church has always been a part of my life. Faith was something I practically inhaled from my parents and the world around me, rather than something I was taught. Going to all church activities had the same (or greater) priority as the routine trips to the grocery store. There was never a question about participating in the many activities of my home congregation, Locust Grove, in Big Valley, Pennsylvania.

My parents always taught Sunday school. Mom taught children's classes in the earlier years, but then shifted to leading women's classes. Dad taught either the high school boys or a men's class. My preacher uncles came to our house regularly to discuss issues of theology with Dad even though he was not a minister. It was routine for my brother and me to wait impatiently while someone talked with Dad after a service so long that we were one of the last to drive out of the parking lot.

As an early teenager, I had many questions about our Mennonite practices and traditions. Helping to milk the cows became an opportunity for me to discuss theology and religious traditions with Dad, such as these issues: What does baptism mean? Can church membership and baptism be separated?

I even had a favorite question: Why do Mennonites need to be so different from other Christian denominations? Mennonite girls were required to wear some clothes that I thought were ugly. To my way of thinking, God does not intend for us to be ugly! Since the

Bible clearly states that all creation is beautiful, why can Mennonites not be beautiful as well? I particularly wanted to wear a nice Easter bonnet! Dad's answers to my questions did not always satisfy me. But he was patient in trying to deal with my persistent queries.

God's Special Purpose for Me

Over time, the adults in my life gave me the clear message that God had a special purpose for me. Dad instilled in me the desire to find the unique role that God intended for me. He did this by encouraging me to focus on opportunities I was given and not to compare my journey with that of my peers. I sensed that my task was to continually search for that purpose as my life evolved.

The pastors of my congregation, some being my uncles, always affirmed my abilities, encouraging me to try new opportunities. I did not feel comfortable doing some things, such as leading Bible studies, teaching Bible school classes, and giving "talks." My mentors seemed to believe my abilities to be greater than I understood them to be. With their encouragement, I timidly tried new challenges and learned to be more comfortable in leadership roles.

I marvel at the willingness of my father and uncles to encourage me to be open to God's call in my life, regardless of where that would lead. I have no memory of any hint from them that certain activities were unacceptable for women in the church. Was that message never given, or did I simply disregard it?

My father's older brother was a bishop in the Conservative Mennonite Conference. In my last conversation with him before he died in 1991, he gave me encouragement and support. He had just learned that I had been asked to be moderator of the Mennonite Church. He assured me of his prayers and support, stating that things were changing in the church of today, and that he could give his blessing to those changes.

My mother passed on to me the messages she had received throughout her life. They were much more traditional: conform whenever possible and to the greatest extent possible, and do not make waves. My tendency to ask questions and push the edges kept Mom a bit anxious, wondering what I was up to next.

As my leadership roles in the church increased, Mom voiced her support for me even though she did not understand exactly what my work involved. She often said she had her opportunities to be involved in church life in her younger years through teaching and helping in conference events, and now was my time. She was among the partners-in-prayer who surrounded me over the years.

From Where Does My Help Come?

An important piece of my spiritual development has been Scripture, specifically the verses I learned as a child. Psalm 121:1-2 has been with me from early Sunday school days. I memorized the words from a little cardboard "ticket":

> I lift up my eyes to the hills—
> from where will my help come?
> My help comes from the Lord,
> who made heaven and earth.

Growing up on a farm, I learned to love and respect the world God created. Today I draw strength from our Creator God through the enjoyment of the ocean, woods, grass, and gardens.

Long, regular walks out-of-doors provide balance in the stresses of committee work and the frustrations of human relationships. Meeting God under sunlit skies or storm-threatening clouds is a persistent reminder of my God, who is a much bigger force than anything I am experiencing. My God is loving and nurturing, caring for my spirit through communion with her Spirit. The caring comes to me as I shout, cry, laugh, or walk quietly in God's presence. The joy of being in God's presence during these quiet times keeps the center of my being in touch with God, who provides me with strength and confidence to tackle the work ahead of me.

Music has always served as inspiration for me. From my early years, I have participated in special music groups. My times of greatest spiritual connection with God have been through singing the great music of the church. Classical music, particularly choral pieces, reaches my soul in ways that refresh and restore me spiritually and emotionally. I also have a good selection of folk and jazz music in my collection as well. High school and college choir experiences are high points of those years.

A Holy Kind of Question

A vital, life-giving part of my journey has been taking significant blocks of time to discern the voice of God when making critical decisions. When I was a young wife and mother in Souderton Mennonite congregation, my pastor asked me to consider serving as coordinator of the education ministry. Then he asked me an odd question. "Do you feel God calling you to this position?"

God calling me! That was language used for men being called to the ministry, not for me! I could not answer. This was a holy kind of question. To find an answer, I needed time to search my depths, with God's help. This was my first step toward a new awareness of the awesome call of God in my life.

Another significant time with God was discerning God's voice in the call to be moderator of the church. Was the church ready for a woman as moderator? What was God asking of me? I spent several days alone by the ocean, reading and praying, but mostly listening for God. The answer that emerged during those hours was that I was to be faithful in responding willingly to the call.

The question of whether the church was open to a woman in that position belonged to the church, not to me. The delegates at the Mennonite Church Assembly in 1991, meeting in Oregon, did affirm me for the position of moderator elect, to become moderator in 1993.

Other experiences have also served as affirmations of God's call through the people of the church. Franconia Conference invited me to serve as chairperson of the Nurture Commission; I now am moderator of that conference. Later I was asked to chair the board of trustees at Christopher Dock Mennonite High School. These three positions were all new roles for a woman to fill. Being part of the General WMSC for the Mennonite Church provided my first experience on a churchwide board and later opened doors to other opportunities.

Working in a World Defined by Men

Struggles have been a critical part in shaping my life. I well remember telling God I did not want to live in "a large Mennonite ghetto!" For years I found great appeal in the church's invitation to go far away, live there, and perhaps plant a church. Because that did not happen, I lived with the frustration of no clear call and of un-opened doors.

One evening I was listening to a speaker expounding on a subject I have completely forgotten. He referred to John 14:6: "Jesus said, . . . 'I am the way, and the truth, and the life.'" All I heard was the message that Jesus would provide "the way" out of my frustration. I chose to relax as much as possible and rely on that word of assurance. But the answer did not come immediately, not till almost a year later. A new direction began to emerge, along with a tangible sense that God's call to me was to work within the Mennonite church community.

Working within that community has meant working in a world that has historically been defined by men. Women as role models have been few. For many situations in which I have worked, such role models have been absent. It is tiring and hard work to plow new ground where the soil has never been turned, the soil of being the first woman in a position!

The words of Jesus in Luke 22:27 continue to challenge me:

For who is greater,
the one who is at the table or the one who serves?
Is it not the one at the table?
But I am among you as one who serves.

Jesus, the leader and the greatest among his disciples, chose the lesser position. It is a model of leadership which I continue to ponder and from which I continue to learn.

Another Way to Say That

With the church and business world being defined mostly by men, the style and manner of functioning is male. Women bring different styles to leadership roles, styles that are not always understood or appreciated. The times of greatest frustration to me are when my comments and style of leadership are devalued.

With some frequency, a statement I make will be followed by a man saying, "In other words . . . ," or "another way to say that . . ." Because of such experiences, for years I doubted my ability to speak or communicate. After a meeting, I would spend hours reviewing what I had said, why it was not understood, and how I could have stated it better. And my self-esteem would take another beating.

It was an enormous relief to learn from other women that they had similar experiences! To know it was a gender difference and not a personal flaw was something I could deal with! That understanding still gives me new confidence in myself and courage to speak for the value of different styles, God-created styles!

The words of Paul in 2 Timothy 1:7 provide fortification at such times to speak this truth:

> For God did not give us a spirit of cowardice,
> but rather a spirit of power and of love
>   and of self-discipline.

Our work as a people is enhanced when women and men work together in complementary ways. The strengths of each gender build on those of the other, creating a unique and whole dynamic. We are much less than what God intended when we stifle use of the unique gifts of either gender.

The Love of God Has Taken on Human Faces

Low self-esteem issues have plagued me all my life. Since I am an introvert, my pattern is to look inward for the cause or source of deficiency. I have received years of encouragement from mentors; advice and affirmation of counselors; support from husband, family, and friends. Through all this, the love of God has taken on human faces, and the inner voice of inadequacy has diminished.

Mistakes can be forgiven and tossed aside with less time spent in agony and self-critique. Some advice from a friend was helpful: "Oh, you will make mistakes. Just learn to anticipate them and ask forgiveness!"

I have learned to be more realistic in my expectations for myself. This change in mental habits has been helpful and has made self-forgiveness possible.

Loneliness and Exhilaration of a Leader

Some experiences in leadership have brought the greatest "aloneness" of my life. Giving leadership is quite stressful when issues that divide become the agenda. The pressures mount, giving rise to forces that tend to work like buffeting winds, pushing and pulling from all directions. It is difficult to be true to one's own convictions and find the space to be oneself while giving leadership to the group.

Good leadership involves directing the group to find its own way in a time of difficulty. It does not mean having the leader define the solution for the group. However, all the forces tend to pull toward having the leaders define the answers and setting leaders up to carry the responsibility for the group. It is a lonely road to go against those forces. The current struggles on the issues of homosexuality illustrate this well.

Most times the journey in leadership has been exhilarating and exciting for me. Those are the times when God has provided persons to be companions, to walk with me in difficult responsibilities. They have been there with prayer, support, and presence at critical times. Truly they have been angels of God for me.

In other exhilarating times, God has been with me as I have been stretched to the limit of my abilities and found God there to supply what I needed. As I have been willing to take the leap of faith and jump into the responsibility, God's wings have been underneath to provide the critical support (as in Exod. 19:4).

I celebrate the diversity of races and ethnic groups and the wide variety of traditions in our Mennonite churches today. We enjoy a wealth of spiritual and cultural color in our denominational life. My leadership roles have given me incredible experiences of meeting many dedicated, gifted people in the Mennonite Church across Canada, Puerto Rico, Mexico, and the United States. I have been blessed by the many people in our congregations who give so freely to the work of the church, and do so out of love and dedication.

Joys of Integration

The work of integrating the Mennonite Church and the General Conference Mennonite Church has been most invigorating. I found good, hard work in being part of the Vision and Goals Committee and more recently the integration committee! Many perceived differences melted away as we worked side by side in common efforts with a common mission.

We were developing a vision statement that emerged as "Vision: Healing and Hope." This was an authentic outgrowth of the Vision and Goals Committee's joint work and worship, directed by God's Spirit. At the end of our four-year experience, the committee spoke hopefully and eagerly of the prospect of integrating our denominations. I felt highly privileged to be part of that process. It allowed me emotionally to become a member of the new denomination that is being born.

A great personal joy for me was leading the business sessions at the 1995 Mennonite Church General Assembly held at Wichita, Kansas, and then reporting the result of the vote on integration to the delegates. The General Conference delegates were meeting in another hall across the street. By previous agreement, we had arranged to have both delegate bodies vote on the question of integrating at approximately the same time.

The results of our respective votes were communicated by telephone to the moderators of each assembly. As moderator of the Mennonite Church assembly, I received that telephone call and was thrilled to announce an affirmative vote by both groups. Many prayers and much careful planning had led up to that time in our collective histories. What a privilege it was to be part of that moment! The joint times of singing, prayer, and communion that followed were a memorable celebration.

If we can come together as two denominations, surely we can also come together in our understandings of persons of other races, cultures, and gender. We are becoming more inclusive, but we must continue to work hard for even greater mutuality.

A look at the past fifteen years will show that we have taken some positive steps to involve women in leadership roles. But there are more changes in attitudes, understandings, and practice that need to be made.

Models for Our Daughters and Sons

The ministry of leadership in the Mennonite Church is work for both women and men, for both our sons and our daughters. For me, there is no more compelling reason to continue in leadership than to pave the way and to serve, by the grace of God, as a model for these, our daughters and our sons.

Those who have been models for me, my parents, teachers, pastors, and friends, have illustrated through their lives that fulfillment comes in being faithful on the journey God calls us to take. In responding to God's leading for my journey, I am grateful for and humbled by opportunities that have become available to me.

Over and over again, I have seen God's gracious leading in the adventures I have experienced. It is the anticipation along with the excitement of the next steps of the God-led journey that compels me to continue to say yes to leadership when God and the church call.

Donella M. Clemens

I Can't Make That Much Potato Salad

MARIAN CLAASSEN FRANZ

John Eisele

MARIAN CLAASSEN FRANZ is the Executive Director of the National Campaign for a Peace Tax Fund in Washington, D.C., and Executive Director of the Peace Tax Foundation. In pursuit of peace tax legislation, she interprets to Congress the conscience-driven values of persons who assert their right not to participate in killing other human beings through their military taxes.

Marian has experience in areas theologically, socially, and politically diverse. Her journey has taken her from Kansas wheat fields to the crowded poverty of Chicago, then to one of the world's power centers. Over a decade of experience at Woodlawn Mennonite Church on Chicago's impoverished south side, in a neighborhood with more than two thousand people per square block, helped to form her values and direction.

She is Vice Chair of Conscience and Peace Tax International, an organization with authorization to lobby foreign parliaments about issues of conscience and war. In addition, she has provided leadership for international conferences of Peace Tax Campaigns and war tax resisters in Germany, the Netherlands, Italy, Belgium, Spain, and London, England. She speaks from national and international experience.

In her book, *Questions Which Refuse to Go Away*, Marian asks ancient and current questions: What belongs to God, and what to Caesar? When does divine obedience call us to civil disobedience? If we pray for peace, how shall we find ways not to pay for war? How do Christians stir government to provide justice and well-being for all?

She has written chapters for books such as *Seeking Peace: True Stories of Mennonites Around the World*, struggling to live their belief in peace (ed. T. and L. G. Peachey); and *Godward: Personal Stories of Grace* (ed. T. Koontz). Marian has also published articles in several journals.

Marian serves on the board and is an active participant in the Faith and Politics Institute chaired by two members of Congress, a Democrat and a Republican. The Institute's mission is to provide settings for moral reflection and spiritual community for political leaders through reflection groups and forums that contribute to healing the nation's wounds.

She is a graduate of Bethel College, Newton, Kansas; and Mennonite Biblical Seminary, Chicago, with a master of religious education degree. Marian taught in Chicago schools and in a prison for girls. In Washington, D.C., she has directed Dunamis, an organization providing prophetic and pastoral roles for religious people relating to persons in power.

Marian serves on the General Board of the General Conference Mennonite Church (soon to merge with the Mennonite Church). She has served several terms on the GCMC Commission on Education, and on the Commission on Home Ministries.

Marian is married to Delton Franz, who served for over twenty-five years as director of the Peace Section Washington Office of Mennonite Central Committee. The Franzes have three children: Gregory, Gayle, and Coretta Franz Eby.

Marian enjoys Washington, D.C., for its natural beauty, places of historic interest, and museums. She is fascinated by governmental decision-making structures and personnel. Her favorite recreational activities are swimming, *Washington Post* crossword puzzles, and her one-year-old twin grandchildren, Justine and Adam.

EXPERIENCES THAT SHAKE us, shape us.

Not much shook my peaceful childhood years. We had a routine of chores: milking cows, feeding chickens, gathering eggs, and walking two miles to our one-room country school made up almost entirely of children in our church community. Yet this peace had an ingroup quality. I now regret that adults did not prevent us from teasing one or two Catholic children in our midst.

The white-steepled church was the center of life in that rural Kansas Mennonite community. On Saturday I memorized the prescribed answers to theological questions posed in the catechism book so I could recite them flawlessly on Sunday.

The deaths of a five-year-old sister and a twenty-three-year-old brother by the time I was age eighteen were shaking and shaping events. In surprising ways, such experiences mold us as they teach us about the seriousness of life, and paradoxically about the love of God. These family deaths came from disease, however, not from intentional violence.

A War Comes on Stage

One Sunday evening in December 1941, we were visiting my aunt in "town," Whitewater, Kansas (population, 500). Sober relatives gathered around her radio to hear the report of the attack on Pearl Harbor. The country was now at war with both Japan and Germany. Tragedy, not from natural causes but from calculated violence, slowly reshaped our lives.

The community remembered World War I. Several Mennonite pastors were nearly lynched. Some of our churches were burned because we did not take part in war. So our community made adjustments. Our summer Bible school was no longer taught in German, the language of our immigrant ancestors.

The war weighed heavily on us. Grown-ups worried aloud that bombs might eventually fall here. My father kept a map on the dining room wall and traced for us the troop movements. Mother grieved over daily newspaper photos of fine young men being killed.

Not mourned in the local press were the thousands of injuries and deaths of enemy soldiers and civilians. Those victims, however, received a good deal of our attention during the war years. We received a series of letters from Europeans having little access to relief agencies and desperately needing clothing and other basic supplies.

My father cataloged their letters and requests for help. With our mother, we plunged into tables full of secondhand clothing. She found good warm coats, while my sisters and I found fancy gowns. If the price was well under a dollar, she occasionally gave a nod.

Packing days excited the several families participating in the project. Each completed package seemed to reflect the personality of the persons to whom they were sent. We put in shoes, baby clothes, tins of food, socks, coats, sweaters, long underwear, and coffee. Coffee was rare in wartime Europe and was valuable as barter for other necessities. So were cigarettes, but we never sent those.

The Enemy Arrives at Our Home

German soldiers arrived at our Kansas farmhouse door. They came not as combatants, but as prisoners of war. Housed in a small nearby town, they were available to work on local farms during the day. I had no fear of these enemy soldiers. What terrified me were the U.S. guards who accompanied them. They were the ones with guns. In total terror, I watched as one demonstrated how to attach his bayonet. No weapon intended to kill people or spear stomachs had ever before been near our home.

At first the guards were tense and the prisoners wary. At noon on the first day, after washing up out-of-doors with the rest of the harvesters, they waited outside to be served. Perhaps they expected to be served in the yard from tin cans. My mother stepped out on the porch and in perfect German invited them in to her table as graciously as she would have called any other guests. Overwhelmed by the unexpected kindness, several wept.

As time passed, the tension between the German and U.S. soldiers was eroded on both sides by the hospitality that our Mennonite home and community extended equally to friend and foe. Guards no longer brought their dreaded guns to the table (to my enormous relief), but left them out on the porch.

These enemies, who on the battlefield would have been visiting unspeakable horrors on each other, swapped photos and stories of their families back home. To facilitate communication, my father translated. One joke was about Italian tanks having one speed forward and four in reverse. Not knowing of Italy's brief participation in the war, I did not understand what was so funny.

One afternoon, to escape the broiling Kansas sun, the guard was napping under the shady trees along the creek, leaving the prisoners in the field with the farmers. Suddenly excited chatter erupted amid a frantic flurry of activity. The prisoners had spied a fast-approaching Jeep. It was loaded with military superiors, coming to inspect the guard on duty. Several prisoners rushed to awaken the guard, who hastily rubbed sleep from his eyes and regained his watchful post.

There were stiff salutes, the clatter of weapons inspection, and intense conversation. Satisfied that the prisoners would not escape under such careful watch, the officers boarded their Jeep and disappeared as quickly as they had arrived. The silent tension of the field broke into laughter as guards and prisoners alike enjoyed success in dealing with that close call.

What was a child to think? If the German and U.S. soldiers were not each other's enemies, who was the enemy in the war that was killing and maiming so many? On our farm, the soldiers of these warring countries had made common cause against the real enemy, the system of war. *War is the enemy*, I thought. *People are not.*

Anabaptists and Inner-City Chicago

The same week we graduated from Bethel College, Delton Franz and I were married. We served two brief pastorates in Kansas, while I was teaching school. Then this idealistic couple was off to Chicago to attend seminary and return to rural or small-town pastorates. We had not the remotest idea of how our decision would thoroughly shake and forever reshape our lives.

Eight years before we arrived in Chicago, Mennonites had found good investments for their dollar. They had purchased several apartment buildings (and later a church building) for seminary students on the city's south side.

They may not have fully understood "white flight." As African-Americans moved in large numbers to northern U.S. cities in the 1940s and 1950s, whites sold their apartment buildings and fled, moving further from the city centers. Landlords seized the opportunity to subdivide apartments into tiny units, thus doubling and tripling the population (and their rental income).

A cramped community squeezed into multistory tenements. The community grew to more than two thousand persons per square block, a major change from the fifteen persons per square mile I had known as a youngster. This was a drastic change from the rural life we had known. We called it a baptism of fire.

Murder

We seminary students traveled daily to the west side of Chicago for classes at the Church of the Brethren seminary. One morning our bus was full as usual with diligent students innocently engaged in cramming for exams in biblical studies. Abruptly the bus stopped.

Lying on the sidewalk, in front of Woodlawn Mennonite Church, was a woman who had just been stabbed. The knife handle was protruding from her chest.

Never again do I want to see a nine-year-old girl awakened from her sleep to find her mother murdered.

The police were shockingly casual. In a matter-of-fact manner, they felt for a pulse and declared, "She's dead."

Prematurely, I thought.

We were relieved to learn this was a motive-driven murder rather than a random killing that could have happened to any of us. Nevertheless, there were heightened calls to move the seminary to calmer pastures. Delton and I argued against relocating the seminary and closing Woodlawn Mennonite Church. After all, church members from the community were beginning to join.

Mennonites, we insisted, had something to teach in the inner city—and much to learn. Others insisted that if the church would stay, it would need leadership. We stayed.

Our biblical studies were immensely richer in this inner-city context, I am convinced. As I was studying the sixteenth-century Anabaptists, I could look out of our apartment window and see youngsters using drugs. A mental skirmish ensued as I tried to relate clashing worlds. Working for social justice while studying theology, balancing biblical texts with concrete experience—these shakings shaped our theology and made the Bible relevant.

Relatives urged us to consider serving churches with names like Pretty Prairie. But we embraced our neighborhood and its wonderful people. Naturally, with so many cramped into crowded tenements, tensions sometimes ran high. Infant mortality was well above the norm, and 40 percent of our neighbors were on welfare.

Two of our children, Gregory and Gayle, were born in this setting. They were two of the seven white children in a school of 2,400. I taught in local schools, including a prison for girls. Delton and Vincent Harding, a Ph.D. candidate at the University of Chicago, became copastors at a time when interracial partnership was unusual enough to get pictorial coverage in Chicago newspapers.

Riots

The civil rights movement, the war on poverty, and U.S. immersion in the Vietnam War all coincided in the 1960s. Martin Luther King spoke about all three, then he was assassinated and riots ensued. I arranged for a place outside the neighborhood to take our children if violence and burning came too near. Truckloads of army troops passed our homes. Army encampments were nearby.

Our African-American neighbors phoned to say, "A crazy white man has just killed King. A crazy black person, filled with grief and rage, might want to get even. Please stay indoors. We will buy your groceries. Let us know what you need."

Some of our friends expressed pity and regretted our choice to stay in the city. They did not know and sadly could not share the richness, friendship, and fellowship of that congregation. Grandma Hicks was the child of slaves and had picked cotton much of her life. Now at an advanced age, she lovingly took in a troubled boy to raise. When I handed her a hymn book in church, she smiled sweetly and said, "I cain't read."

In the same pew were likely to be Ph.D. students from the nearby University of Chicago. Others had vocations in medicine or education, housekeeping, etc.

Sadly, the church building was burned by a local gang. However, we former members of this diverse congregation stay in touch. To a person, we agree we have not since found a church that compares in warmth, closeness, caring, and love. Perhaps the diversity helped us to better understand our common bond in Christ. What a pity it would have been to miss that lesson.

Tiny Caskets

During our dozen years in the inner city, we witnessed needless deaths of many, including four two-year-olds—one each from faulty wiring, rat bites, an apartment fire, and lead poisoning. Mercedes Reed had a two-year-old son named Manuel. We enjoyed visiting as Manuel played with my two-year-old Gregory.

One day when she came to visit, her face told me something was terribly wrong. For months Mercedes had pleaded with her landlord without success to remove the loose plaster from the ceiling of her one-room apartment. Manuel had died a horrible death of lead poisoning from the paint on plaster that had fallen into his crib.

Now her son was in a casket and mine still happily at play. Did each of us deserve our bad and good fortune? Not at all. Even though our incomes at the time were roughly the same, the difference lay in my access to affluence and resources that she did not have. Her husband had left, and she had no relatives to help. The fault lay in the laws which allowed landlords to charge exorbitant rents without having to make the housing safe for habitation. This is murder by neglect.

My rural Mennonite upbringing had taught me what to do when people die: one visits their families with Scripture and potato salad. These tragic, needless deaths occurred so rapidly, however, that I could not make enough potato salad.

To tend "the least of these," one would have to go to the government. As we examined city codes, we realized that the touch of Christ was not on the drawing board when those laws were made. The laws needed repair.

Lobbying in Washington, D.C.

In 1968 we made another dramatic move—to Washington, D.C. We opened a Capitol Hill office for Mennonite Central Committee (MCC), an international relief agency with seventy years of experience in fifty countries. Our mission was to address flawed government policies that contribute to suffering. We set out to build bridges of understanding between those on one hand who suffer from want and war, and legislators on the other hand who make decisions affecting them.

My road to becoming director of the National Campaign for a

Peace Tax Fund was accompanied by a nagging question that would not go away. Who would turn off the tap of free-flowing money for military use and divert it to feeding, clothing, and sheltering the needy?

After a time in the MCC office, I directed Dunamis, an organization seeking to fulfill a prophetic voice about suffering *and* to be pastoral in relation to persons in power.

The National Campaign for a Peace Tax Fund was sponsored by dozens of religious bodies and peace organizations. As director, I had an opportunity to work with issues of conscience and war. I now walk the halls of Congress as a registered lobbyist.

God or Caesar?
Questions of Conscientious War Tax Resistance

Many citizens feel it a harsh violation of their religion or moral beliefs to contribute to suffering through paying taxes for military use. Conscience is pained and distressed by the double violence of military spending. First, these deadly weapons are used. Second, even if the weapons are never used, their cost bleeds resources from desperate persons whose lives could be saved with that money.

I am perpetually astonished by the staggering statistics of misplaced national priorities, the imbalance of tribute to God and to Caesar. The military gets the lion's share. Think of the potato salad needed just for these grieving families alone: according to UNICEF, 33,000 of the world's children die *daily* from preventable causes such as lack of vaccines and nutrition.

The money wasted on just one Seawolf nuclear-powered submarine ($2,500,000,000) would fund an immunization program with added vaccines and nutrients for *every child in the world*, according to studies on world military and social expenditures.

The size of today's world arsenal of weapons is 727 times the *entire* fire power of World War II and the Korean and Vietnam wars combined. U.S. military spending alone exceeds the total military expenditures of the *twelve next-largest spenders combined,* including Russia, France, Great Britain, Germany, and China.

There is a danger that, even with these staggering and unavoidable statistics, we become numb and lose our capacity for moral outrage.

Fallible Decision Makers

Fallible women and men in positions of power make decisions that result in war or peace and justice or injustice for millions of people. I find many exceptions to assertions that "all members of Congress are alike, and as political animals seek only selfish ends." On Capitol Hill, I have found a few conscientious objectors. Among them is a congressman who was on the board of the American Friends Service Committee.

As a member of the board of the Faith and Politics Institute, I meet with members whose stated goal is to maintain their moral compass in the heightened tempo and temptations of public office. As a nice surprise, the relationship with some has become a two-way street. Some have become the agents of God's love to me, and bolstered me through their pledges of prayer and support.

I hear diverse comments:

- The Christian love you have shown me means more than I will ever be able to express.
- I cannot understand why any citizen would not want to pay for a B-1 bomber.
- I was almost a conscientious objector during the Vietnam War, but I'm a Jew and I can never forgive Hitler.
- I understand the concept. I went to a Quaker school.
- The issue of Peace Tax Fund legislation is an issue of greater moral magnitude than other issues.
- I never could figure out where you people were coming from. Now I understand that while I am not a conscientious objector, I must support your right to be one. Religious freedom is at stake.

The topic of taxes for war or peace does cause people to examine their own beliefs about participation in war.

Nice Surprises

However life shakes and shapes us, it will also amaze us, I have learned. "Seek ye first the kingdom of God and God's justice, and nice surprises will be added unto you." That is my paraphrase of Matthew 6:33.

One of my many surprises has been the opportunity to travel to a different country in Europe every two years for an international Conference of War Tax Resisters and Peace Tax Campaigns. In other countries, I have been able to visit with parliament members interested in our efforts for conscientious war tax resistance.

Our work for the Religious Freedom Peace Tax Fund Bill has gained allies far beyond the historic peace churches. Nonpacifists understand that a conscience against killing or paying to kill has the stature of a religious conviction. Failure to find accommodation in law for this belief is a violation of religious freedom.

I can now summon a delegation of persons to accompany me to the White House and the Department of the Treasury. They include representatives from the National Association of Evangelicals, The Christian Legal Society, the National Council of Churches, the United Methodist General Board of Church and Society, the Presbyterian Church (USA), the Baptist Joint Committee on Public Affairs, a Catholic sister, and a Jewish rabbi, as well as Mennonites, Quakers, and Church of the Brethren. In fact, some of these visits are possible *because* of this broad delegation.

One Step Prepares Us for the Next

"How do you explain your path from country roads and inner-city streets to the marble halls of Congress?" I'm sometimes asked.

"Because God is tricky," I hear myself saying. One step of obedience leads to another. The next step does not become clear until the current step is taken. In the economy of God, one step prepares us for the next. "And nice surprises will be added unto you."

Life's most rigorous shakings and shapings are still to come, I presume. I now know there will also be nice surprises. I am most grateful for this: God accepts our gifts and our sometimes half-hearted faulty faltering, and crafts them into something both useful and beautiful.

Marian Franz

How Will I Learn to Dance?

SHIRLEY BUCKWALTER YODER

Sʜɪʀʟᴇʏ is Vice President of Health Services at Mennonite Mutual Aid, Goshen, Indiana. She is a registered nurse with a master's degree in public health from the University of Pittsburgh.

Troyer Studios, Inc.

"Never in my wildest dreams did I think I would work with health insurance when I was in school," she said. "But women are always fitting things together in new and amazing ways. It is exactly what our mothers and grandmothers did with quilts! They made something whole from bits of this and that. Actually, it is a perfect job for me since it links my interest in health, administration, and the church. In public health you must think of populations of people: it is the same in insurance."

Shirley also taught nursing, has been a public health nurse in rural Virginia, and supervised regional offices of Church World Service's educational and fundraising programs.

She and her husband, Ron Yoder, lived and worked in Haiti with Mennonite Central Committee and later in India with Church World Service. Shirley also worked with the United States Agency for International Development (USAID) on a large maternal and child nutrition project while in India. She and Ron are the parents of two sons, Branson and Michael.

Shirley's community involvement includes being a member of

Goshen's City Planning Commission and its board of Parks and Recreation. She also teaches youth Sunday school.

"I am happiest when I am near or on the water. We have a small sailboat, and if the wind is up just a little, I feel a strong urge to drop everything and head for the lake. My roots still run deep in Virginia. My vision of retirement is a home in the Shenandoah Valley and a sailboat on the Chesapeake Bay. From there, I'll surround myself with friends and garden, and I'll write and thank God for all the seasons of my life."

THE ODDS were against me, it would seem to a casual observer.

I am just barely one of those baby boomers, born right after the war, in 1946. Neither of my parents had much formal education. While I was growing up, we never talked about "going away to college." Graduate school was simply unheard of. Women in my home community who took jobs, usually before marriage, were secretaries, teachers, or nurses. Some were marketing farm produce or their own baked goods.

Grades one through ten of my education were in a three-room schoolhouse that sat inside the perimeter of the A. D. Wenger peach orchard. Lenora Wenger was my teacher for grades two through six. She was my first model of an educated, professional woman, and I owe her a debt of great gratitude.

My own mother, Roberta Wenger Buckwalter, was a quiet, nurturing woman whose own life story was told over and over in our home. She had been orphaned at the age of seven, when the great flu epidemic of 1918 swept through Virginia's Shenandoah Valley. Though her life had been hard, she was determined to undergird her own children with the love she felt she had never experienced. She was the one who most guided my early moral and spiritual development.

I was surrounded by strong southern women: aunts and neighbors, who worked hard and laughed much. These women were wise. They knew how to make something out of nearly nothing, and they had great courage in the face of tragedies that arose from farm accidents, untimely deaths, an occasional wayward husband, and economic hard times.

All the children of that tightly knit, somewhat isolated, Mennonite community were known by all the adults. We were truly raised by the whole church-based community, not just by our families. Thus, as a young child I knew I was part of something much larger than myself or my family.

If my shoelace was untied, there was someone else who cared about that. Neighbors helped keep an eye on me. My school bus driver was one of my mother's good friends. I learned much from these women. I had to leave that place to learn that some women felt these Chesapeake women were deprived and discriminated against. Some of them were.

Early Leadership Lessons

Our congregation, located on the south side of the Chesapeake Bay in Virginia's Tidewater region, was somewhat cut off from the larger Mennonite Church by geography. This contributed to a characteristic of rather independent thinking by church members. That bay, a barrier to relationships and reliance on the larger church, also offered me some of my earliest lessons on leadership.

My father had an unusual occupation. While his brothers in the church were plowing fields and running milk routes, Dad was a captain on the state-owned ferryboats that crossed the bay. The captain of any ship, regardless of size, is a leader. If he is not, he does not remain captain for long. From my youngest childhood and up through teenage years, I observed my father face many leadership challenges in a world of work that reached far outside our rural farming community.

In these years before "Take Your Daughter to Work Day," my dad often took me to work with him. He sat me up on a stool in the pilothouse of the ferry and said, "Help me keep the boat on course, Sis. We're steering for the light on top of the Chamberlain Hotel. Tell me if we aren't where we're supposed to be." Leaders need to know where they are going and what the most effective way is to get there. It helps when the whole crew knows, too.

I watched Dad navigate in thick fog, across heavily trafficked international shipping lanes. Who of us in leadership today has not needed to make our way through fog! In the gloom, he called on the entire crew to pay special attention with their powers of observation. They needed to listen for the horns of other ships. Someone was assigned to watch the radar, and the windows were opened so that there was absolutely no obstruction of vision or hearing. How tempting it is to do the opposite in administrative fog. The tendency is often to close the windows and wait for the fog to lift.

I did not realize until much later in life how unusual my experience was. Mennonite girls in pigtails and bobby socks just did not have that kind of opportunity in the 1950s and 60s.

However, another important lesson came from those years. Because Dad had shift work on Sundays and had to wear a uniform that included a necktie, he was once denied communion by a conservative bishop. Dad took it in stride.

He did not leave the church as a result of the discipline. He also refused to leave his job. He stuck to his goals and rode out the turmoil in the church. The bishop finally left, Dad was able to take communion, and he retained his love for the church. What an example of hanging in there!

How Will I Learn to Dance?

As a four-year-old I wanted to raise cats when I grew up. *The perfect job,* I thought, *would be to have a cat farm.* But dreams evolve. In my early teen years, I remember lazy, sweltering hot summer afternoons in a hammock held by a strong, sheltering oak in my parents' yard. There I daydreamed of travel and career over *Life* or *National Geographic* magazines and washed away any of my doubts with sweet iced tea. I knew I wanted to be a journalist some day. I just needed to know how to access the system.

As a junior at Eastern Mennonite High School in the early 1960s, I took a standardized career test that was to help the guidance counselor direct me. My results came back strongly suggesting that I go into drama or journalism. Eureka! Now someone else could confirm my own internal sense of direction. I would become the first Mennonite woman reporter for a major national magazine, or maybe a photographer. Eagerly I walked into the guidance counselor's office. An hour later, I walked out with an application for nurse's training.

With parents proudly supporting my so-called nursing decision, I enrolled in a three-year diploma nursing program. It was 1964.

Within months, I found myself on a big stage, trying out for a major role in a little theater production of *Sound of Music*. After the first cut, I was assured of the lead role, Maria. I carefully planned how I would study for my freshman nursing courses and for the theater role as well. I remember the tremendous feeling of accomplishment, of urgency in planning my overall schedule, and of knowing I had been given an unusual opportunity for that time.

This was a rather daring thing to do since I had absolutely no Mennonite role model for acting. We weren't even supposed to go to movies! Clearly, my heart's energy was the theater opportunity. Studying also to be a nurse was just "work." My only worry was, "How will I learn to dance?"

Then came a second encounter with a guidance counselor. "Miss Buckwalter . . . ," she began. Her enormous presence exuded through the pupils of her eyes and out across her desk, piled high with science textbooks. "There is simply no way I can allow you to pursue involvement with the Peninsula Little Theater. Your chemistry grades are too low, and besides, we must enforce curfew. The theater will demand that you stay out too late. Your parents have paid for you to study nursing, and . . ." Thus ended my theater career.

I accepted losing the opportunity, though not happily. I was not a rebellious youth; I generally followed what was expected of me. I pushed at boundaries, but not too hard. I loved my parents deeply and also felt rooted in the church. I knew I was in the consciousness of God. Some parents draw a line and rigidly set rules. My parents never did that. Perhaps it was because they too had pushed at Mennonite boundaries early in their married life, even to the point of leaving the church for a few years.

It is hard to rebel when there is unconditional love and acceptance, and it is easier to excel when there is unconditional support. I feel I had both from my parents. I was always pulling toward something, not pushing away from things. At the same time, I did feel I was somehow different from other girls my age who married, settled within a mile or two of home, and continued the rich nurturing life of that community. I did not feel I was better than others; it was just that I was pulling toward another reality, toward a different vision of who I could be.

The Years of Becoming

When I was twenty-one, I married the great love of my life. I had a nursing diploma and no college degree. For many women, the story of personal growth plateaus here, but for me it became a launching pad. Ron has been my strategic adviser, empathetic listener, and chief cheerleader throughout our wonderful thirty-plus years together. He has helped me nurture my dreams and has always been there for me when I crashed.

We married during the Vietnam War. Like other conscientious objectors before the draft was abolished, Ron's number came up. So we left for two years of service under Mennonite Central Committee (MCC) and Church World Service in Haiti. That was absolutely life changing for me. I discovered the whole arena of public health research and intervention and loved the feeling of making a difference at a community and a national level. I found I was respected for what I knew and for the decisions I could make.

Service in Haiti was a far cry from hospital-based nursing, where we still needed a doctor's order to wash a patient's hair. When we came back to the United States, I worked for the county health department and then finished college. I was in the first graduating class in the degree completion program for registered nurses at Eastern Mennonite College.

With the memory of Haiti still fresh, Ron and I enrolled in graduate studies at the University of Pittsburgh. He entered the School of Public and International Affairs, and I the health administration section of the School of Public Health.

We often studied together and always wondered where our next meal would come from. I remember wondering how one would go about catching and cooking the pigeons that nested outside our bedroom window. But we were building a strong, supportive marriage and learning to encourage each other. Since we were both in a steep learning curve, we found each other to be fascinating friends.

In winter 1977, I returned to Haiti alone to do research for my master's thesis. In the coastal town of Petit Goave, I lived with two physicians, research professors at Harvard. We spent many late nights discussing the rigors of scientific inquiry. I was also six months pregnant with our first child.

Back in Pittsburgh, all my energy poured into finishing my thesis before the baby came. Ron and I had been married nine years, and I was not fooled as to how this blessed event would change my life. My goal was to finish the thesis completely and have a few weeks just to enjoy life before the big change.

At eleven on the eve before Easter, I struck the final key on my typewriter, with carbons, and with satisfaction put away the clean white pages representing the culmination of my graduate education. Three hours later, as though he had heard the silence and knew his mother could now turn her attention to him, I began the labor that gave me my firstborn.

The next five years were some of the best of my life. We moved to India under an assignment with the National Council of Churches and Church World Service (CWS). I was free to find my own professional involvement. Together we taught project management to Indian development workers, and I also had a contract with CWS.

Later I also received a contract to join the design team of a forty million dollar project run by the U.S. Agency for International Development (USAID). During the maternity leave of my supervisor, a career foreign service officer, I was placed in charge of the project. I negotiated fine points of the project with Indian government officials and wrote portions of the project paper going to Washington for funding approval.

The chief of mission asked me to help resolve a contract dispute between USAID and CARE (Cooperative for American Relief to Everywhere). The strategy I suggested helped avoid litigation. About this time, one of the officers learned I was Mennonite. "That explains it," he said. "I knew there was something different about you."

Those were incredibly productive years. I did program evaluation work for a church organization in the Netherlands and for the Lutheran church. It never entered my mind that because I was a woman, there might be fewer opportunities for me. I did not observe women being limited in that environment. I was accepted as competent and capable, and commended for my energy, thoroughness, and willingness to do the hard fieldwork needed to support quality results.

I was surrounded by male and female role models who simply took charge and moved forward. The missionary women I met throughout the ecumenical spectrum were undaunted. I served under a dynamic woman, the chief of mission at USAID. I met courageous Indian women who were working to end the misery of the under-class of that society. Sometimes they seemed able to move mountains.

We could have stayed. Opportunities were there for us in the ex-citing world of international development administration. Ron was offered a UN job. I was asked to join a consulting firm in Boston that would have taken me all over the world. But we wanted to raise our two sons in a Mennonite Christian world. We wanted them to have the kind of nurturing community we had experienced. We wanted them to know their extended family and to grow up in the church.

Reentry

On return to the United States, we moved to Indiana, and I be-came the administrator of the already-failing continuing education in nursing program at Goshen College. Reality hit me when a new administration decided to close the program only a few months after I began.

As an administrator, I believe it was the right decision. But the lack of professional courtesy in that process was far beyond what I had experienced in the secular or even ecumenical world. Cutting this program was the first strike of putting the ax to the budget. After that, other programs fell, but I felt quite alone. I was avoided as though contact with me would cause others to get the ax, too. It was not the nurturing community of my youth or what I remem-bered and longed for.

I started looking for administrative work. A Mennonite adminis-trator advised me, "Be willing to scrub floors, Shirley. Cream rises to the top. If you're any good, you'll be noticed."

My prior education and experience seemed to count for nothing. He intended to give friendly advice, I learned later. But with the ex-perience I already had and at age forty, his comments felt blatantly sexist. I was not about to start over.

Happily, Church World Service had not forgotten my years with them. When they heard of my availability, I was offered full-time work in Elkhart, Indiana, supervising nine of their state education and fundraising offices.

For nearly five years, I again became immersed in ecumenical church life and honed my management skills. I directly supervised a diverse staff, mostly male, many of whom were ordained in mainline Protestant denominations. I traveled to Indonesia with an ecumenical consultation team. My roommate was head of a major agency for the Episcopal Church. She and I talked late into the night about our spiritual pilgrimages. I was impressed with the openness of her conversation on her spiritual life. When the staff came together, they gave a high priority to worship.

Some congregations in my own denomination were trying to rid themselves of the "somewhat meaningless practice of foot washing." At the same time, my Roman Catholic friends were just discovering its deep spiritual meaning and connection to servant leadership.

Conferences in my own denomination were arguing over women in leadership. Meanwhile, I was working for a church agency whose chief executive was a woman.

My denomination often tried to avoid overt conflict. Yet my colleagues within Church World Service entered into vigorous but fair confrontation on issues.

I found these ecumenical contacts to be new windows for my soul. During that time, I set another goal for myself. I wanted to be in a top management position, set corporate strategy direction, and make leadership decisions. I believe our gifts are God given, and that when we exercise those gifts, we honor our Creator. Since Mennonites were not officially members of the National Council of Churches, I knew my chances of progressing further at CWS were limited.

The First

I became the first female vice president at Mennonite Mutual Aid (MMA) in 1990. That same year, *Fortune* magazine advised women who wanted to succeed, "Look like a lady; act like a man; work like a dog."* During this decade, other church organizations also opened executive positions to women. Each of us has her own story. But I can truthfully say I chose this position because of its challenge and not because I wanted to be the first anything.

---

*Quoted in Chris Lee, "The Feminization of Management," *Training*, Nov. 1994, 25.

I had come from work settings where women leaders were accepted as normal, and I did not want my femaleness to be an issue. However, I entered an all-male management team at MMA that was at best welcoming and at worst simply reserved and cautious.

On my first day at work, a male asked, "What makes you feel you can do this job?"

It was a direct question, and I gave an honest response. I reminded him of my supervisory experience, my board leadership, as well as my vision for creation of a new team.

Later I heard a male manager say, "Well, she might be okay if she doesn't smile too much."

So I learned that in this setting, soberness should be added to my decorum. I took this in stride. But when I learned that a peer with whom I needed to work directly said he just did not feel women should be at this level of management, I knew there were rough days ahead. Building a bridge of trust would take some time. Maybe *Fortune* magazine was right.

Some say gender does not make any difference in leadership, that leadership is a set of qualities and skills. Either you have them or you don't. Others argue that women really do have different ways of leading that complement the styles of men. I do not know which side is right. I only know what my experience has been.

There is a core way of managing or leading that I observe to be the same for both genders. Yet I know that sometimes I come at the same issue from a different angle than do my male peers. I do not feel my way is superior or inferior. I only know how I think.

I find myself asking more questions than they do. I am always trying to understand linkages to other agenda, or how one decision will tie itself to another. When I receive information, I instinctively think immediately of my staff and what they will need to know to feel connected to the larger organization and its strategy.

A study of women executives observed that women are less concerned with hierarchy and more concerned with networks and how things fit together. Sally Helgesen calls it a "web of inclusion."* Carol Gilligan notes one of the differences between men and women: In a

---

*Sally Helgesen, *The Female Advantage: Women's Ways of Leadership* (New York: Doubleday, 1995), chap. 2.

society where men are defined by their independent judgment and their separation as an empowering feature, women tend to define themselves and are empowered by attachment and relationship.*

I find being excluded a difficult struggle for me. I observe that it does not appear to affect my male peers the same way.

When I began, I was expected by our board of directors to develop a plan enabling women to advance in the organization. In a letter of support to me, MMA board member Bill Dunn wrote, "My experience says that an organization can develop female leaders if it will: (1) work to identify potential leaders, (2) create an individual plan which isn't bound or limited by policies or fear of setting a precedent, and (3) lend support and encouragement."

I found that Bill's second point needed some attention. The prevailing culture required that new hires be able to "hit the ground running." The business pressures of the time made this a pervasive philosophy. In the world of insurance and finances, we did not have many women candidates who fit this hit-and-run definition. The implication was "We can't wait to bring someone up to par."

One of the first changes I made was revising our education policy. It had been written so that assistance for college or advanced degree work was available only to top management. Since there were few women in top management, it was, in practice, a gender discriminatory policy. Since that change, more women have completed their degrees or obtained organizational management certification from Goshen College.

One more woman came up through the ranks and joined me on the executive management team. The percentage of women in the next layer of management grew both in actual numbers and in percentages. This was accomplished even at a time when we were flattening the organization and there was an overall decrease in the number of managers.

At present my days are filled with routines of strategy implementation. That includes helping other staff members realize their potential. On most days I do not think about my gender or anyone else's. There is work to do, and I just do it.

---

*Carol Gilligan, *In a Different Voice* (Cambridge: Harvard Univ. Press, 1982), 156.

Two Standard Deviations from the Norm

I am where I am today because of God's incredible grace and love for me. I also have been able to take a whole string of life experiences and in each situation look for opportunities that could be used to build up my capacity to work meaningfully. I am a risk taker and a goal setter. Like the apostle Paul, "I press toward the mark."

A friend of mine, Judy, could write the ultimate book on goal setting. One day Judy burst into the student lounge at the university and announced, "While on the city bus coming here, I met the man I will marry. He doesn't know about it yet, but he will." A few years later, they did marry, and our families have stayed in touch over the years. She created and now owns her own highly successful business, is prominent in her community, and is vice president of her temple.

When I feel claustrophobic, like a frog trapped in a well, I give Judy a call. She can see things in my world that are not immediately apparent to me. Recently, when I felt my life was slipping into a daily, grinding routine of little significance, and when I felt that I really was outside the norm, I happened to go to temple with Judy.

While community life is important to both of us, the Jewish community also tends to give high value to individual expressions of gifts and affirms debate. For more than thirty years, the Reformed Jewish community has ordained women. My Mennonite community still values consensus, endless processing, and sameness—no longer sameness of dress, but sameness of behavior, of politically correct thought, and where one is placed on the liberal-conservative spectrum.

After the temple experience, Judy and I talked about issues of religious faith and our own practical day-to-day existence. I told her I was reflecting on the whole sweep of my life and how I got to where I am today.

She listened and responded, "This is exciting. Your life really has not been the norm for Mennonite women of your generation. You can describe your life in terms of a statistical model. You're in the tail of the bell curve. You're two standard deviations from the norm."

Judy never lacks words to express ideas. But at that moment, I wasn't sure I wanted my life to be thought of as a deviation from anything. Then I caught the implied point of her statistical musing. If my life and work are outside the norm, they must be significant! Thank you, God! Thank you, modern Jewish woman, gifted friend, daughter of Sarah!

Significance is also what I want from my church. I am sometimes frustrated because I expect more than the blandness that is seeping in as a way of keeping us all together. I am disappointed that in our rush to put a more conservative past behind us, we seem not to be conserving what is of value. In embracing professionalism, we forget to be just plain ordinary people who care.

We seem to be more preoccupied with the sexual orientation of a few than with the spiritual health of the many. We seem to be seeking answers to questions for which there are no answers and are ignoring what should be obvious.

Thomas Merton wrote:

To hope is to risk frustration.
Therefore, make up your mind to risk frustration.*

If that is the price of living in hope, then I accept it. What is the point of living if there is nothing more than the frustrations of the present?

I have to hope that my church will become more alive than it is today. I have to hope that we'll make it through the fog. I have to believe we will all learn to dance somewhere on the tail of the bell-shaped curve. That's why I still hang in there.

Shirley Byrder

---

*Thomas Merton, *New Seeds of Contemplation* (Abbey of Gethsemani, 1961), 104.

Six Decades in God's Global Family

ALICE M. ROTH

Wayne Gehman

ALICE WAS the fourth child in Pastor A. J. and Alta Metzler's home in a western Pennsylvania mining community, Masontown. She was a year old when the family moved across the hills to Scottdale. Five years later, twins were born into the home. Family life centered upon Mennonite Publishing House and Laurelville, the first Mennonite camp, now Laurelville Mennonite Church Center.

When Willard Roth came for a summer internship at Mennonite Publishing House, a friendship began between Willard and Alice that flourished into their 1956 marriage. Alice earned her B.A. in English at Goshen College.

During two and a half years as church planters in Des Moines, Iowa, their daughter, Carla Joy, was born. A son, Kevin Roy, was born while the family lived at Akron, Pennsylvania (1959-60), maintaining the Iowa-Pennsylvania balance.

From 1961-68, the Roth family lived in Scottdale. Again, the Publishing House and Laurelville were significant hubs of family activity. Before the children were in school, Alice did freelance and volunteer editorial work. From 1964-68 she was news editor for Scottdale's weekly paper, *The Independent Observer.* In 1966 Willard and Alice coauthored *Becoming God's People Today—The Church's Mission in an Urban World.*

A planned two-year term as Mennonite Board of Missions workers in Ghana stretched to five years. They were involved in the beginnings of MBM's teaching ministry with African independent churches. That service sparked Alice's interest and led her to graduate work at the University of Ghana. A decade later, she resumed formal study and earned an M.A. in history of religion at Northwestern University.

The Roths have lived in Elkhart, Indiana, since 1973. Alice worked three years as communications coordinator with Mennonite Board of Education, ten years in administrative faculty posts at Goshen College, and nine years as a vice president at Mennonite Board of Missions, retiring in August 1998. She has occasionally written for church publications.

On the question "What will you do in retirement?" Alice responded, "First, spend a couple years rediscovering who I am when life is not defined by my job." She and Willard hope to spend part of their early retirement years closer to the granddaughters, Becky and Maggie, and their parents in Colorado, and to their daughter and son-in-law in England.

In 1863, the Yankees won at Gettysburg and my paternal grandmother, Katie Kreider, was born. A year later Abraham Lincoln was reelected president, bicycles were first commercially manufactured, and my maternal grandmother, Anna Baker, was born.

When Grandma Annie Baker Maust died in 1950, Hiroshima was five years behind us. My first granddaughter was born in 1989, the year Voyager 2 reached Neptune, sometimes the planet most distant from the sun. In the middle of this five-generation span, in the year of my retirement, I purchased two machines for the decade ahead: a wide-tire bicycle and an IBM ThinkPad.

While this span of technology fascinates, I find more joy in the span of faith traditions in these five generations. Grandma Annie grew up in the Church of the Brethren. Mother, Mennonite all of her life, is now ninety-two.

When our daughter, Carla, was a young adult, her father and I participated in her baptismal service during Easter vigil in an urban Episcopal parish. Last Easter we worshiped with our son, Kevin, and his family in the growing urban evangelical, independent congregation where they are active members.

I have chosen to remain with my own faith family, flowing with the stream in which I was born. Mennonite institutions have shaped most of my life.

I learned to talk as I named Mennonite Publishing House employees walking by our front porch on their way to work each day. We played hide-and-seek around skids of paper destined to become Sunday school quarterlies or the *Gospel Herald*. In 1943 my parents helped to found Laurelville Camp, the first Mennonite camp, against resistance of some in the church.

During my sixty-four years, I have worked for seven Mennonite institutions or agencies. More important, the congregations where I have been a member have each provided spiritual nurture, a circle of friends, and a safety net in times of crisis.

Like my biological family, my church family has given me both roots and wings. The church is home for me, the base from which I participate in the global ecumenical family of God. That larger global reality, and my participation in it, is as important to me as the home base.

Reflecting on six-plus decades in the church, I am grateful for mentors, friends, opportunities, a worldview, and hope. Certainly the church has no monopoly on any of these realities, but in the context of the church, I have experienced them as rich gifts of grace.

The Gift of Mentors

For my senior year, I enrolled at Eastern Mennonite High School in Virginia. There I made the shocking discovery that my western Pennsylvania home setting, Scottdale, was not a typical Mennonite community. The Mennonite population was small, and none of us had cousins, aunts, and uncles nearby. Not being farmers, we seldom cooked with butter and cream.

Years later I realized a great benefit of growing up in Scottdale:

Mennonite professional women taught my Sunday school classes, took me to concerts in Pittsburgh forty miles away, cared about me and my friends, and expressed that care by being involved in our lives.

I grumbled when Elizabeth Showalter, a Publishing House editor, expected us to study and prepare reports for Wednesday night mission classes (while our parents were in prayer meeting upstairs). The only time I was ever asked to leave a classroom was when Elizabeth decided that my whispering disrupted a sixth-grade summer Bible school class. But Elizabeth believed in us and in our abilities. She cared that we developed these abilities to the fullest. After a short-term mission assignment in Africa, Elizabeth returned to found Books Abroad.

Ruth and Rhoda Ressler were educators, Ruth in a local school system and Rhoda at a school for the deaf. As our Sunday school teachers, they included us in their wide-ranging interests and creative activities. I was a teenager when the Ressler sisters went to Japan as missionaries, part of the time self-supporting as English teachers. During a recent visit in their Ohio home, I found eighty-eight-year-old Rhoda and ninety-two-year-old Ruth still brimming with humor and stories.

"We've had a lot of fun," Rhoda declared. "Of course, there have been hard times, but we've had fun."

To earn money for college, I worked a year after high school in the Mennonite Publishing House bookstore. A long-time neighbor and family friend, Lois Yake (now Kenagy), was bookstore manager, my supervisor. I admired Lois's ability to discuss and recommend books with any customer—ministers of all denominations, businessmen, and Mennonite tourists of any stripe.

As I left for college, one of Lois's parting words of counsel was a reminder that college offers new worlds to explore. She advised me to think twice before closing any of these doors by a quick rush into marriage.

These persons are examples of many single women whose lives seemed to me to be rich and full. Their example, their personal interest in me, their commitment to the church—all influenced my childhood and youth. Little did I realize the pain they might have experienced. It did not occur to me to ask why they were not preaching or leading departments at the Publishing House.

The Gift of Friends

Through these decades, my home congregations and the church schools I attended have provided a rich and lasting network of friendships. In a world of increasing mobility and transient, shallow relationships that often result, this network provides sustaining continuity in the changes of my life.

Some of these friendships are based partly on common ethnic heritage, but more importantly I believe, on shared values. As a young mother of small children, with a spouse often traveling, the companionship of other young mothers helped me keep a sane and healthy outlook. It's hard to imagine parenting through the teen years without close ties to other parents of adolescents.

With friends, I have critiqued, chewed, and digested important books. I remember the startling impact during my young mother years of Betty Friedan's *Feminine Mystique* (I don't have to *enjoy* vacuuming?) or Bishop Robinson's *Honest to God* (he believes *that* about God?).

Toward midlife, I appreciated studying and praying around the biblical story of Esther, using Marjory Bankson's *Braided Streams,* with a group of women.

In my work as an administrator in Mennonite institutions, women mentors have been few. This has made it especially important to have peer friendships with other women in similar situations. At the bimonthly gatherings of Mennonite women administrators in our area, I find courage and hope in our shared stories, tears, and laughter—lots of hearty laughter.

Some twenty years ago, when my congregation encouraged intentional prayer partnerships, I began to meet regularly with a friend. Through the years, the joys and problems of family, work, church, and the world have surfaced at our biweekly breakfast meetings. Thanks to e-mail and telephone, that relationship continues today across thousands of miles.

Willard and I have needed to intentionally cultivate friendships outside the church-related circle. Sometimes our friendship network seems confined; we are too much alike. Part of the special joy of our years abroad was the enrichment of work, worship, and social life outside the Mennonite context. In retirement, I expect my friendship network to expand in surprising new directions!

The Gift of Opportunity

As part of reentry after living in Ghana for five years, I enrolled in a Life Choices course at a women's center. It was a useful time of considering work and education options in light of my interests and abilities. But I never caught on to the charting-your-future exercises.

Unable to pinpoint a career goal ten years ahead, I could not chart steps toward such a goal. I was a responder to opportunity that came my way rather than being proactive toward a career goal.

I am grateful for opportunities in church structures for meaningful work with competent, motivated colleagues. As a teenager, my first employment was at Laurelville Mennonite Camp. We worked long, hard days. I was a waitress but accepted without question the expectation that we all would pitch in till the work was finished.

As a student at Eastern Mennonite High School and Goshen College, extracurricular activities—writing, speaking, organizing—developed important skills for future responsibility. In my senior high school year, I was uncomfortable with the apparent preoccupation with dating and boyfriends. A happy exception to that atmosphere was the debating club, where we competed and worked together without gender consideration.

During my college sophomore year, a conversation happened several times as I was learning to know the extended family that later became mine through marriage:

"You're studying to be a teacher?"

"No," I would reply.

"Oh, then you'll be a nurse?"

"No."

Silence.

Why, in the mid-1950s, would a woman be in college unless she planned to be a teacher or a nurse? I wasn't sure myself, but finally settled on an English and journalism major, with no thought of graduate study.

Twenty-five years later, after two satisfying administrative work experiences with Mennonite Board of Education and at Goshen College, I weighed the hardest vocational decision of my life. I was completing a master's program in history of religion at Northwestern University. Should I move ahead in doctoral studies?

Facing that decision then differed from possibly facing it twenty-five years earlier. Sitting in the Northwestern library one sunny spring afternoon in 1982, I found myself wishing that I were in a committee meeting! It was a moment of insight. At age forty-eight, I was not motivated for the discipline of more academic years.

I never regretted my decision of returning to administrative work. I remained a generalist rather than pursuing further specialization. In retrospect, however, I believe I could have worked with more confidence through the decades if I had taken out time for study to enhance my administrative skills. Experience is a great teacher, but I and the church agencies I served would have done well to supplement experience with training.

I am grateful for many supportive, encouraging male peers and supervisors through the years. I have missed gender balance in my work teams. Female perspectives are different; women's voices are still often not heard with the same weight as those of men. Being part of a work team more nearly gender balanced is simply more comfortable.

The Gift of a Global Worldview

Although Mennonite Publishing House is in a small town off the beaten track, it attracted international visitors to learn about church publishing. I was in sixth grade when two Mennonite leaders from India visited. Since I had studied India as a mission field, I was awed and impressed as these brothers preached and led Bible studies.

My parents welcomed international visitors into our home like family members. Not having extended family nearby, perhaps we were more able and eager to extend the family circle. As Dad traveled internationally, his accounts of fellowship with Mennonites around the world reinforced my impressions of a global family.

On a visit to India, Dad participated in sessions of a World Council of Churches Assembly. It was life changing. God spoke to him about the relevance and urgency of Jesus praying "that they may all be one, . . . that the world may believe" (John 17:20-23). He called that experience a second conversion.

That global, ecumenical perspective was shared and deeply felt by my spouse. It prepared us for five years in Ghana as Mennonite Board of Missions (MBM) workers. We were relating to the historic churches in the Ghana Christian Council and to African Independent Churches, so different from our own church background.

We experienced the paradox I dealt with as an MBM administrator the last nine years: Mennonites are invited to serve in places and in particular ministries *because of* our Anabaptist faith perspectives. Yet we often do so without a surrounding Mennonite church community to help us live out those convictions. As a family in Ghana, we found ourselves "at home," nourished and nurtured, by very different faith communities.

Hope Wavers, Hope Sustained

The story of Mennonite women's rest-room graffiti should be preserved for our granddaughters. In preparation for Bowling Green 1981—the Mennonite Church biennial Assembly—congregations were asked to consider a study paper on church leadership. At issue for many conferences and congregations was the question of women in leadership. A dozen women in the Elkhart area took this opportunity seriously.

As we studied the biblical and theological material prior to Assembly, we longed for a missing dimension. We wanted to hear the actual experiences of our sisters in the Mennonite Church across America. How could that happen at Assembly, now only a few weeks off?

The Assembly planners said a Wednesday breakfast meeting would not conflict with scheduled activities. But it was too late for any pre-Assembly announcement.

Assembly began on Tuesday evening. How could we announce an early Wednesday meeting? A simple solution surfaced: we would post notices in the women's dormitory bathrooms. While we were at it, we decided to put up newsprint for comment during the week, a good graffiti conversation among women.

I anticipated the fun and female fellowship. However, I was unprepared for the threat these actions posed for many of the men in positions of church leadership.

Those 49 newsprint pages from the rest-room doors, transcribed later in 15 single-spaced typed pages, are a wide-canvas picture of women's experience in the Mennonite Church in 1981. Joy in being a woman and a Mennonite was a theme through the comments.

Nevertheless, experience and concerns varied widely:

- "Women should stop trying to assume leadership and authority."
- "Just this piece of paper here shows how unique and creative we are as Menno Women."
- "How different my life might have been had today's options been open to me."

The Bowling Green event was a time of both hope and despair for me. I was discouraged by the eye-opening reality of challenges to women's full participation. I found hope in the commitment of many women and men to work for change. And change has characterized the intervening seventeen years.

Finally, though, my hope rests in God's intention for all humankind, dramatically pictured in Revelation 7. With John, we live by the vision of every tribe and nation around the throne, praising and serving God, secure in the presence of God, who wipes away every tear.

Meanwhile, there is surprise and mystery: the church is God's choice for a sign of that reality. That choice is enough for me.

Alice M. Roth

Blazing the Leadership Trail

CAROL J. SUTER

CAROL SUTER is Executive Director of the Center for Management Assistance in Kansas City. She served three years as Vice President and Legal Counsel for Mennonite Economic Development Associates. Before that, Carol was engaged in legal practice for fifteen years, with special emphasis on corporate law and employment law.

Carol also spent three years with the General Conference Mennonite Church as Director of the Call to Kingdom Commitments project. Before law school, Carol was a high school English and speech teacher. She spent three years with Mennonite Central Committee, teaching school in Jamaica.

She is Vice Chair of the Mennonite Mutual Aid Board of Directors, and a trustee for the Western District Mennonite Conference. She has served on a variety of task forces for Mennonite Mutual Aid and Mennonite Central Committee, and in a variety of roles in her local congregations.

Carol is a member of Centurions (Leadership Development Program) of the Greater Kansas City Chamber of Commerce. She has served on a number of local boards and foundations.

She is a Fellow in the American Bar Foundation, an honorary association recognizing no more than three-tenths of one percent of American lawyers for outstanding community and professional service. She chaired the Ohio Joint Task Force on Gender Fairness in the Law, a working group commissioned by the Ohio Supreme Court and the Ohio State Bar Association.

Carol and her husband, Eugene, are the parents of Leanne and Tracy. Her personal interests include swimming, scuba diving, travel, home decorating, and reading.

I SAT ON THE BENCH in stunned disbelief! I had just been elected to a churchwide board. How could this have happened? It was late July 1980, at Estes Park, Colorado. Eugene, our young daughters, and I were attending our first Triennial Conference of the General Conference Mennonite Church (GCMC) as our family vacation.

An Election That Changed My Life

Early in the week I attended a workshop on women and theology. During the session someone commented that there were four churchwide boards with all-male slates of nominees. The group discussed the issue. Many shared their feelings of frustration that women had not yet broken the gender barrier to church leadership roles.

Someone encouraged all those interested in the problem with the nominating slates to remain after the workshop for further discussion. Though I had no background in the politics of the GCMC and knew none of these women, I decided to stay. I had a great deal of interest in leadership opportunities for women.

For a while we vented our frustrations. Then we focused on what action we might choose to protest the lack of female nominees. Someone who knew GCMC politics suggested that we nominate women from the floor, just to make a statement.

We met several more times in following days, devoting ourselves to selecting four women to nominate for slots on four boards. We also chose the right man to actually nominate these women. It was fairly easy to identify women to nominate for the General Board and the boards for missions and the seminary. Highly qualified women were well-known to many.

However, we couldn't think of someone to nominate for the Division of Administration, comprised of accountants, lawyers, and businessmen. We were adamant that we would nominate only qualified women.

As we polled the group, my status as a third-year law student emerged to make me the one closest to being qualified. I was hesitant to let my name be used. But the others gave strong assurances that there was no way I would be elected. This effort was to make the point that women were absent from the ballot. We had no expectation that anyone could actually be elected from the floor. So I capitulated.

Well, we made our point—so well, in fact, that all four of our nominees were elected! Many delegates did share our concern about the lack of female nominees.

That election changed the way things were done for the GCMC. Immediately thereafter, the rules for nominating were changed, effectively eliminating the possibility of nominating candidates from the floor. The nomination process was improved to guarantee that real effort would be made to identify women for leadership roles. And women were guaranteed a place on the nomination committee itself.

That election also changed my life. For me, it was the door to leadership opportunities in the Mennonite world.

The Absence of Women Is Still Overwhelming

In the almost twenty years since, my journey as a Mennonite woman leader has been interesting, enriching, and often frustrating. During those years, gender relations have changed considerably in North America and, to a lesser degree, in the Mennonite world.

In the secular world, I see women almost reaching parity in many arenas. Leadership opportunities abound, and in many ways being female is now an advantage.

Sadly, that is not yet so in the Mennonite world. To approach parity in this community of faith, we still have a distance to go. We have become politically correct with our language. Our policies and procedures are gender neutral. But when I sit with a leadership group of any Mennonite organization or institution and look around the table, the near absence of women is overwhelming.

Many men have worked diligently to become aware and enlighten themselves. I feel the results of that collective effort mostly on a personal level. However, professionally and in leadership circles, I find people still need to be reminded that all segments of the community are not represented. So many men and even some women still do not "see" the absence of women and minorities.

Recently I sat through a board meeting of a Mennonite organization where the subject of appropriate gender representation on the board was raised. Not one person in the group, male or female, identified a single reason why the organization should be concerned about the lack of women on the board. That was a disappointing and discouraging occurrence.

Observations While Blazing the Leadership Trail

As I look back on the past two decades, several observations strike me. Two outrageous confrontations with Mennonite men are vivid reminders of the challenges presented as I blazed this leadership trail.

Once a church administrator accosted me as I arrived for a board meeting. I had spent the morning in my law office before catching a plane for the meeting, so I was dressed accordingly. In private law practice, I always dressed in a more formal manner in both my personal and professional lives. Every person I encountered everywhere I went could be a current or potential client, juror, judge, or opposing counsel. I was focused on building my business and my reputation.

This church administrator took great pride in his wardrobe of ragged blue jeans and well-worn sandals. "Carol," he said, "Don't you own a pair of jeans?"

"Sure," I replied, "but I never wear them off the farm."

He scowled at me. "Boy, you always look so perfect. Hair done, face made-up, dressed to the nines. . . . *Yuck!* You remind me of a Mary Kay woman."

When I was directing a fundraising effort of the General Conference Mennonite Church (A Call to Kingdom Commitments), I was also accosted by a pastor, church leader, and self-appointed prophet. He launched into a fiery tirade, accusing me of leading the conference "to hell in a handbasket." My "ultraconservative political and social leanings" clearly indicated that I was the devil's handmaiden, dedicated to destroying the denomination.

I asked him what had given him the impression that I (of all people!) was ultraconservative.

He responded, "Just look at you. You look like all the other pro-business, Republican, right-wingers."

I gave him a litany of information about my religious, social, and political beliefs. I listed all my community, professional, and church involvements. But it was to no avail. This man was convinced I was a "Jezebel," without redeeming value.

Later both men lost their ministerial credentials as the result of sexual misconduct.

At times, I have been accused of being too slick, too flashy, too flirty, too sexy, and too earthy. Observation: *Women with strong personalities and identities are perceived as very intimidating and threatening.*

I remember many occasions when my opinions, suggestions, and comments were discounted and disregarded. I have not experienced this phenomenon in the secular world for many years. But in the church world, the phenomenon continues.

My most-extreme example of this was at a recent Mennonite meeting where I was the only female and the only lawyer present. A legal issue arose in the discussion. The chair asked an accountant for advice, then several others chimed in. No one asked me for advice or even for a response to the "legal" advice given by all the men.

Some may say I'm overreacting. But there seems to be no explanation for such behavior other than because of my gender. Observation: *While women have made great strides in professional arenas, in church circles, our opinions and expertise are sometimes discounted. Often a male concurrence is needed for validation.*

I love language and respect its power. I have come to understand how differently men and women use it. That causes problems for us. Because we use language differently to express our feelings or outline our thoughts, it is often presumed that we operate out of motivations different from men. These motivations are often suspect.

I still find myself in settings where Mennonite men question women's ulterior motives. They don't have the same suspicions of men. Men are presumed to operate out of logic and concern for the good of the group. Women come from "someplace else." Observation: *Women's motivations are suspect. We are assumed to operate out of emotion. Our concern is assumed to be personal rather than organizational.*

Stewardship of Human Resources

So why go on? Why do I not back off and reduce my frustration level? For a number of reasons, I am even more motivated to proceed now than I have ever been.

The truth is, for every negative experience I have encountered, I have experienced many more positives. Leadership experiences in the church have enriched my life, honed my skills, broadened my horizons, and increased my confidence.

I have had opportunities to speak widely, to write for publication, to create programs and materials, to give legal advice, to give management advice, and to travel the world. For the most part, I have felt that my contributions were appreciated and valued. I now know that church leaders do seek out my advice, opinion, and expertise.

God has gifted me for leadership and calls me to use those gifts in service to the church. I love the imagery in 1 Corinthians 12. That chapter touches me, inspires me, and motivates me. We each have a role to play in the life of the church, just as each part of the body has its own role. The body needs all the parts to be a healthy whole. The church needs all its members and all their skills to be a healthy organism. For we are the body of Christ, and each of us is a part of that body.

My motivation for leadership is not to even the score with men or to prove a point. I want to be a good steward and use all the resources with which God has endowed me. As more and more women respond to the call for leadership in the church, we can help the church understand its responsibility of stewardship. The church is called to use all the human resources God has made available to it, "as the Spirit chooses" (1 Cor. 12:11).

My many mentors and supporters encourage me to press on. My husband, daughters, and sisters have always believed that I could do anything and everything life offers. I have been privileged to know outstanding women leaders in the church, in my profession, and in my communities. I have learned from their successes and from their challenges.

I am blessed with a wide circle of female friends who encourage, support, and listen to the whining! I am also blessed with a wide circle of male friends—men who have worked successfully to unlearn gender-biased socialization. They accept me as equal and encourage and support my personal and professional development.

I hope I haven't lost any of my sense of humor over these years. It has been one of my best defenses. A light touch has often helped make a point without damaging relationships. So much of what frustrates and disappoints us becomes quite humorous with the passing of time.

Recently a group of women gathered for a late-night "session" during the board meetings of a Mennonite organization. There were few women on the board or on the executive staff, so we didn't have any trouble fitting into a hotel room for a party. We whined, we vented, we told horror stories. But mostly we laughed—and laughed!

Becoming Mentors

The tide is turning in North America and in the Mennonite world. We have already reached critical mass. Now there is no turning back. Women are catapulting into significant new leadership roles in the twenty-first century. I wholeheartedly believe that this new century will usher in the Era of Women. Political, economic, and business power is changing hands—from men to women.

On some matters of fairness, the church seems to trail society, but it always follows along. So let's not grow weary just as the tide is ready to crest (cf. Gal. 6:9).

That late-night women's session reminded me how important it is for women to continue to be supportive of each other. We must share our experiences with those coming along behind and beside us. We must encourage and exhort less-experienced and younger women to follow their own callings to leadership.

Some of us have spent our whole lives searching for mentors. In the process, we didn't notice that we ourselves have become the mentors needed by others.

A best-selling book by Robert Fulghum reminded us that all we really need to know, we learned in kindergarten. We learned to hold hands when we cross the street. I have a dream of hundreds, thousands, millions of women hand-in-hand, crossing the street to the new millennium. Gifted by God, called to lead!

Carol J. Suter

Red Poppies

LEE SNYDER

SINCE 1996, Lee Snyder has been President of Bluffton (Ohio) College. In 1987-96, Lee was Vice President and Academic Dean of Eastern Mennonite University, Harrisonburg, Virginia.

Lee earned a B.A. in English and a Ph.D. in English Literature from the University of Oregon, as well as an M.A. in English from James Madison University.

She and her husband, Delbert, spent 1965-68 serving as Overseas Missions Associates in Nigeria with Mennonite Board of Missions.

Lee enjoys the Midwest setting after living most of her life on either the west or east coasts. She finds it to be a new experience to live in a small Ohio town which still has a real main street, where the locals gather for coffee and conversation, and where movies cost only three dollars.

She finds being part of the academic world and the mission of the church to be a wonderfully rewarding opportunity. She says preparing and calling young people for service and Christian leadership in the next century must be one of the most exciting and daunting challenges imaginable.

Lee has been a leader for many academic task forces and workshops, and has made presentations to many academic groups as well as churches. In 1996, the Council of Independent Colleges gave her the Annual Dean's Award, and in 1993 named her a Dean's Fellow.

English literature is her discipline, and books are her passion. She enjoys working with people and has never managed to repress an irreverent curiosity about most anything. Her time with family and friends, reading, travel, and entertainment are her sources of personal renewal.

Lee and Delbert have two daughters, Lori Garrett and Judith White, and two grandchildren.

> We shall not cease from exploration,
> And the end of all our exploring
> Will be to arrive where we started
> And know the place for the first time.
> (T. S. Eliot, *Four Quartets*)

> For you, O Lord, are my hope,
> my trust, O Lord, from my youth.
> (Ps. 71:5)

DR. GRIFFITH, the shuffling, grizzled professor, was the one who gave me the words. I had been studying for comprehensive exams. That day I found my seat a few rows from the back of the class. The lecture was pure Griffith, with a cryptic outline on the board for his introduction to American poets: Edward Taylor, Ralph Waldo Emerson, Longfellow, and Poe.

Of all my graduate school professors, the most intimidating was Dr. Griffith. He had seen much of life and found most of it wanting. I still see the yellowed whites of his eyes and straggly hair, his bowed shoulders, his worn and ill-fitting jacket. I hear his booming voice and sense his wisdom and vast knowledge. Among his graduate students, fear blended with near worship.

"The function of poetry is to defamiliarize the familiar and to express the inexpressible." To underscore that observation, he turned and scrawled out the words on the blackboard. There they shimmered—capturing something of life itself.

That day they were words to express what I had dimly felt and known: the strange and wonderful journey which mingles elements of the ordinary and the extraordinary. What I saw and felt that day continues to give shape and substance to my life. Books, reading, poetry, Scripture—words—have provided glimmers of the mystery and surprise of the Word.

First Encounter

I think I must have always believed that God was there somewhere, but I have been surprised continually when God actually interrupts my life, when Word becomes flesh. My first direct encounter with God was when I was five or six years old. That experience is also one of my earliest memories of the importance of books in my life.

My most prized possession was a maroon Gideon New Testament. One day I lost it. I was devastated. When it did not turn up after much searching, I began praying that God would give it back. My prayers were pleading and demanding.

I knew that God so choosing could simply open up the heavens, reach down, and return the New Testament. It was as simple as that. So my prayers continued with a fierce insistence and an unshakable belief that God would intervene.

I have no idea if my parents knew about this desperate drama going on between their oldest child and God as she prayed night and day, walking to and from school, for the return of the New Testament.

What would Heaven do with a six-year-old who believed literally that God was going to give back the Gideon Bible?

God gave it back. One day a car pulled into our driveway. A man got out and knocked on the door. From the other side of town, he showed up with the New Testament in his hand.

The Edwards had found the Bible sometime after our family had stopped in to see their new home. My parents were hoping to build a house to replace our tiny, four-room farmhouse. They were interested in the Edwards' floor plan. When we had gone to see the place, I had taken along the Gideon New Testament.

This is my first memory of God honoring faith and paying attention to me, personally. It was as though the heavens had opened and God had handed me that little Bible.

While that experience appears to an adult as a naive and simplistic view of things, I have never doubted that God answered my prayers. I remember that God encounter with the same kind of awe I experience when I reread the story of Moses and the burning bush, or of Samuel hearing God's voice in the middle of the night.

A Room Called Remember

There was also Grandpa and Grandma's living room. On the bookshelf, the *Martyrs Mirror* propped up the Bible concordances and hymnbooks. It was the biggest book we grandchildren had ever seen. We looked at the gruesome sketches but never read the martyr stories.

Instead, we preferred looking at the old Sears and Roebuck catalogs stacked in the musty compartment under the window seat, or the Little Red Riding Hood puzzle Grandma stored in a high chest of drawers in the front bedroom.

Only years later did I discover the *Martyrs Mirror* printer's device and motto, "Arbeite und hoffe" (work and hope), which appeared on the title page of early editions. That motto—with its balance and neatness—explained a lot to me about the spirit of the place where I grew up. Hard work and unbounded hope were the two pillars that sustained the community of faith.

However, my memories of growing up in Oregon also include green fields and the splendor of summer nights when the farmers burned ryegrass stubble. The fragrance of salmon smoked in Grandma's smokehouse, steam from the apple butter kettle in Grandpa's back yard, or slippery eyeballs sucked from their blue Concord skins—these were tastes and smells and sensations of the valley.

Our world was the Willamette Valley, bordered by Cascade mountains on the east and the Coast Range on the west. Circumspect and circumscribed, it stretched from Eugene at the south end to Portland on the north.

I remember night rain, bee stings while going barefoot, and old oak puffballs we stomped on to release their breath of dry dust. The cycle of the seasons ordered the work. Each harvest brought hope and anticipation: Would it be a good crop? Would the rains hold off?

We lived in fullness, attuned to rhythms of planting and harvesting, but fully aware that nature was sometimes harsh. We knew bounty. But if the seed sprouted in wet fields or the market price was down, we knew hardship.

In this Amish Mennonite community, life was lived simply, work was held sacred, and everyone's place was clearly defined. Yet extravagances of beauty still color my memories. There was Grandma Kropf's exotic peacocks, her speckled guinea hens, and the strange Muscovy ducks.

She was called "Frank Annie," according to the custom of that community where women were known by their husband's names. So common was this practice that I never stopped to think twice about the fact that my mother was called "Lloyd Ruth" and three aunts "Loras Ruth," "Merle Ruth," and "Lafe Ruth."

Grandma loved the gaudy poppies, glistening an enormous redorange with beady black eyes, and the money plant, with papery white ovals she dried for the house. The magnificent tulip magnolia presided over the north yard. The ivory plumes of the pampas grass by the front walk evoked Bible storybook illustrations of Moses and the bulrushes, and the court of Pharaoh.

Grandma was not a petunia-and-geranium person. Neither did she wear the usual Mennonite head covering. Instead, she chose to wear a black kerchief, on Sunday and for everyday.

Without knowing it, I was absorbing the extraordinary in the mundane. I was learning how one might be an individual within the boundaries of a rigidly defined community.

Being Different

It was one thing to be part of a community that stood for difference. "Nonconformity," the preachers called it. It was another to feel that difference alone. On one hand, the Amish Mennonite community provided a strong sense of "us," with everyone else an "outsider." Yet a shaping reality for me was the fact that as a child, I was unusually small. "Puny" was the word the aunts would have used.

I heard comments of relatives about my size, or unfavorable comparisons with my sister, who would "catch up" with me if I didn't hurry up and grow. These remarks contributed to a dawning realization that something was wrong with me. My greatest wish, never spoken and dimly perceived, was that I could just be normal, for once like everybody else.

Not till high school did I begin to be aware that being small could have its advantages, that size need not determine one's destiny. What that destiny was to be was not clear, but there were hints that the journey would be an adventure. One memory stands out, mostly of place, sensation, and feeling, of colors and textures.

I was a junior or senior at Western Mennonite High School, a small boarding school among the tall firs. I remember nothing about that day, except coming out of the main office and classroom building. In it I had classes in English, Spanish, Bible, chemistry, algebra, and home economics. There we also ate our meals in the basement dining room, and went to chapel in the west wing.

That day I was wearing a dress my mother had made, a print shirtwaist which the stylish young English teacher had noticed. Leaving the building, heading out the door and off the porch toward the dormitory across the yard, I had an overwhelming sense that some great adventure lay ahead. With an inexplicable sense of exhilaration, I knew I was ready to embrace whatever that should prove to be.

Whether prompted by the sheer beauty of an autumn day (or was it spring?) or by the hormones of a seventeen-year-old or something else, I no longer remember. Yet that scene remains fixed in memory. No doubt embellished by time, that memory represents another intersection of the inexpressible with the ordinary.

Why does that experience stand out now? Because without words, that moment of being has gathered to itself the power of the ineffable, of mystery, of the sureness of the transcendent mediated through the commonplace and the unremarkable.

Work and Worship Are One

As with my mother before me, life takes shape in routines, in the everyday. On some days, "work and worship" are one. But most days one does not think about it until much later.

It was still dark when I stepped out the front door to head for the office. I was nine months into my first year as president of Bluffton College. I was still surprised at being there. But that Monday morning, heading down Brookwood Drive, over to Elm and then Spring Street, I had a lot on my mind.

The unrelenting pace was beginning to tell. I had been on the road for a succession of weekends. I was keenly aware not only of what happens when I miss my "Sabbaths," but of urgencies at work.

We were at a critical point in the process of hiring a new dean. There had been media criticism and community misunderstanding of a student demonstration on behalf of the Palestinians. A key employee had just resigned. There was a sermon to prepare, a speech to deliver. I tried to pray, as I often did while walking to work. I desperately sought some sense of inner peace.

As I tried to form the words, I discovered I could not pray. Each time I began, "God . . . ," my mind was racing off in many directions. Here it was Monday morning, and I was already so frazzled I could not even focus long enough to pray.

Sometime that day or the next, I checked my e-mail. There was a message from Maggie, a new friend I had just met in a neighboring state: "One of the thoughts that came to me as I was praying for you is that God will give you the gift of discernment, as you are constantly faced with more to do than you can do."

In that moment, I knew that the Holy Spirit through Maggie was praying for me when I could not pray for myself. And I knew that the work which was threatening to overwhelm me was not my work.

The Laundry

The events which had brought me to Bluffton College as president were not flashy or dramatic, nor were they predictable. Following graduate school with a master's degree in English literature and linguistics, I had no clear sense of what would be next. I had not prepared to teach. Instead I chose, with my husband's encouragement, to study what I loved—literature. With degree in hand, it made sense to apply for an office job at Eastern Mennonite College, where Delbert taught mathematics.

I accepted a clerical position in the registrar's office. One day, before beginning work, I decided to tackle a major job at home, shampooing the carpet. The telephone rang while I was on my knees, sponging the rug the old-fashioned way. That call marked a turning point.

I was asked to give up the position in the registrar's office and step into an administrative assistant vacancy in the dean's office. There mentors would teach me much about higher education and about my aptitude for the challenges of administration.

Twenty years later another call came, this time while I was doing the laundry. After twelve years as academic dean and vice president at Eastern Mennonite, I had decided it was time for a change. My husband, Delbert, who had moved from teaching to business, also was ready to consider other ventures. We were just beginning to consider possibilities.

That Saturday when the telephone rang, I picked up the extension in the basement. I had to excuse myself to turn off the washer so I could hear the two gentlemen on the other end of the line. I was unprepared for the question: Would I consider being a candidate for the college presidency at Bluffton College?

For me, that Saturday in August, doing the laundry would take on new significance. The laundry had long been my favorite household chore. Folding the clean towels and smoothing the sheets provided a sense of something worthwhile accomplished. As one of the household rituals, doing the weekly "wash" (as my mother would say) was also a way to gain a sense of order and control.* That day doing the laundry would prove, once I had worked through many doubts, to be the setting for God's interruption again in the everyday.

My mother and grandmother never envisioned or wished for me a college presidency. Yet they understood rituals of home and family that provide sustenance in the most unexpected circumstances. Their lives depended on the belief that hard work and faith and hope and persistence mattered.

The weather of the soul and the landscape of the spirit were perceived and expressed for my mother and grandmother as they were for me: in outward forms of cleaning and cooking, planting and harvesting, sewing and preserving, practicing the art of hospitality, respecting expectations of community.

"Will You Have a Good Man to Work For?"

Expectations, particularly of women's roles, were clear in the Mennonite community. When I told my mother I had been urged to consider the college deanship, her first question was "Will you have

---

* "Laundry is one of the very few tasks in life that offers instant results, and this is nothing to sneer at," says Kathleen Norris. For a wonderful meditation on laundry, see "At Last, Her Laundry's Done," in her book *The Cloister Walk* (New York: Riverhead Books, 1996), 283-286.

a good man to work for?"

I assured her I would have.

It was still fairly startling for a Mennonite woman to be an academic dean. "I don't think of you as a woman," one of my mentors told me. He meant it as a compliment.

"Why would you want to do this?" asked a sympathetic but incredulous trustee wife, when I appeared at the interview for the college presidency.

Delbert and I often laugh—the only possible response—at hints voiced on occasion that he must be strong for me in the difficulties of the presidency. We smile because we know we must be strong for each other in each of our jobs.

Meanwhile, we still marvel at the intricacies of lives lived together when calling means taking risks, when the simplest joys provide the greatest rewards: faith in God's plan for our lives, a church family that matters, rare and rich friendships, seeing the world again through the eyes of a four-year-old grandson or a two-year-old granddaughter.

The poet Rilke says, "Love the questions themselves. . . . Live the questions now."[*] Married at nineteen, I am still with the man who is my best friend. We have two daughters and their families. They continue to teach me much about God's surprises, about the eruptions of grace in our lives.

I used to say I was lucky. Now I say I am thankful. I am grateful for meaningful work, for the sacrament of calling; for the unfolding adventure of the journey with God, who has a plan that includes ordinary persons.

I am grateful for the memories of red poppies and peacocks, for a grandmother who taught me something about the extraordinary, whose living and being were a form of poetry expressing the inexpressible, introducing me to the wonder and mystery of the commonplace.

Lee Syd

---

[*]Rainer Maria Rilke, *Letters to a Young Poet*, rev. ed. (New York: W. W. Norton, 1963), 35.

The Alabaster Jar

MARILYN MILLER

MARILYN MILLER was the first woman ordained to the congregational pastoral ministry in the General Conference Mennonite Church (GCMC).* She was ordained at the Arvada Mennonite Church, September 19, 1976. Marilyn is presently Director of Outreach Ministries for GCMC.

Before taking this assignment, Marilyn copastored for nine years at Arvada Mennonite Church and then spent five years in church planting at Boulder Mennonite Church.

She received a B.S. from Bethel College, North Newton, Kansas; an M.Div. from Iliff School of Theology, Denver, Colorado; and a D.Min. from San Francisco Theological Seminary.

Marilyn and her husband, Maurice, who works for the National Park Service, enjoy hiking and camping in the mountains. They have two married daughters, Michelle and Monica; two sons-in-law; and four "granddogs." Their son Michael tragically lost his life in a kayaking accident in 1996.

---

*Ann J. Allebach was ordained in 1911 at First Mennonite Church, Diamond Street, Philadelphia, by Eastern District Conference. She pastored the Sunnyside Reformed Church in Long Island, N.Y., from 1916 until her sudden death in 1918. *Full Circle: Stories of Mennonite Women*, edited by Mary Lou Cummings (Faith & Life Press, 1978), 8-10.

As a young child growing up in Hesston, Kansas, I thought I had the gift of preaching.* I would gather my sisters, brothers, and neighborhood children together and hold evangelistic services for them.

When they grew tired of listening, my sister, Joy, and I would move out to the hen house. A roost there looked like chorus risers. Joy would put the chickens on the risers and lead the "cackle choir," and I would preach to those hens.

I Didn't Dream I Would Preach to Real People

The "amens" from the hens came as lots of cackling. My parents were bewildered as they wondered about the sudden loss in egg production. As a result, I had to quit preaching to the hens. But I remember thinking, *If I were a man, I would be a preacher.* In those days I didn't know of even one female pastor, so I didn't dream that one day I would preach to real, live people. I did decide to marry a minister so I could do church work through him.

In the late 1940s, when I was in elementary school, I heard our minister pray fervently for God to open the ears of more young men so they would hear the call of the Lord. I remember going home, standing in the backyard, looking up at the stars, and asking, "God, if you need more pastors, why wasn't I created a man? I would love to be a pastor."

Again, the solution seemed to be to marry a minister.

No Greater Joy Than Pointing Someone to Christ

As a child, I was influenced by my pastor-teacher-father. He wrote books about evangelism. But it wasn't the books that influ-

---

*This chapter includes excerpts from articles in *The Mennonite*: "Laughter in Heaven," by Marilyn Miller, June 27, 1995, excerpted and edited by Mary E. Klassen; "The High Threshold: Reflections on the First Two Mennonite Women Pastors," by Anne Stuckey, Aug. 4, 1998; and "Celebrating a Woman's Gifts," by Jan Lugibihl, Jan. 18, 1977. The main thrust of the chapter comes from a sermon by Marilyn Miller at a Women's Missionary Organization Meeting, Buhler, Kansas, Oct. 22, 1997; at the 29th Annual Woman's Fellowship, at Camp Menno Haven, Tiskilwa, Illinois, Nov. 15, 1979; and at Associated Mennonite Biblical Seminary, Nov. 9, 1982. Rhoda Keener and Mary Swartley edited this chapter in consultation with Marilyn Miller.

enced me. It was his life. I saw him intentionally befriend unchurched people. I remember him taking time to go fishing regularly with an unchurched man in town. Like Jesus, my father didn't associate only with good church people. One of the greatest joys in his life was helping people have a life-changing relationship with Jesus Christ and the church.

My grandmother was another person who had a great influence on me. As she lay on her deathbed, reviewing her life, she told her children, "There's no greater joy in life than pointing a person to Christ."

I saw how important it was to my father and grandmother to help others know Christ, and I saw the joy that came from it. So I, too, wanted to do evangelistic work.

When I was in elementary school, several neighbors and my younger sister and I formed an evangelism club. Our clubhouse was a large outbuilding in the yard of a local church. We sat on the cold gray cement floor and made plans for how we could help save all the sinners in Hesston, Kansas. We didn't have any great successes to report, but we did have good intentions.

When I was a student at Hesston College, every Sunday I taught at a mission for African-Americans in Wichita, Kansas. I was more comfortable sharing the gospel with people of different racial backgrounds than with the lost in the dominant white society.

I Decided to Marry a Minister . . .

I also found much learning and joy in that work. It brought me to the conclusion that I wanted to continue in mission work. Because I didn't know it was possible for a woman to be a minister, I again decided I would marry a minister so I could do mission work with him.

Then my "shining knight" came riding up in his new Ford, and I fell in love. But Maurice Miller said he did not feel called to be a minister or missionary. My heart ruled over my head, and we married.

I taught school for five years while Maurice finished his degrees. Then he worked as a city planner. For nine years I stayed at home, busying myself with homemaking, three children, and various church activities.

During these years I was active in Christian education work and led a Bible study group. I became interested in going to seminary, but there was no seminary in our area. I learned that Iliff Theological Seminary in Denver was the one closest to us, but I saw no way for me to go there.

I Said I'd Go Anywhere

One Sunday my pastor, Melvin Schmidt, gave a sermon illustration about a monk named Brother Lawrence. He practiced the presence of God among the pots and pans of a kitchen. Since I was spending a lot of time myself those days among the pots and pans, I decided to do some more reading about Brother Lawrence. One story I read about his life really struck me.

On a winter day, Brother Lawrence went out for a walk. As he strolled along, he came to a large gnarled, barren tree. It was just an ordinary tree. Probably many people had walked right by it without a second thought.

As Brother Lawrence looked at the tree, however, he thought about how it soon would be breaking forth with buds, then beautiful leaves and new life. A revelation hit him. "If God can bring about such changes in an ordinary tree, what could God bring about in me if I would be open?"

Brother Lawrence's story so challenged me that I decided to open my life and ask God to work through me in a new way. I remember kneeling beside our bed one morning years ago in Wichita, Kansas, and saying, "Lord, I give myself completely to you. I'll go anywhere, do anything. Just let me know your will."

The answer came much sooner than I expected. That evening when Maurice came home from work, the first thing he said was "Marilyn, how would you like to move to Denver?"

I felt completely astounded and humbled by this question. I thought, *My devotions this morning! I said I'd go anywhere.* I had experienced the grace of God; I had given myself to God. Now I needed the courage and strength to leave our many close relatives and friends and move to Colorado.

We moved to Denver with our three school-age children. I decided to start seminary studies. I chose to go to seminary because the Christian gospel was important to me. I wanted to be in work where I could be free to use the concepts, words, Bible study, and prayer that were important to me.

I also wanted to be a good mother to our children. I felt that the most important thing I could do for my children was to help them have a meaningful faith. The more I could learn how to teach children and bring them up so they could have a good relationship with God and humanity, the better it would be for them.

When I started seminary, I told my adviser, "I'm a woman and a Mennonite, and there are only four Mennonite churches in the Denver area. I know of no Mennonite church anywhere that hires a woman for anything except secretarial or janitorial work. So I really doubt whether I can get a ministerial job in the Mennonite church when my seminary training is done."

After two years of study, I was asked by a person from an area Mennonite church if I was interested in an interim pastoral position. From that time, I began thinking seriously of pastoral ministry. Later, the Arvada congregation, where our family attended, issued a call for me to become a copastor, working part-time.

When I was questioning whether it was necessary to be ordained to pastor, a saint from the Arvada congregation climbed the hill behind the church with me, just to talk. She said, "Maybe if you allow us to celebrate the gifts God has given *you*, then we can celebrate the gifts God has given *us* a little better."

Relationships Are Most Important

My children have always been an important part of my ministry. When they were younger, they sometimes went with me to visit our oldest members or to see newborn babies. On Sunday, they participated in the worship service through children's church. They also helped with the offering and childcare in the nursery. Before it was popular to do this, we had regular "take your child to work" times.

It felt to me that what I was doing as a pastor at church was often the same type of ministry I did as a homemaker. I was meeting people's needs, providing hospitality, listening, and trying to create a family spirit centered in God's unconditional love as we see it in Jesus. In the home and in the church, relationships are most important, relationships with God and with others.

This belief about relationships took on dimensions I could never

have imagined after our thirty-two-year-old son, Michael, was tragically killed. On Mother's Day 1996, we received a phone call—the
type of call that parents most fear. Our son, Michael, had drowned
in a kayaking accident.

Right when the phone call came, I was preparing a sermon for
our daughter's wedding. We were all involved in candles and flowers and wedding clothes. After Michael's death, none of these were
important—including the eloquent words I was hoping to speak at
the wedding sermon. What was important was the people who
would be there. Could we realize the precious gift that these relationships are and treasure them while we have them?

Another aspect of relationships came home to us on Father's Day,
five weeks later. Our family had gone to the high school where
Michael had been a teacher, to clean out his things. Even though
Michael's body had still not been found, we all decided to go to the
river together, to be at the place where he had died.

While the younger people climbed down to the water's edge,
Maurice was thinking, *Michael, what message would you want to
give me on Father's Day?*

I was thinking about a sermon one of my pastors, Steve Goering,
had given about Jesus' death. He said the disciples were confused
and grief stricken. Inside I said, "Yes, yes. I know what that feels
like." Steve went on, "They knew how to relate to someone who
was physically present. But how do you relate spiritually to someone no longer physically present?" That was my big question.

I spent some time in prayer: "Lord, if this beautiful river canyon
is to be Michael's burial place, I can be at peace. It seems to be more
fitting for him than a casket in the ground since he was one you
couldn't box in. However, if his body is going to be found, it would
surely be nice if it could happen today so we could experience some
closure while we are all here together."

At about that time, Mike's body floated past on the swift river
current. It seemed a miracle that, after five weeks, the body dis-
lodged just when all of us were there. We took it as an answer to
prayer and a message from God that the spirit world is much more
powerful than the physical world.

It also seemed like a message from Mike, telling us not to worry
about the physical body, because his spirit is exploring even more

wonderful canyons in another world. Mike was one who always was ahead of the rest of us on hikes or whatever. So it is a comfort to know he will be there ahead of us in the next world.

Through the experience of Michael's death, I learned in a new way that relationships are the most important things in life. How could we have gotten through this time without our relationship with God and our church family? This made me see again why we need to invite and welcome others into the church family and into relationship with God.

She Has Done a Good Thing

Once I preached a sermon on grace, giving, and gumption. I talked about the woman with the alabaster jar (Mark 14:3-9).

In that story, Jesus is sitting at the table of Simon the Leper when a woman comes in with an alabaster jar of very costly pure nard. She breaks it and pours the ointment over Jesus' head. Some of the dinner guests criticize, "Why this waste? This perfume could have been sold for a large sum, and the money given to the poor" (NAB, adapted).

However, Jesus says, "Let her alone. . . . Why do you make trouble for her? She has done a good thing for me. . . . She has done what she could. . . . She has anticipated anointing my body for burial" (NAB, abridged).

The people scolding the woman see only dollar signs. But Jesus sees beyond the ointment and the money. He sees a person, a woman giving her love, giving herself, wanting to relate to him. The perfume is merely a sign of that love, of that self-giving, of that relationship.

In those days, such giving was especially hard for the woman to do. A proper woman did not break up a meeting of men with their words and acts. This woman knew she would be condemned. But she had experienced grace, and in response she wanted to give of herself. The grace she had received gave her the energy to act, to give of herself, despite the harsh rebukes.

And Jesus still says, "She has done a good thing."

Finding the Grace to Risk

I wish I could say to all of you women, "Just trust God. If God is calling you to the ministry, the doors will open for you, just like they did for me."

However, I can't truthfully say that. I know too many women who are as capable (or more capable) than I, who have sensed God's call to the ministry and yet have had no job offers. I thank God that people in Arvada and in the Western District Conference had open minds and open hearts to test God's call.

My experience in the ministry has been quite a rewarding and growing time. But it has not always been easy. There have been criticisms.

My mother-in-law wrote and asked, "Isn't it unfeminine for a woman to be a pastor?"

My very own mother came to Colorado for my ordination. During sharing time in the morning worship service, she stood and held up her Bible. She stated that she believes the Bible teaches a woman to stay at home and be a helpmeet to her husband. She said she knows I (Marilyn) believe differently, and that I have her blessing. But she did want the congregation to know where she stood. She did not want to be a hypocrite.

She went on and on. When she finished, the congregation gave her a big applause. All I could say was "Mom, for a woman who doesn't believe in women preaching, you have certainly given a tremendous sermon."

Although Mother and I could both laugh at this, there have been times when it has taken considerable courage to face the criticism, frustrations, and struggles that come with pastoring and church administration work.

I experience grace and giving as a cycle. I experience grace, and with the grace comes an urge or call to give of myself. But often, to respond to the call, I must risk and sacrifice. When I do so, it often leads to a new grace experience, and the cycle goes on.

One Whispering Voice

Each of us, like the woman in the Bible story, is gifted with an alabaster jar. In it we carry a very precious perfume, our own unique personalities. We can choose to go through life carrying that precious perfume in an unopened jar, waiting for a time when there won't be much risk in opening it and sharing it.

We can choose to measure that perfume out little by little, sharing it only with those we think will appreciate it. Or we can do as the woman in the Bible story, and offer it all to Christ.

If we pour it out as an offering, there are apt to be mixed reactions. Some people will say, "What a waste! . . . This isn't proper! . . . What kind of woman would act this way? . . . We didn't say you could do that. . . . You're wrong!"

Nevertheless, there will be one voice, perhaps only whispering, yet saying to those who will listen, "Let her alone. . . . Why do you make trouble for her? . . . She has done what she could. . . . *She has done a good thing for me.*"

Marilyn Miller

Epilogue

Let this be written
for a future generation,
that a people not yet created
may praise the Lord.

—*Psalm 102:18, NIV*

Little Girl in Pigtails

RHODA KEENER

Little girl in pigtails
    Swinging high
    Swinging far
To reach the sky
Pigtails flying . . .
How high little girl
How high
How high *can* you fly?

When I was a little girl,
I took my Bible
With colored pictures of Jesus
And a zipper that closed the whole Bible
    all the way around
With my name written on the dedication page:
    "This Bible is presented to Rhoda Jean Shenk
    From the Sunday school department
    Of Souderton Mennonite Church."
I took my Bible
    To Sunday school,
    And Bible school,
    And Christian day school.
I read my Bible often,
And followed the daily schedule of readings,
Crossing off the long sections of Ezekiel and Leviticus
With relief—having dutifully read every vision and law
So I could say I read the Bible through in a year.

When I was a little girl,
I never dreamed that women could be
Anything but happy wives and mothers and missionaries
Or teachers of children or pastor's wives—
    To serve God.
I never heard a woman preach;
I never met a woman seminarian;
Or professor of theology,
Or president of a college.
I did not think this odd—
That's how it was.
    I did have a great-aunt, however,
    Who was a bit outrageous.
    When we went for dinner,
    She, and not my uncle, decided who would pray.
    Once, she even had the audacity
    To ask my mother to say grace.

When I was a little girl,
There were no women leaders
    Who walked in front.
They led surreptitiously, from behind the scenes,
So that, unless I looked closely,
I did not even know that they were there.
But now, today, I hear their voices . . .
Coming from the laundry
    The pulpit
    The office
    The classroom
    The podium
    The boardroom,
With images of trees firmly rooted
And a grandmother's bright beautiful red poppies
And a loving father teaching his little girl
    to steer through the fog.

I hear their voices
In these stories of women
      who have done a good thing.

Little girl in pigtails
      Swinging high
      Swinging far
To reach the sky
Pigtails flying
How high little girl
How high
How high *will* you fly?

Rhoda Keener

I say to you,
wherever the gospel
is proclaimed to the whole world,
what she has done
will be told
in memory of her.

—Jesus, in Mark 14:9

The Editors

MARY SWARTLEY has been a business educator and educational administrator, spending most of her years of teaching and administration in Mennonite institutions: Christopher Dock High School (Lansdale, Pa.), Eastern Mennonite High School and E. M. College (Harrisonburg, Va.), and Bethany Christian High School (Goshen, Ind.). During the last five years at Bethany, Mary combined teaching business with being business manager, and eventually was interim principal.

Mary's education includes: Sacred Heart University, Fairfield, Connecticut (Certificate in Advanced Administration); James Madison University, Harrisonburg, Virginia (M.S., Business Education); and Eastern Mennonite College (B.A., Business Education). Mary is studying at Associated Mennonite Biblical Seminary.

Mary was a member of Mennonite Mutual Aid board of directors (1979-91) and chaired this board in 1990-91. Mary has also been on the board for Church Community Services in Elkhart. As a leader in the Belmont Mennonite Church, she has served in various capacities and now is congregational administrator.

At at Eastern Mennonite College, Mary met Willard Swartley, and they were married in 1958. Both Mary and Willard grew up in the Franconia Conference of eastern Pennsylvania. Since 1978, Mary and Willard have lived in Elkhart, Indiana, where Willard is Professor of New Testament and Academic Dean at Associated Mennonite Biblical Seminary.

Mary and Willard have a daughter, Louisa; a son, Kenton; and six grandchildren. Mary's interests include church organization and administration, reading novels, playing piano, and entertaining friends.

Steven Keener

RHODA KEENER has served as a psychotherapist, English teacher, and mental health administrator for fourteen years. Rhoda's work in the Goshen, Indiana, area has included nine years at Bethany Christian High School, counseling for Pleasant View Mennonite Church and for a battered women's shelter, and serving as an administrator at Oaklawn Psychiatric Center.

Rhoda's education includes studies at Associated Mennonite Biblical Seminary, Elkhart (Certificate of Theology); St. Francis College, Fort Wayne (M.S., Mental Health Counseling, National Counselor Certification: NCC); and Goshen College, (B.S., English)—all in Indiana.

She and Brandy Burt are coauthors of a training manual for use with adults having serious and persistent mental illness (for Oaklawn Psychiatric Center), *Training the Trainer: Individual Adult Daily Living Skills*. Rhoda has also written dramatic readings for public worship, and has published pieces in *Christian Living* and *With,* and a poem in *Daughters of Sarah,* "A Mennonite Story" (1993).

Rhoda met her husband, Bob Keener, in Voluntary Service in New York City, and they were married in 1972. For nine years Bob served as pastor of East Goshen Mennonite Church, Goshen, Indiana. He is a chaplain at Menno Haven Retirement Community in Chambersburg, Pennsylvania. Rhoda is working as a counselor at Fairfield Mennonite Church, and as a consultant for a local mental health agency.

Rhoda and Bob are the parents of three adult children, Jean, Gloria, and Steven. Favorite activities for Rhoda include swimming, reading, watching movies, meeting with friends and family, and drinking good coffee.